THE LAST CROCODILE HUNTER

THE LAST CROCODILE HUNTER

BOB IRWIN

with Amanda French

ALLEN&UNWIN
SYDNEY • MELBOURNE • AUCKLAND • LONDON

First published in 2016

Allen & Unwin
83 Alexander Street
Crows Nest NSW 2065
Australia
Phone: (61 2) 8425 0100
Email: info@allenandunwin.com
Web: www.allenandunwin.com

Cataloguing-in-Publication details are available
from the National Library of Australia
www.trove.nla.gov.au

ISBN 978 1 76029 237 9

Set in 12/18 pt Sabon by Midland Typesetters, Australia
Printed and bound in Australia by Griffin Press

10 9 8 7 6 5 4 3 2 1

The paper in this book is FSC® certified. FSC® promotes environmentally responsible, socially beneficial and economically viable management of the world's forests.

For Lyn and Steve

Contents

Epigraph

Below is a letter from Steve to Lyn and me that he wrote a long time ago. I've lost a lot of precious memorabilia along my journey, and have very few photographs of Steve and our family to reflect on, so I particularly treasure this.

Envelope inscription: *Please be happy to know that your strength and wisdom has been passed on.*

Dear Mum & Dad,
Probably one of the most unfortunate things in a bloke's life is that it takes over 30 years to realise how essential you have been to build my character, my ethics and, most importantly, my HAPPINESS.

At 32, I am finally starting to figure it out. In good times and in bad, you were there. Your strength and endurance to raise me will not go unrewarded. My love for you is my strength!

For the rest of my life I will reflect on the unbelievably GREAT times we've shared and will continue to share. You're my best friends!

Thank you,

Steve

Foreword

Bob Irwin

'My dad, just the legend of the universe. When I was the tiniest little kid, I'd look up to my dad and he was larger than life; he was just this action hero. He was everything I wanted to be. And all I've done in my life is follow in his footsteps, mimic him and try to be him. And nowadays, I just try to make him proud, mate.'

Steve Irwin, from interview with Andrew Denton on *Enough Rope*, ABC TV

Certainly the proudest feeling I've had about building the zoo was giving Steve an outlet to harness some of his energy. Because in a very short period of time he managed to inspire millions of people around the world about nature conservation, using one animal that wasn't all that easy to fall in love with—the crocodile, and yet crocodiles are incredible animals that date back to over 80 million years ago when there were no humans on this planet.

I can't imagine having lived a life without wildlife or having had the opportunity to connect so frequently with our natural world. To me, it doesn't matter how often I see a black-headed python, or a crocodile, or whatever animal it may be, I always get excited. To understand how the bush has taught me so much, you have to realise that nature is communicating with us whichever way we turn. These days, in our busy lives, with such advancements in technology, we tend to forget the things that came so naturally to our ancestors. We've become oblivious to the whispers that are there to be heard. We can no longer be guided by a starry night, or smell danger blowing in on the wind, or migrate with the seasons, or track unwoven paths beneath our feet. But the animals can. We are the only species that has ever lived on this planet that destroys its own environment. No other species devastates the home in which it lives.

When the script was written for nature, humans weren't in the picture at all. We weren't involved, we weren't asked to be involved either, nature simply didn't require us to be part of it. But unfortunately, since our short time on this planet, we've become the most dominant species and now we impose our will upon every living thing out there. And until we get to the point where we start to ask the question whether we intend to be successful and sustainable in the long-term, then we're going to always have a big problem.

For me, and for Steve, crocodiles were colossally misunderstood. They're an animal that's survived ice ages and some pretty catastrophic climatic changes over all these years, and they're still doing well in our world today.

When it comes to animal intelligence, the unfortunate thing is that we tend to look at it from a human perspective. We say that an animal is intelligent only when its actions make sense to us. And yet it is very hard to judge the difference between instinct and intelligence. Steve, because of his inquisitive nature, was able to get a better understanding of animals. He had an animal instinct right from an early age. He was never satisfied with learning about a species from a book or a scientific paper; no, Steve had to be out there amongst it observing the natural world around him.

Through Steve's passion and enthusiasm he was able to shine a spotlight on our natural world that wasn't there before he came along. He had a unique way of connecting people with wildlife that was contagious. His success in the end was not something that I can necessarily take credit for either. But I guess, getting him into it as a kid and encouraging his interests was something that I was able to do as his dad. While I may have been the teacher in the early years, I certainly became the pupil later on. In Steve I found a likeminded friend with whom I could share my passion. Because it was Steve in the end who was able to teach me that passion alone has the ability to ignite a spark in others and send a warm glow over the rest of the world—and that's exactly what he achieved. And yet it started out reasonably unsophisticated, getting muddy catching crocodiles in the mangroves and swamps of Far North Queensland. To have had the opportunity to venture to some of the most remote areas of Queensland over the years, and to be able to experience that with someone like Steve, who had the same interests and understanding that I have, that's the part that I treasured most of all. That's called passion, and if you ever lose that then you might as well get out of the wildlife industry all together, go and do something else. Because it doesn't matter what you encounter out there, if you don't get excited about that experience and feel something profound for that animal, then it's probably time for a career change.

I'm constantly reminded of his boundless energy, infectious humour and unrestrained passion for wildlife. When the world lost Steve, the animals lost the best friend that they ever had, and so did I. But he's still here, still with me, and I'm able to gain strength from him, and harness the same passion and drive that we had together. What he stood for and what he was able to achieve means just as much now as when he was here in this physical world. There are so many people who have been inspired by, and are still being inspired by, Steve Irwin. That's something that makes me feel really, really proud.

I only hope that sharing some of these stories reminds people of his enormous legacy, teaching not only the importance of reconnecting with our environment, but to be passionate in doing so. We can no longer live in isolation from the environment that nourishes us so well. We are interconnected with every single strand of it. Our own survival depends on its very health.

Author's note

Amanda French

Take one look at him. He's a slight man, small in stature, pretty much guaranteed to have a smoke hanging out of the corner of his mouth, no doubt his tenth for the day. But I'd challenge anyone to underestimate him. Although this wildlife warrior is pint-sized, his inner strength is giant.

It's not brute strength and muscle that have got Bob by during his lifetime capturing some of this country's largest crocs, it's his endurance and drive. It's ironic that his favourite animal has been the crocodile, an animal that's survived many millions of years and seen out the world's most drastic natural events. Because that's what Bob is too: he's a survivor. He's battled from tragedy to triumph, time and time again, and yet he's still got that get-up-and-go, is still a voice for our wildlife. Where most of us would probably have thrown in the towel, he's drawn strength from helping animals that have no voice, in a time in our world when we constantly place them under threat.

I've been on many outback adventures with Bob supporting his advocacy work with his current platform—the Bob Irwin Wildlife & Conservation Foundation Inc. One of my first trips was to an arid property in outback New South Wales. Looking out over the cracked, dry, red soil plains, I privately wondered why on earth we'd travelled for sixteen hours non-stop to see nothing but a desolate landscape. I loved wildlife, but usually the big kind, the kind that demanded your attention. It's all too easy to overlook the smaller, often forgotten, creatures. It was on this trip with Bob that I suddenly realised I had been guilty of this.

He pointed out the type of finch flitting by, the grip on a gecko's hand, or the way a spider was waiting in its web. He knew every reptile we saw by name, and precisely how many days it incubated its eggs. He understood how everything fitted together in that entire ecosystem. It became clear to me that nothing out there survives in isolation from its environment and every little creature plays a vital part. His passion was undeniably contagious, and before long I had caught it too. I had never experienced a shift in myself as rapid as that.

He'd be up at the crack of dawn, more excited than a kid on Christmas morning, to see what wildlife he might stumble across. Day after day, he stood up there on the back of our moving vehicle, looking for a sign of anything that had slithered or burrowed just out of sight and he'd be out of the truck like a flash the second he saw it. I wish I could have bottled that passion. I worry about the world of conservation when he's gone, well aware that it won't be long before Bob is not physically able to do the things he does now. I have also never met someone with more compassion than him, even for the tiniest little lizard.

When we set out one afternoon to dig up some ant burrows, he apologised to the inhabitants for digging up their home. When he had identified the ants, he replaced it all to the best of his ability, putting things back the way he had found them.

Bob is the last of his breed of bushman. He can tie any knot, track animals by instinct, survive in the bush and tell a bloody good yarn by the fire. But try to connect him with today's technology and you're in for a challenge. He eats only meat and three veg and drinks only Bushell's tea. 'Water's for showering in,' he says. He'll walk out of any restaurant serving native wildlife, happily get arrested for standing up for what he believes in and won't be seen driving anything but a Toyota Landcruiser ute.

At forty years Bob's junior, I have lived in a very different time for our environment. I've only known a life where rainforests are vanishing and animals are endangered. Bob's right when he says that my generation are equipped with the knowledge to make a change. Let's hope we haven't left it too late.

Bob is the first to admit that he doesn't do people all that well. But I disagree. He's everyman's hero, recognised in some of the most remote places across Australia, and welcomed by other down-to-earth bushies who want to shake his hand and have their photo taken with Bob. Despite tiring on his long tours to spread his environmental message, he insists on giving time to each and every person he meets who wants to talk about how much Steve inspired them, or what they're doing for our wildlife. Bob always tells me that you had to be pretty genuine to work with Steve, and throughout the time I've been fortunate enough to spend in Bob's company, I've learnt that's Bob through and through as well. Never tolerating a fool, the way to his heart is really quite simple: hard work, humour, Bushell's tea.

Writing this story has been an adventure in itself. We travelled twenty thousand kilometres, criss-crossing the east coast of Australia. It wasn't for the faint-hearted. There weren't always showers or flushing toilets in the isolated places where we ventured. We didn't sightsee, we were on a mission. Along the roads less travelled we encountered native wildlife I never even knew existed, cried as we saw parts of our Great Barrier Reef dying right before our eyes, and rejoiced as we unearthed a community of dedicated, steadfast individuals working tirelessly to save our environment and the precious wildlife that call Australia home.

These long-haul trips also earned me a special friendship with this grandfather of conservation, and along the way Bob entrusted me to capture his story. His stories were told to me exactly where Bob needed to be to tell them. By the campfire. Beside a crocodile-infested river. In the middle of nowhere. The wild is where Bob comes to life, it's where he belongs. For Bob, a very private man, writing this book could only happen long after the events depicted. Time and distance have allowed him insight into the unbelievable losses that have come his way.

The man's got 77 years' worth of stories to tell that paint a picture of an ordinary man who has lived an unlikely extraordinary life. It's time for Bob Irwin to tell his story: the story of the man behind so many great things for Australian wildlife, the last of his kind. 'Who is Bob Irwin?' you might ask. Well, he's just Bob, and that means more to the everyday Australian who thought that they couldn't make a difference. If Bob did it, so can you. He's every bit the father of the man and finally . . . this is his story.

Prologue

I have always felt the weight of the environment on my shoulders, metaphorically speaking of course. But the story of how I found my true way in this world starts more literally: I was buried alive. My story starts not six but fourteen feet underground.

I was entombed down a shaft, with earth bearing down on my trapped body. The mud and dirt enveloping me was suffocating. Every second that passed transformed the oxygen trapped in a tiny pocket around my face into dense, asphyxiating anguish. If I had been able to move them, my hands could have cut the thick, suffocating air with a knife. The only thing keeping me alive was another pocket of air trapped beneath my hunched-over body. The load of the compacted clay earth was crushing and it thrust me uncomfortably down on the handle of the axe I had been holding when the cave-in happened.

The wooden handle was stuck upright beneath me, slowly winding me as it pushed further into my stomach. My short breaths became gasps as I rapidly ran out of precious oxygen.

I could hear muffled shouting from above but I couldn't call out. I couldn't move a muscle. All I could do was wait there, unresponsive and limp, my life in the hands of my quick-thinking father-in-law, Pa, on the surface. I waited anxiously, with nothing left to do but contemplate my likely fate. I pictured myself discovered like a Palaeolithic specimen fossilised in the viscous clay. *This is it*, I thought, *I'm not getting out of here alive. Here is where it ends for Bob Irwin, at the bottom of a hole that I've literally dug for myself.* And as I pondered the irony of the situation, concluding that this wasn't what I'd signed up for, I passed out.

On the surface, Pa panicked as he realised that he wouldn't be able to manually dig me out before I suffocated. We had been 'shaft and tunnelling'—where you dig two shafts and then tunnel at the bottom in between them—by hand with a pickaxe and shovel. After digging the first fourteen-foot shaft, I had been standing at the bottom when the whole thing caved in, burying me alive.

Pa was an older man with injuries sustained from a bullet to his back in the war, so he wasn't physically capable of digging me out by hand. The machine he was operating could have done the job, but it would most likely have dug me up as well, most likely in bits. So he made the astute decision to jump into the car and hastily pick up my young brother-in-law and plumbing apprentice, Graeme, from trade school to get me out. He frantically dug me out by hand, eventually dragging my lifeless body to the surface.

As I lay there coated in thick mud as though the earth had just given birth to me as a grown man, I drew what felt like my first proper breath. If I'd been down there a moment longer, it would surely have been my end. Saying that I felt ordinary was an understatement as I slowly regained my faculties. I should have gone to the hospital, but protested and insisted on being taken home. I felt near death, fatigued and defeated by a job that I had slowly but surely started to detest.

When I got home all I could do was lie down on the kitchen floor inside the front door, resembling some kind of creature of the swamp, mud and all. I stared up at the ceiling feeling sorry for myself. I had grown to quite simply hate the type of work I had found myself doing, and that day it had nearly cost me my life. And to make matters worse, I knew that tomorrow I would only have to dig that bloody hole again from scratch.

I was thirty years old with three young kids, a thriving business and a house. I had ambitiously worked three hundrerd and sixty-five days straight in order to pay off the mortgage. In the evenings, I was playing professional badminton; my competitive approach had won me the title of Victorian state champion.

I had all the notches on my belt that a man of my age was supposed to have. I'd done everything by the book. I'd followed the grain. But the truth was that life in the city had grown to be something I no longer felt a passion for. I was working hard, providing for my family, but something was greatly amiss. While we were reaping the rewards of our hard work, inside I didn't feel rich at all. In fact, I felt empty, as though I had wound up on the wrong path, having chosen practicality over what truly made me tick. But that's just what you did. In those days you didn't do what you loved, you worked hard to make a living.

I worked tirelessly around the clock, knee-deep in mud in the relentless Melbourne weather, and as a result I spent little time with my young family. I knew these were valuable years that you never get back, no matter how much I might try to make up for it later in life. It was time, I thought, for a radical change. I couldn't have gone another day without making a decision. For too long, the safe path I'd trodden had worn me down.

Lyn was shocked when she returned home to the unfamiliar sight of her husband lying motionless on the kitchen floor. She asked what had happened and I told her everything, including my desire to give it all away. 'I've had enough,' I said. 'I've reached the point where I absolutely despise it. If I continue this kind of work, it's quite simple: it's going to be a very short life.'

Without much hesitation, Lyn said, 'Okay then, let's do it. Let's start your reptile park. If you have the will to do it, then we'll all go, the whole family.'

So it was on the kitchen floor of our inner-city Melbourne home that I made a really clear, finite decision: a promise to myself that I wasn't going to lead a life I no longer felt any passion for. I decided then and there, with Lyn's reassuring backing, that I'd give my long-held dream of opening a reptile park my best shot, despite not having the slightest bit of experience in running a zoological facility. I knew I could always go back to plumbing, but I hoped like hell I'd never have to. Up until this point Lyn and I had fashioned a very safe existence, but everything from here on was going to be flying by the seat of our pants.

I got sick of sitting on the fence. We just knew that we wanted to get involved with wildlife, and so we did it. It was time for us to chase a dream we really wanted, rather than doing what was required to make ends meet. There was more to life than following the herd. Queensland, here come the Irwins.

1

A father figure

Most people would be surprised to know that I started out as a plumber. An ambition I had from a young age was to be just like the man I most admired, my stepfather Les. I only knew him as Dad. I can still remember being an enthralled little boy as I watched him work in his blacksmith shed, my eyes as wide as dinner plates. He was a man of few words and we had very few frank conversations, Dad and I, but I'll always remember the day he gave me a rare piece of resounding fatherly advice: 'Son, as you get older and you go through life, never expect any reward unless you work hard for it . . . and always be nice to your mother.'

My biological father died in a prisoner-of-war camp in Burma along with my uncle when I was just four years old, leaving my widowed mother to care for my older brother Ron and me during the hard times following World War II. I have no recollection of my dad, and wasn't aware back then about the adversity our mother would have faced in simply making ends meet despite her broken heart. As a child, you rarely consider the wellbeing of those who selflessly bring you into the world.

But in hindsight our humble abode was a stark example of just how tough times were: our home was basic, with a dirt floor in the kitchen and very few material things. We never had the luxury of keeping pets; they would have been just another hungry mouth Mum couldn't afford to feed. As young boys, our job was to make sure that the hessian sides of the Coolgardie safe were always damp to keep the food inside cold; this was well before the days of refrigeration. We took on many of the physical jobs around the home, in place of the man of the house. But none of this mattered to us kids. Money stuff didn't cross our minds so long as we could get outdoors and find some fun. We improvised and relished in our childhood adventures.

It must have been difficult for Mum to raise two boys on her own, particularly livewires like us. Ron and I were only two years apart, and we fought like cats and dogs. We always seemed to be bluing or getting into mischief. If we weren't getting the cane or a lashing of the leather belt in the classroom, Mum used to whack us with wooden coathangers at home to pull us into line. When the wooden ones broke on our backsides, she changed to wire ones. They didn't break, they just bent a little and left a lasting sting. We never received that kind of punishment unless we deserved it, and it never did us any harm.

Sometime later, Mum married Les and we moved into his much more comfortable home. I don't know how they met: from as early as I can recall he was always in the picture. Les quickly became a strong male influence for Ron and me: a sturdy, incredibly tall man who was nevertheless remarkably tender, a true gentle giant. He was always Dad to me. When he spoke, Ron and I always listened, captivated.

No matter how much I used to trail him around, getting under his feet, he was endlessly patient with me. I used to adore watching him at work in his smithy making picks and shovels, crowbars and horseshoes. When he'd get steel splinters in his big calloused hands, I'd spend hours removing them with a pair of tweezers. To my eyes, each hand seemed the size of a leg of ham as I diligently worked away at them. I liked to think I could help him and he knew it would keep me busy.

He had a fit, muscular physique without an ounce of fat on him. He worked too hard for that. Dad was all about physical work. Like the good teacher he was, he always had the time to stop and show me how to do things properly. In Dad's book you never did things by halves: it was a hundred per cent or nothing at all. 'If you take the time to do it properly the first time, then you'll save time later.' I grew up emulating his vigour and appetite for hard work.

We lived in a tiny country town called The Basin, situated at the foothills of the enchanting Dandenong Ranges in Victoria. Our house was on Mountain Highway, a winding narrow road that saw little traffic. Vehicles were so infrequent that Ron and I would use the middle of the road as our cricket pitch because it was perfectly flat. If a vehicle happened to approach, no one ever seemed to mind waiting for us to move the wickets to let them pass, then we'd pick up our game where we'd left off.

For a restless boy like me, school was completely uninteresting, and I struggled to learn anything from a book. The Basin Primary School consisted of one room and felt just like a prison to me—and I found my stern teacher to be boring and uninspiring.

Trapped at my desk, I couldn't wait for the hours to pass so I could race home and get back down to the creek to see what creatures I could discover.

Being just about the smallest kid in the district, I used to cop a fair bit of bullying. As the years went by, I realised I had to either learn how to fight or run very fast. Being the size I was, I mostly did running. Whenever I had the chance I'd lose myself in the bush, engrossed in my own untroubled world. I felt at ease in my own company. I thought humans were a peculiar breed. But with animals, on the other hand, I'd grasped from a very young age that you always received honesty, you always knew where you stood. If you mucked up, they bit you. But if you respected their space, they'd respect you too. It was as simple as that in the animal world and a lot more complicated when it came to humans. The more I observed things out in the bush, the more insatiable my appetite grew to know more. The bush became my school of life. When the school bell sounded, I'd run out of the front gates as fast as my little legs could carry me, back to my sanctuary.

Our house was adjacent to a vast open paddock, filled with blackberry bushes and butting up against miles and miles of dense bush that sloped down to a flowing creek. The bush was full of all kinds of creepy crawlies that fascinated me no end. It was an idyllic place for a curious boy to grow up. It became my habitat, where I felt a sense of belonging. The day would turn to night before I'd run home to my worried mother, after eking out every last moment of light, always pushing to stay out there later and later.

It was the start of my fascination with the environment. I'd follow every critter to see where it lived: in the hollows, in the mud, below the surface of the water. I'd come home so excited because I'd found something different: a frog, an eel, or a little lizard. 'Mum, look at this!' I'd exclaim. And every time her horrified reaction would be exactly the same: 'Yeah, okay, son, but now you can go right back where you came from and let that go again.' Which I'd do, relishing in the excuse that gave me to return to my favourite place.

One particular day, Mum wanted to bake her famous blackberry pie, so I headed out in my lace-up workboots to pick blackberries; I knew secret spots flush with berries that no one else had found. But unbeknown to me, as I stood picking berries I had parked myself in the middle of a raging bull ants' nest. None of them bit me until there were dozens filling each boot. Suddenly I received hundreds of agonising bites from the irate ants, and I instantly dropped the blackberries and ran home screaming. Thankfully Dad was home. He saw me wailing as I came running down the driveway, tears streaming down my swollen red face. He immediately picked me up and put my feet in the laundry trough with a solution to help reduce the swelling. My feet were so inflamed that he couldn't get my boots off, so he cut them down both sides with a leather knife. Mum rubbed a soothing mixture on the bites. I was in agony. And it was the end of my boots too. But none of it stopped me going back to the same spot the next day, barefoot, to curiously observe those ants move about their bustling city for hours.

I was one of those fortunate kids in the world in that I was able to grow up in a place where I could virtually do what I liked when it came to exploring. I gloried in the bush for years and years. And then the time came when I had to grow up, earn myself a living and put the environment thing to bed for a while.

The closest high school was Box Hill Technical College, a trade school a long way from where we lived. In my first year of plumbing theory, learning again from a book, I failed miserably. But in later years, when I got to spend more time working hands-on in the field, I passed with honours. I had decided on a plumbing apprenticeship so that I could help Dad with his business.

I eventually landed an apprenticeship with a great bloke named Fred Moore. My final year of the apprenticeship was in Melbourne, which was even further to travel from The Basin. I bought a pushbike to ride between home and work; it took a couple of hours each way. If I timed it well enough of a morning, a friend of mine travelling to work in his car would wait for me at the bottom of the hill to tow me behind his car on my pushbike. When I finished my apprenticeship, I finally realised my dream of working for Dad as a plumber. That was a gratifying day.

Dad eventually had a career change to building septic tanks. I continued to work with him in this new endeavour because I loved the physical activity and the test that came working on the hillsides of the Dandenong Ranges. We'd build tanks in some unbelievably challenging places, where we'd have to mix the cement on the top of a hill, and send it down to the bottom via a series of corrugated-iron chutes, wheelbarrowing the cement between one chute and the next. I used to love digging the septic tank holes. I wanted to prove to Dad that I could dig those holes as quickly as him, and in the end I could, despite the fact that he was double my size.

To make a bit of extra money, I started digging graves for the local council. It was just me digging down to the bottom of a six-foot hole, digging with a pick and a shovel. There were no machines to do it in those days. I used to challenge myself to dig each hole faster than the last.

As we grew from boys to men, there came a time when alcohol became part of the scene. I'd get together with the boys from the local area. Living in a small country town, about the only place to go was the milk bar. I'd watch as they'd drink and drink, and then the fights would break out. If there was another group of teenagers from a different area it would end up a total riot. I associated with these guys for a fair while before I realised that alcohol was so much a part of this scene that it had become unenjoyable. I tried a beer once but vomited almost immediately. And so drinking never became something I chose to do. I decided that I always wanted to be aware of what I was doing, would never be in a situation where I didn't have my wits about me. I thought there were better things to do with my time than wake up with a sore head or a split lip. I don't have any regrets about living my life without alcohol; I don't feel as though I've missed out on anything there. I've managed to get through life without it. But I won't lie; I missed the explorations of our childhoods in the bush, once everyone had grown up and their interests had turned elsewhere.

***

Our childhood family holidays were spent at Mum and Dad's holiday home in the seaside town of Port Lonsdale. The long expanses of uninhabited sandy beaches were more wonderlands for me to endlessly explore. As kids we'd play around the old lighthouse on the headland and trawl the beaches for whatever washed up with the tide. As I got older I learnt to spearfish and became quite good at fishing in the surf. I eventually built my own surf ski because I wanted to go further out into the ocean to spear bigger fish. But I very quickly learnt not to tie my catch to a long line from my belt so that they were trailing twenty metres away when I was underwater. Because quite often I'd feel an unnerving tug on my line and the next thing I'd know a shark would have got hold of my fish and would be staring me down for more. I wouldn't say that I particularly enjoyed the company of sharks in such close proximity.

At Port Lonsdale we'd often get together with a lot of other families staying at a caravan park close by. Us kids would stay out all hours of the night playing beach cricket and football. On one of these holidays I met Lynette, a pretty brunette who liked to fish. She was my kind of girl, and I was instantly smitten. It wasn't just about her looks but the kind of stuff that made her tick that I prized the most and she was really into everything that I enjoyed. For years, I'd look forward to being reunited with her on our holidays by the sea. We were only young teenagers when we met, and as we got older we'd often return there as a group without our parents. As we grew, our relationship grew too. We became childhood sweethearts and were married when Lyn was just eighteen and I was nineteen. I had proposed to her a fair few times before she finally accepted. Lyn was pregnant at our wedding, when it wasn't all that accepted to have a baby out of wedlock. But I knew that I was going to marry that girl one way or another, and I couldn't wait to start a life with her. I had always wanted to be young enough to grow up with my children, and to keep up with them when they were young adults.

Lyn's parents, Nanna and Pa, were wonderful people and really good about the whole thing. Like my own mum and dad, they couldn't do enough to support us as we started our young lives together. Lyn was living with her parents when we got married, and then she moved in with my mum and dad before we set up on a block of land Dad owned in a town called Boronia. Our first home on that block could only be described as a glorified shed. I was determined to make a good living and promised Lyn that we'd own a home of our own one day and that I wouldn't stop until we did. It was hard to start with, but we managed to get by. When you have children young, it increases all of your responsibilities, but it teaches you a lot about yourself too.

Lyn had a lot of trouble with the birth. She was in hospital for three weeks prior to having the baby. I used to drive down to the hospital in the city every night after work to visit her, concerned about her and our unborn child. But soon we had a beautiful healthy baby girl: Joy Lesley Irwin, named after Lyn's older sister who had passed away as a young child. She was our firstborn, and I thought that she was exquisite indeed. I was fascinated by her, and she was cute as a button, even if I say so myself. I'd take her everywhere with me, pushing her along the Yarra River in her all-terrain stroller, crossing cow paddocks. We'd go off camping as a young family, just the three of us, sleeping in the back of my work truck.

Those early years with Joy were a huge learning curve for me. Lyn was a trained mothercraft nurse so she had a hell of a head start on me as a parent; she knew all about babies and what they required. She was an exceptional mum. But kids don't come with a manual and much of the time no one can say exactly what your child needs, so it was often about finding our way and learning as we went and I enjoyed that part immensely.

By then I was busy being the provider for our young family, trying to make ends meet. I would have been happy with just one child at that stage, but Lyn wouldn't have a bar of that.

Two years after Joy was born, our lives profoundly changed again when our son arrived in a hurry on Lyn's twentieth birthday in 1962. We were at home, and Lyn kept saying to me, 'I'm not ready to have him yet!' But after the trouble she'd had with Joy, I wasn't willing to risk it. 'I'm taking you to the hospital right now,' I insisted, as I virtually forced her into my work ute.

I couldn't get to Upper Ferntree Gully Hospital fast enough. That drive was the longest fifteen minutes of my life. Her waters had already broken at home and I wouldn't have coped very well if she'd given birth in my ute. I must have broken some speed limits that day, I don't mind admitting it. When I arrived, the nurse wheeled Lyn into the delivery room and I went and sat outside. I was trying to pull myself together; I felt helplessly concerned for Lyn and the baby. But there was no way I was going to watch the carnage going on inside that delivery room; I would've been a mess because I'm not good with blood.

Eight short minutes after we arrived at the hospital, Lyn gave birth to our little boy. I couldn't believe it. Out came the nurse with this little bundle: Stephen Robert Irwin. It was clear that he couldn't wait to come into this world; his enthusiasm to be on this planet was evident from day one.

'Congratulations, Mr Irwin! Here is your beautiful son,' the nurse said as she handed him over to me, all wrapped up tight in a light blue baby blanket. I was always frightened to hold babies because I was scared of breaking them, but I eagerly took him into my awkward arms. *Beautiful? Talk about an ugly bugger*, I thought to myself, but I made all the appropriate noises for the nurse's benefit. All I could think to myself was that anybody who says newborn babies are cute has got to be kidding. He looked more alien than human.

But I was stoked to be a father to a son, and felt like punching the air. We hadn't known we were having a boy, and I immediately started dreaming about all the things I would teach him, the way my dad had taught me. I instantly knew that we were going to have a great adventure.

Thankfully as the days went by, he changed from blue and wrinkly to a pretty damn good-looking blond-haired baby. And he was a tornado, wired to the eyeballs, right from the start. He came in a hurry and he never stopped from then on. He was into everything that it was possible for him to be into. From the age of two onwards, whenever he went missing you'd just look up the nearest tree and there he'd be. I never tried to stop him, it would've been useless. You had to let him go merrily on his own way. That kid just couldn't keep still.

By this stage, I'd learnt a bit about quoting for different jobs and I'd helped Dad to expand his business for many years. But eventually he had to retire due to poor health, the beginning of debilitating emphysema. So I decided to go out on my own.

Lyn and I moved to Essendon, one of the inner-city suburbs of Melbourne, where I knew I could get ample work. I took out a mortgage to purchase a modest family home on a comfortable street in suburbia. It was nothing special, but it was a start: somewhere to live and run a business from. I made a promise to Lyn that I would pay off the home in just five years. With this goal came a lot of work, and before long the business picked up and we were run off our feet.

Eventually we were so in demand for work that Lyn took on the bookkeeping as well as being a full-time mother. She would do all of the quoting, running around to different government departments. We made a great team, and it would have been impossible without her: bookwork and me never got along.

I was lucky to be in an industry where the harder I worked, the more hours I clocked up and the more money I made. We were becoming financially stable. But I hated living in the city. The steel and concrete jungle was a world apart from the quiet and calming effect of the bush where I felt such a deep-rooted connection. I was never home, working day and night, so I didn't spend time with the kids and I missed a lot of that little kid stuff. By the time I'd get home they'd usually be in bed. You don't always realise the cost at the time, of course. Your mind says, *You've got a family to support, it's your responsibility*, so you work like buggery. That became our life from the day we arrived in the city.

But every now and then, Lyn and I would escape from the city for the day and take off down south to do a bit of trout fishing on the Goulburn River. We had a permit that allowed us to catch six trout per day and would rarely come home empty-handed. We had quickly learnt that the best bait for trout were frogs we'd collect from the banks of the river. In my opinion trout made for terrible eating, but these trips got us out into an isolated part of the world. I always enjoyed watching the scenery evolve from concrete and bitumen to reviving greenery as we waved goodbye to the city.

Out there everything was alive. Tall river red gums lined the banks of the creek, home to cockatoos, galahs and parrots, which flitted in and out of hollows in their broken branches. Occasionally we'd catch a golden perch or freshwater crayfish. Most of the time we'd put them back, but there was always that anticipation of what we might find next. No two visits to these parts were ever the same because the wild is such an unpredictable place.

One day I was walking the length of the creek on my own, searching under fallen logs for frogs. As I overturned the first log I expected to see a bunch of frogs, but instead found a startled banded brown-coloured snake. I identified it as a mainland tiger snake, one of Victoria's best-known snakes, often with distinctive tiger-like bands along the length of its body. His ragged stripes varied in colour from pale yellow to black along his solid, muscular body. I wasn't all that shocked to find him, just annoyed that the little bugger had eaten all of my frogs. I went to the next log only to find another tiger snake and no frogs. By the time I got to the fifth log with the same frustrating sight, I was getting so grumpy that the snakes had taken all my bait that I just sat there looking at this snake until I finally thought, *Oh well, I'll take you home instead.*

I was far from experienced at handling venomous snakes, so I observed him for quite some time before planning my move. I knew enough to be aware that it wasn't an intelligent thing to be doing. Mainland tiger snakes are high on the list of Australia's top ten most venomous snakes, and they can inflict fatal bites. If I made a wrong move, I'd likely pay for my inexperience with my life. With just one strike, within minutes, I'd have trouble breathing, and paralysis would take hold soon afterwards. And I guess I didn't have much in the way of common sense because I weighed all of that up and I still proceeded with trying to catch him.

As I approached him, he gave me a warning, raising his head in a threatening pre-strike stance. I hadn't seen a snake do that before and I was fascinated to find that he flattened out the entire length of his body in his aggressive posture. Duly warned, I gave him a wider berth and continued to observe him. I realised he had no intention whatsoever of harming me if I could just show him that I wasn't a threat.

In my attempts to interpret his defensive behaviour, I was reminded of the advice of my self-defence instructor at a time when I'd been finishing my plumbing apprenticeship. I'd become tired of being knocked around by boys twice my size and I wanted to learn how to stand up for myself a bit more. The class taught all forms of self-defence, with the teacher making it clear that these skills weren't to be used unless you absolutely had to. The ideal situation, of course, was to just walk away from a bully. 'But if the worst comes to the worst, Robert,' my teacher told me, 'don't wait. If you know something is going to happen, then you need to become the aggressor.' Applying that same understanding to the snake, it was clear to me that as I had cornered him it was in fact me who had become the bully. I knew he didn't perceive me as food, I was far too big for that, and if I was bitten it wouldn't be out of malice but self-defence.

After quite a while of warily watching each other, the snake chose not to become the aggressor but instead to walk away. Well, in his case, slither. Carefully watching how he manoeuvred, I grabbed him by the tail and cautiously lowered him into the pillowcase I had been carrying to collect frogs. I tied a very tight knot to close the opening and stood frozen for a moment, my adrenaline soaring. *I can't believe it. I did it.* I was excited to realise that I'd read the snake well enough to capture the animal with minimal stress to him. As I returned to the car, I'm sure I triple-checked that knot before letting him ride with me on the floor of the cabin.

We weren't equipped for a new family member of this nature, but I hunted around the house and found an old glass aquarium and set him up on the kitchen bench. I was really rapt with my catch. Now that I had caught my first wild snake, I wanted to immediately go out and do it all over again.

Lyn wasn't too happy with our new housemate. 'Either that snake goes or I go,' she told me. 'Well, off you go!' I replied. But before long her fascination matched mine. She helped me breed mice to feed to him, cleaned out his enclosure and read any literature available on how to care for him, of which there wasn't much in those days. Ever since that day I had a certain fascination with tiger snakes. I used to wander along the rock fences around Wirroughby and catch them just to look at them, then put them back, honing my catching technique.

It wasn't long before our snake collection had expanded so much so that I had to build an extension to the house—we called it the Snake Room—to accommodate them all, from venomous varieties to the non-venomous like tree snakes and pythons. From the outside our home looked just like every other residence on Primrose Street, but inside it was beginning to tell another story. Keeping reptiles in Melbourne was always a challenge during the wintry cold. The thought was always there, in the back of my mind, that it'd be much easier to care for them in a warmer climate further north. But it wasn't just the snakes that had trouble with the temperature. Even though I'd grown up in Victoria, I simply hated living in a cold climate. At times I considered myself coldblooded too.

Lyn was naturally very maternal, and I suppose that's what made her such a good wildlife carer as well as a mother. After taking an interest in the reptiles, Lyn started to get involved with all kinds of Australian wildlife. She began caring for orphaned and injured animals from time to time: native birds, possums and snakes from the local area that had been hit by cars or attacked by dogs. She absolutely loved it and had such a wonderful affinity with the animals. As time went on, our small family home seemed more like a zoo.

But our human family was not yet complete: four years after Steve was born, we completed our litter with the arrival of our youngest daughter, Mandy, at Moonee Ponds Hospital in Melbourne in 1966. We'd had a lot of trouble having her and were thrilled to finally welcome her into the world. Steve was in awe of his little sister and newly appointed playmate, and over the years they became as thick as thieves. She was nicknamed Grub, as she shadowed her older brother through creeks and mud. And although he was sometimes tough on her, he generally liked to look after her and get her involved in his boyish games. Mandy was into everything that Steve was into, always seeking the approval of her intrepid older brother, whereas Joy grew to be more studious and into the intellectual side of life.

To me, having girls was a totally different experience to having a son. I loved them equally, of course, but I learnt very quickly that you have to treat your daughters differently to a son. I taught my son to be strong and resilient. With Steve, we had to teach him to toughen up if he fell over or pushed the boundaries a little bit too far, which he frequently did because he was just unstoppable. Given his tremendous energy, we had to teach him to be pretty tough to survive.

Steve tormented the girls endlessly; he'd annoy the hell out of them with pranks and drive them up the wall. At times he went too far, and I'd have to step in and put a stop to it. The only place that was suitable to give him time-out was the toilet.

It was the only place he couldn't escape out of the window. But as he grew older he became fiercely protective of his sisters, and everybody in his family.

At the time, the kids were city kids because that's all they'd ever really known. But Steve was lucky, because our home backed onto Moonee Ponds Creek, a tributary of Melbourne's mighty Yarra River. He'd be out there exploring for hours on end and come back with his gumboots full of water, soaking wet, but thrilled with little lizards that he'd caught, excited to show me and always seeking my approval. Nine times out of ten, though, he wouldn't come home on his own at all—I'd have to go out searching for him at dusk. So his attempts to try to impress me often backfired because I'd have to go out and find him.

I realised that from very early on he enjoyed the same kind of things that I did as a kid and so I started to take him with me out into the bush. Even at his young age, I could see he had that same curiosity about the natural world that I had as a young boy. He was a great observer of animal behaviour and driven by a natural curiosity. But he was just never where he was supposed to be: Steve came with a guarantee from birth that if he could go missing, he would.

When he was just four years old, I took him out to Sunbury, on the western periphery of Melbourne. I was headed there on a mission to catch eastern brown snakes. Its hilly boulder-lined paddocks with very little undergrowth supported a large population of these particular snakes. I was catching them for subcontractors to Eric Worrell, founder of the Australian Reptile Park in Gosford, who would then milk them for their venom and send it to the Commonwealth Serum Laboratories—an

Australian government department researching antidotes to Australia's venomous inhabitants.

The brown snake antivenom had only been around for ten years or so then. It had been introduced in the mid 1950s, and it took a lot of venom milked from a lot of brown snakes to develop it, and then to keep the antivenom on hand around the country. And it was sorely needed: brown snakes were responsible for more fatal snakebites in Australia than any other snake, and the antivenom would go on to save many lives.

Catching snakes was a hobby; I wasn't paid for it, it was just something I liked doing. I started getting to know people in the industry and made a lot of friends from whom I learnt a lot about reptiles.

I would always bring Steve with me if it was practical. We both got a lot of satisfaction out of these trips—it wasn't a one-sided thing. It was a good exercise for me as a young dad. I taught him bush skills, and he relished learning all about the environment and how it all worked in the wild. He was a good learner because he was just so naturally inquisitive, a little sponge soaking it all up, asking more questions than I had the answers for.

But similar as we were in that respect, we were also totally different in others. I was measured and relaxed, and would always take my time. Steve was the polar opposite of that, completely hyperactive. I would go so far as to say that he was a monster child at times. Steve was not your ordinary toddler.

This made field trips a nightmare on occasion. I'd be trying to creep up on snakes out sunning themselves, and before I'd get close enough to catch them they'd take off down a hole in the ground because he'd have scared them away. So I was trying to concentrate on the job at hand, while also looking after a child who couldn't stand still for more than two minutes. On this day he was in sight just over a slight rise, not far away. But then I must have lost concentration for about a millisecond, because he suddenly vanished.

Then I heard him shout out, 'Dad, I got one, I got one!'

I knew straightaway that this wasn't going to be good. I raced in the direction of his exhilarated voice. 'Where are you?' I shouted, struggling to catch my breath.

'I've got a big brown snake!'

I thought I had been running as fast as I could but those words doubled my speed. As I clambered over granite boulders, I finally saw him on the side of a hill. My heart was in my mouth as I caught sight of him. He didn't have one snake. He had two. Two of the biggest eastern brown snakes I had ever seen, one in each hand. He had no catching bag, wearing only sandals, the skin on his feet fully exposed. It was another lesson in parenting that I knew I needed to be more attentive to in the future—in particular, workplace health and safety.

Brown snakes are the second most venomous snake in the world. But worse than that, they're also some of the most nervous. Most snakes seem to tolerate human interaction without a great deal of agitation, but common brown snakes get displeased very quickly indeed. And here was my four-year-old son, only knee-high to a grasshopper, holding two of them by the tail. They were longer than the kid was tall, with their heads still on the ground, hissing in anger as he held them up. They could quite easily have swiped him. Either of these snakes could have killed him with just one drop of their lethal venom.

As I reached him, I gave him a backhand and he immediately dropped them. 'You bloody idiot!' I shouted. I had hit him with such force that he rolled down the hill backwards. He didn't cry, and I'd hit him hard enough to make any kid cry. Afterwards I felt really bad about hitting him so hard. In the intensity of that moment I felt I had no other option. I had to act instantly to remove him from the immediate and very real danger. If booting him halfway across the paddock meant he wasn't going to get bitten, then I was okay with that. I was just so angry with him. And I was even more angry with myself, that I'd let him get that far from me because I had been focusing only on the job at hand.

He eventually got up and dusted himself off. I went down to him and explained that my reaction was due to the risks he'd taken. His knees were skinned and bleeding but I knew his pride was hurt more than anything else. Then I walked over and caught the snakes correctly, showing him the safest way to do it, all the while reiterating how it was not something that a boy his age should be doing. As I did, I reasoned with him. I told him how dangerous it was. That we were a long way from the truck, and from medical help. That because he was only a little fella, if either of those snakes had bitten him it would have killed him. He'd have been as dead as a doornail, it was as plain as that. And that would have been a bad day to be his father.

I learnt a valuable lesson there and then about how the dangerous field I was working in could be perceived by someone his age. My risky hobby was commonplace to him because he knew no different. I guess to most children, your parents are your action heroes: you just want to imitate them and follow in their footsteps. *Well, this is how Dad does it, so I can do it too.* But after that day, I realised I had to try to teach him care, and that even superheroes can make mistakes. It's hazardous enough for an adult to deal with a brown snake, let alone a kid who has no idea what he's doing, just fuelled by gusto and enthusiasm and an inability to perceive the risk.

In the car on the way home, after my heart rate had returned to normal, I turned to him and said, 'Steve, this is one of those things that your mother doesn't need to know.' And he never told her. It was definitely on a need-to-know basis and this was one of those situations where Lyn didn't need to know, if he was ever to be allowed out with me again.

After that experience, I realised I needed to teach him how to handle himself with snakes, and he was keen to learn. We started back at the basics, handling a non-venomous variety. For Steve's sixth birthday, I bought him his first snake: a tropical amethystine python thereafter known as Fred the python, or Big Fred. I had wandered into our local pet store and there he was, an exquisite specimen unique to the rainforest areas of Far North Queensland.

Amethystine pythons are the largest non-venomous snake in Australia, and this particular fella was twelve feet long, far too big for that kid to handle on his own at first. But Steve was awestruck. He had to care for Fred on his own, learning what he needed to stay alive, what he ate and how warm his enclosure needed to be. He loved every minute of it and got him out every chance he had, when finally he grew big enough to handle Fred alone.

Which brings us up to the day I nearly died on the job site, buried in that hole like a wombat in a burrow, and the catalyst it became for our family to pursue a new direction. Certainly after that day it was vivid in my mind what I really wanted to do. Wildlife was on my mind constantly.

Dad taught me to work hard, but also to enjoy the work you do. I had become a plumber because I admired him and

I wanted to work alongside him. But when he retired, so did my enthusiasm for the job. I realised it wasn't the job that had been motivating me but the quality time I got to spend with my dad. After all those years, there came a time when there was no more challenge, no more goals to achieve.

And in those last few years of plumbing, I had moved into rock blasting because there was more money to be made there. It enabled me to pay off the house a lot quicker. But the weather made doing that kind of work in Victoria simply awful. I'd come home covered in mud and soaking wet from sewage and rain, boots full of sloppy mud, and absolutely freezing. Some days, I'd come home three or four times and change. And as happened that fateful day, the trenches I was digging would quite often cave in and then I'd have to dig them out a second time, and I'd be silently cursing with every single shovel-full of wet, thick mud.

I'd had a few other minor accidents in the lead-up to the cave-in, and I came to the conclusion that if I kept going the way I was going, it could well be a short life. When you're regularly using compressors, drilling rock, blasting with explosives and using a lot of heavy machinery, it can be all too easy to become complacent. Even just fatigue would easily lead to accidents, and there was no such thing as workplace health and safety back in those days. Then, one day, one of my good friends made a fatal mistake while blasting rock, detonating the explosives too early, and he didn't survive. That shook me up. It once again brought home to me just how unnecessarily risky that kind of work was, particularly given we were more or less financially stable by then.

So our decision to leave Melbourne and follow our dream was a culmination of many things that had built up over time. It just takes one thing to start you off thinking, and then there's some other little incident which sets you off again, and it escalates from there, until one day you are forced to make a decision. Financially, we would have been better off staying in Melbourne—that was the safe option. But at the end of the day we had to weigh up what was more important: money or our happiness.

Our early discussions about starting a reptile park had been a bit pie-in-the-sky, just a farfetched dream. But as we returned again and again to this idea, and started to research it a little, it grew increasingly plausible. We knew we'd have to build the reptile facility in Queensland, because it was far too cold in Melbourne. And we knew it would have to be on a traffic thoroughfare to put us on the map.

Lyn had such a wonderful philosophy. Her advice was always the same, with our kids and for life generally: 'If there's something you can't do, you just don't want it badly enough.' Her ethos had a really positive influence on me and it was perfectly true. If you wanted something badly enough, you pulled out all the stops to do it. The most important thing is to ignore all the nay-sayers around you. If you can do that, and believe in yourself, then you'll succeed. It doesn't really matter how impossible it seems. You've got to believe that you're going to achieve what you set out to do. If you believe in yourself, there's no reason why you can't do it.

Everyone we spoke to in Melbourne laughed at our idea when I first told them, and I can't blame them: we Irwins weren't renowned for doing anything out of the ordinary. Our every move up until this point had followed a disciplined plan. We heard it all: 'You'll be back,' 'You won't make a go of it,' or 'It won't work.'

But I was determined it would. Our new business venture would not only support the family financially, but also be an exercise in togetherness. In starting a reptile park, we really wanted to achieve something lasting.

In November 1972, on a field trip to catch snakes for snake contractors in south-east Queensland, we found the perfect three-and-a-half-acre property for sale beside the main highway in a town called Beerwah. So we bought it, and that was that. We had made the first leap towards our dream of running a reptile park. We were ready to thaw ourselves, and our menagerie of reptiles, in the tropical sunshine state. I didn't sell the business, I just shut it down. For the first time in my adult life, I felt a fire ignite in my belly.

Big Fred's going to love it here! I thought to myself. *He's going to be the star of the show.*

2

Beerwah Reptile Park

It was one year of hard yakka before the whole family moved up to Beerwah. In those years I drove between Beerwah and Melbourne, building the foundations of the facility. I clocked up that many kilometres along that highway it would've been equivalent to driving the entire distance around Australia. I sold the family home in Essendon, as well as our beautiful brick-veneer beach holiday home down at Port Lonsdale that I'd built with the help of my handy brother-in-law, Graeme. Finally, I sold our prized Dodge Phoenix, which I had bought for Lyn. What a machine it was, an immaculate vehicle that felt like driving your lounge room around town. I regretted the sale of that car most of all. That hurt a lot but we traded it in for a brand-new Toyota Landcruiser, a more practical vehicle for the roads that lay ahead of us. The sacrifices were coming hard and fast as we faced the realities of following our dream. But we were prepared to tackle them headfirst.

My apprehension about whether we'd actually be able to pull this off was building in the background. But I suppressed it, reasoning that while I knew nothing at all about the zoological industry, we did have experience in running a successful family business. We also had a fervent determination to make a go of it.

I firstly built a large shed on the new property, hammering in every nail and screwing together every last sheet of corrugated iron by myself. We planned to live in it until we could afford to build a family home, so I made it homely. It had all the creature comforts, and our creatures could be housed comfortably in it too. The businessman in me knew we had to open the front gates first and start to earn an income before we could afford anything better for ourselves. We were going backwards in order to go forwards.

It was the end of 1972 when we made the final move to Queensland. We took the kids out of school and they had to bid farewell to the only friends they'd ever known. I'm not sure whether the kids were excited at all, or just depressed. Our eldest daughter, Joy, stayed behind in Melbourne with Lyn's parents, Nanna and Pa, to finish her final years of schooling before joining us in Queensland. That wasn't an easy decision, especially for Lyn, but at that stage of Joy's life we felt it was the most practical thing to do.

We loaded up our new cream and green Landcruiser and tandem trailer with all our worldly possessions. We all fitted tightly into the car—Lyn, Mandy, Steve and me, and Trinni, our large white fluffy Samoyed dog—wherever there was available space. Our collection of snakes was simply put in bags scattered at our feet, tightly knotted at the end to stop them from escaping on our two-thousand-kilometre journey north.

We didn't label the bags, so we had to take care not to mistake them for clothing.

We blew four tyres on the trailer in the first hundred kilometres because it was so unbelievably overloaded. Like a tortoise carrying its shell, we were carrying our entire life on the back of that rig. Slowly and steadily, we made our way to our new property. And when we finally arrived, it was a shock for the rest of the family to look at the bare bush block and realise the work that lay ahead. It was a blank canvas, but at least it was our very own blank canvas.

I decided that when I left Victoria I wouldn't go back to playing professional badminton. Time was too precious, with every moment we had being spent on preparing the park for opening. When I'd been playing badminton, training for state titles had been a constant challenge, and I probably made it more time-consuming than it needed to be because I was an aggressive player and I didn't like to lose. I couldn't afford now to keep up that kind of regime. I used to train six nights per week, and it was always difficult to find the time. I'd return home from a long day of physical work, eat dinner, run around the suburbs for an hour and then collapse in bed. It took me away from home and the family that I barely saw as it was. Much as I loved it, I had new priorities now. When we moved to Beerwah, the Queensland selectors came to ask me if I'd represent the state of Queensland. I must have thought about it for about a second before I turned them down. Our sole purpose in moving to Queensland was to spend more time together as a family, and badminton was one of the distractions I was walking away from to make that happen. After eleven solid years, I gave it up, just like that. I didn't miss it and I never thought about it again. I had more important things to focus my energies on, like building an entire park from scratch and making ends meet. We were placing all our eggs into one big basket.

After the family joined me in Queensland, we worked together as a team to finish off the reptile park and open as soon as possible. The first thing we had to do was build an eight-foot-high security fence around the entire three and a half acres. Lyn worked industriously out there with me every day, mixing concrete in the cement mixer while I concreted in the posts. We eventually had another lady helping us too. It was an unusual sight to see in those days, two women mixing concrete, as in that era women didn't typically work such physical jobs, but those women worked harder than any bloke I'd worked with on a job site.

Occasionally a truck would deliver spare concrete left over from other jobs, which I used to build all the paths in the park, barrowing, boxing and screeding them out by hand in the tropical Queensland heat.

When the kids came home from school, they got involved too. It was a great feeling to finally have that intimacy as a family for the first time. The family couldn't have worked together in the same way when I was plumbing. And it was a gratifying feeling to know that ultimately we could all feel a real sense of ownership of this project.

After six short bone-aching months, working through all the hours of the day and night, we finally opened the park on 11 April 1973. Our first unassuming black-and-white advertisement in the local newspaper read:

> Stop! You can't go past without calling in to see one of Australia's largest collections of native reptiles at Beerwah Reptile Park.

Hop in! All venomous species, as well as death adders, pythons, tree snakes, goannas, lizards, in a safe, natural habitat.

We had no grand opening. We unassumingly opened the front gates of our humble facility one day and allowed people in to take a look at our family's personal collection of reptiles. To begin with that's all it was: a basic assembly of a few snake and lizard pits. We'd built a ticket office by the front gate. There was a large mural of a common brown snake near the front entrance that I handpainted with the help of a projector, and a small chalkboard advertising cold drinks on the thoroughfare. I'd toiled away in the shed at night, cutting information signs out of pieces of metal and painting them, along with all of the backdrops for the snake displays. Gate entry was just forty cents for adults and twenty cents for children.

And we were happier than pigs in mud. We couldn't have been prouder to have come this far. It was testament to the whole family, and everyone could take a slice of the credit; we'd seen what could be achieved by working as a team. It was slow to start off with, but people were certainly curious. It was a promising beginning.

As the months passed, the park seemed to grow bigger every day, and with that the workload grew too. At the end of the day when the park was closed to tourists, the real work day began: all the animals' enclosures had to be cleaned and the animals put away, fed and watered. The jobs just seemed endless, and it was a big undertaking for our small family, but we all pitched in and got it done rain, hail or shine. Compared to plumbing, this was a dream, and I found myself enjoying working out in the tropical Queensland heat. I'd be pouring with sweat as

I worked, wearing next to nothing, but for the first time since I could remember I'd come home with dry socks. It didn't feel like work and we seldom got tired of it. Instead we flourished in our new life among the animals. Despite the fact that we didn't even have a proper roof over our heads, it started to feel more like home than anywhere else we had ever lived.

***

I vividly recall my first visit to a zoo as a young lad in Victoria. While the prospect of seeing spectacular animals was very exciting, in actuality I spent the next couple of days crying about the conditions some of those animals were housed in. To see large animals like big cats, bears and monkeys confined to tiny concrete and steel enclosures was very confronting indeed. The animals were so bored they were almost psychotic. But it was the sight of the chimpanzees that moved me the most. They had no stimulation, no exercise, nothing to help pass the time. They sat looking blankly at the ground, depressed. It was an image that stayed with me for a long time.

Zoos to me seemed nothing but freak shows for people to ogle at. I couldn't get over the fact that animals were being used for our entertainment with no regard for their wellbeing, forced to live in enclosures that didn't reflect their life in the wild at all. At that time, zoos didn't serve any educational purpose; it was just a matter of making money by sticking animals in a cage and keeping them alive as long as possible.

And yet animals are actually far more entertaining to see in the wild, in their native surrounds, doing the things they instinctively do. To me, it doesn't get much better than seeing an animal in its own habitat. The intention behind those old zoos may not have been cruelty—in those days there simply wasn't the knowledge for zookeepers to understand the basic necessities those animals required. Research was in its infancy.

Thankfully, by the time our family emerged onto the wildlife scene, that way of thinking was beginning to shift towards upgrading zoos and linking the animals more closely to their existence in the wild. But it remained a difficult time to find out how to care for certain species. Keeping animals was largely a matter of trial and error. Everything we did was considered scientific research because most of the time our methods hadn't been documented before. Research wasn't widely available.

One day at the reptile park I received a phone call from a farmer who had shot and injured a wedge-tailed eagle. In those days farmers considered wedge-tailed eagles vermin that preyed on their livestock. Bounties were paid in Queensland for dead eagles up until they became a protected species in 1974. Over the preceding fifty years or so, it's estimated that over one million of these magnificent birds were culled under this system.

I couldn't believe his gall, asking me to drive up to collect the bird from his farm on the hinterland after he'd nearly shot one of the bird's wings clean off. The bird then underwent an operation to save his life. Afterwards you only had to look at the forlorn animal to realise that he'd lost his regal bearing. This once majestic, proud bird had lost not only his ability to soar across the skies but also his independence to survive in the wild. Wedge-tailed eagles are an incredibly active aerial species, soaring for hours on end without effort, known to fly to heights of eighteen hundred metres, with amazingly large home ranges. He'd gone from being a powerful bird of prey—the largest of the Australian raptors—to a despondent caged creature.

I was determined to do all I could to restore his confidence. I built him his very own aviary, knowing that he would be in care with us for a long time. Following his operation, I had to massage his legs daily for many weeks until he could eventually stand on his feet. To start with, he just wanted to eat me, but in the end I had earned his trust enough that he'd come and sit proudly on my arm, digging in his dagger-like claws and allowing me to stroke him.

I'd marvel at the veneration he demanded, as he nobly puffed out his chest and looked down at me over his beak. He had an impressive crew-cut hairstyle, and the feathers adorning his legs made him appear as though he was wearing an oversized pair of pants. He was an absolutely magnificent bird.

I was becoming so distressed by what people were doing to creatures like him. The more injured wildlife we took in, the angrier I came to feel with the human species in general. With this in mind, I decided to make a sign for his enclosure. With a paintbrush one evening out in the shed, I described his terrible plight.

> This is what happens to our precious native wildlife when people don't care for them. This wedge-tailed eagle, once able to fly long distances, catch his own food, and choose his own mate, has been shot and will be in care for the remainder of his life. He has lost his sovereignty at the hands of humans. Please take better care of our wildlife. It's your responsibility.

Our mission in designing the reptile park had been to educate people about the importance of the wildlife that shares our environment. Because in the 1970s, when we opened the park, the commonly held belief was that the only good snake was a dead one. They were something you'd hit with a stick.

It was a difficult era in which to get people interested in our conservation message. Even the term 'conservation' was such a foreign concept to people, especially when coupled with the word 'snake' or 'crocodile' or anything else with fangs or big teeth. It was almost impossible to change the opinion of that particular generation, where that kind of fear was so deeply engrained.

So we knew we had to work on the kids, to get them involved—to help them to slowly come to appreciate the little bearded dragon or blue-tongue lizard they might find in their backyard. We knew that if we could give people the opportunity to have a positive encounter with something they didn't quite understand, they would have a heightened appreciation for it. We wanted to show people that every creature in the wild was significant and had rightfully earned its place. We were determined to raise the public's consciousness about animals.

As I trawled for more information on keeping birds of prey, I contacted the Queensland government's Parks and Wildlife Services hoping for their expertise. However, instead of receiving information, I was surprised to find myself slapped on the wrist for displaying the eagle. 'Displaying or exhibiting any injured wildlife is against the law,' a department official told me sternly, upon paying a visit to the park.

Threatened with the confiscation of the eagle, I argued till I was blue in the face to keep him. Eventually they backed down, as long as he was no longer displayed to the public. *What's the benefit of an educational facility about wildlife if we can't showcase the plight of animals in the wild?* I thought to myself. In my opinion, they sure had things the wrong way around.

The department was quite happy to read me the riot act but were not so forthcoming in thanking me for the time and expense I'd put into caring for him. Needless to say, I never got the information I'd hoped for.

So the problem remained: how to find the best-practice, up-to-date information on how to care for native animals—or any information at all. I was green starting out. I didn't know much about wildlife other than reptiles and I had to quickly learn how to care for our mounting collection of animals. Before I took on a new species, I would read every piece of literature I could get my hands on, cramming in as much information as I could during every waking minute.

I also started to get in touch with people in the field who were ahead of their time when it came to displaying wildlife. We'd share our findings and observations, and learn from each other. We weren't only learning the right way to do things, but we were also focused on learning from the wrong way. If somebody had made a mistake due to ignorance, then you'd learn from that. It was just as important to find out what not to do.

Lyn and I wanted to run the park as an educational facility, with the ability to care for injured animals and release them back into the wild when they had recovered. Still searching for information on wedge-tailed eagles, I decided to get in touch with David Fleay, an Australian naturalist widely known for his work in rehabilitating native wildlife who kept birds of prey and was a world authority on wedgetailed eagles. David had his own park, Fleay's Fauna Reserve, on the Gold Coast, just a couple of hours away.

David and I immediately hit it off. Talking to David was like talking to a human encyclopaedia. He was painfully shy so there wasn't much small talk, but information on wildlife just flowed out of him. He never wrote anything down, it was all stored in his head. I made it my mission to extract it all.

I enjoyed visiting him regularly, learning as much as I could from him. He always made me feel welcome. He'd make me a cup of tea and we'd go and sit somewhere quietly in the tranquil surrounds of his nature reserve where we wouldn't be interrupted, and he'd give me all the time in the world to answer my questions. Talking to David was better than anything I'd read in a book. I thought he was better than sliced bread.

I regarded him as an elder statesman; he'd been involved in wildlife for so many years and was a true pioneer. Like David, I never wrote down any of the information he bequeathed to me. I guess he and I were a bit alike in that once something in the wild captured our attention we'd never forget it.

One day, while I was admiring his incredibly large bird-of-prey enclosure, David gave me some advice that resonated deeply with me. 'You don't need a university degree or letters after your name in order to be successful in displaying and caring for wildlife. What you need is observation, nothing else. Because that's the only way you're going to learn when it comes to the animals. You've got to think like one.' While it may seem obvious, this ethos was frequently overlooked when it came to working with animals, and I couldn't have agreed with it more wholeheartedly.

I remember once I came across an enormous huntsman spider on the trunk of a rough-barked eucalyptus tree in our park. Huntsmen are harmless garden-variety spiders, common in these parts of Queensland, but they're spectacular: their leg span can grow as wide as the palm of your hand. The large spider, a female, had hold of a male huntsman. They must have just mated—I had missed that bit. Instead, I sat there and watched her consume her mate totally. She ate the whole spider, every last bit, and then washed her face with her front legs as if using a napkin. I was enthralled, thinking to myself, *How good is this?*

Another time, one evening, I was quietly watching a wallaby hanging around on our front lawn. He was loitering by a beam of light trained onto the grass, which was attracting a swarm of insects. Suddenly, with his tiny little hands and some of the best reflexes I had ever seen, he grabbed this rather large moth and ate it, bit by bit, munching on it like it was a stick of carrot. Before seeing that, I'd never have believed that wallabies caught moths. In fact, I'd have questioned the sanity of anyone who told me they did—to me, it was unheard of.

These are just some of those little things that you see from time to time and never forget. You could read it in a book, but ten minutes later you'd have forgotten what you'd read. But when you're in the field and experience it for yourself it's totally different. Observation with your own eyes can be really quite profound.

David was one of the pioneers of the now widespread philosophy that we need to design zoos from the perspective of the animals themselves. His was a lone voice constantly insisting that we make an animal's captive life constructive: not just as an educational tool for people, but for the sake of the animal, keeping its life full of vital purpose. David worked with animals not to provide people with entertainment, but to make them beacons for the survival of the species themselves.

After meeting David I adopted many of his principles in our park. I saw how we could do things better. His work was the higher realisation of a mission that had first ignited in me as a young boy when I saw those miserable chimpanzees. I wanted to make sure that our animals would be not only comfortable but also happy enough to breed so we could eventually reintroduce them into the wild if and when they reached a critical stage out there.

***

It was about this time, in 1973, that I met a terrific bloke who would become my best friend and a big part of our new life up in Beerwah. Peter Haskins was a biologist who'd just emigrated from England with his family, with the aim of setting up a biological supply company. He and his family were driving north from Brisbane when they passed our park and decided to come in for a look-see to get a first glimpse of what were to them exotic Australian animals. What were normal run-of-the-mill things to our family, had captured Peter's attention. He said:

> We saw a man at the entrance squatting next to a bucket filled with water. He was wearing a white-towel hat and no shirt, with a cigarette hanging out of the corner of his mouth. There was a venomous black snake in his hand. He told me he was the owner of the park. Fascinated, I asked him what he was doing. He said, gesturing to the snake in his hand, 'If you don't get its skin off, it'll just die. Snakes need to shed their skin to grow and this guy's having trouble.' I stood there enthralled, not wanting to leave, watching him alternate between soaking the animal's skin and peeling it off meticulously. I considered it a very kind thing to be doing for a snake. That was typical of Bob, you see, the animals always came first.

We struck up a conversation, and immediately realised we were on the same page when it came to our curiousity for animals; this was the kind of thing that made us both tick. And that was it: Peter and his family settled on the Sunshine Coast and we formed a friendship that has now lasted over forty years.

In England, Peter had only seen these kinds of animals illustrated in textbooks, but soon he and I were off on our adventures into far-flung corners of Queensland. We shared a mutual thirst for intrepid adventures, heading out into some of the remotest parts of Queensland to catch things, often for weeks on end without contact with the outside world. Lyn was very good about us going. She realised that without reptiles, there'd be no reptile park.

This new friendship couldn't have come at a better time, because I had started to feel the strain of the financial burden we had taken on. We had rapidly depleted our savings by building and running the facility, and I was beginning to think it might have been a flawed idea. *Have you made the right decision? Are you going to survive? Is it all going to work out?* These questions kept resurfacing the tighter things became. The park could well have folded at any time back then and I would have had to go back to plumbing, which was a sickening thought. We were only just finding our groove as a family and the kids were beginning to thrive in our new life.

Over smoko one day at the park, Peter mentioned that back in England he had grown strawberries as a side business for a while for extra cash and that it had been relatively profitable. I thought about it and then adopted the idea, and we started to grow fruit and vegetables in our down time on our vacant land, to help things along financially. It actually worked out all right.

In the evenings, when the park was closed, Peter and I tended to a strawberry patch across from the front ticket office. We sold the fruit to markets in Brisbane and shared in the earnings. Every evening, I'd be packing fruit in the shed to get it to market by sun up. As I worked out the business side of the markets, I started to grow cucumbers and capsicums too, until we had another idea that was far more appealing: professional fishing.

I invested in a twenty-foot fibreglass fishing boat suitable for conditions offshore. We'd head out to the Barwon Banks, a great fishing location twenty kilometres off the Sunshine Coast where a massive reef system supports large pelagic species. We'd take a big esky and fill it with some of the most incredible deep-sea fish imaginable: kingfish, snapper, red emperor, and so on. The first couple of times we went out we both got incredibly seasick, but thankfully we found our sea legs over time.

We were always so enthusiastic to get out there, and one night this eagerness got us into a quandary. We were twenty kilometres out to sea when we decided to head home, only to discover that the engine wouldn't start. In our haste to get out on the water, I hadn't packed a spare battery, nor did I have any extra fuel; I simply hadn't been thinking properly. Fortunately, we did have a radio and we could just make out the faint light of another vessel in the distance. We radioed them and after an hour or so they finally came to our rescue. They hadn't come any earlier because the fishing was so good that they didn't want to leave their prosperous mark for a couple of clowns who hadn't charged their battery properly. But thanks to these people and their jumper leads, we were able to start our engine and we got home safely in the end.

With a large number of fish out on the reef came a large number of tiger sharks. Hungry tiger sharks were always a hindrance when we were out fishing. Most of the really big fish we hooked were taken by them. Our equipment wasn't up to a battle with a shark: you'd put in quite a bit of muscle reeling in what had to be a really big fish and then you'd see the grey fin surface and realise a shark had stolen it. Those sharks were never far from our thoughts when we jumped over the side of the boat for a swim to cool down in the hottest part of the day, and for this reason we never swam at the same time: one of us would always stay on board to be the spotter. I'd look first, and call out, 'No sharks,' and then Peter would jump over the side, swim beneath the boat, and climb back in. Then it would be my turn. You'd almost walk on water to get back on the boat. It was great to cool off, but we never lingered in the water and we always kept our wits about us.

We'd come home at night, put the fish in the iceboxes, and first thing in the morning Peter would take them up to the fish auction at Mooloolaba. Our catch would be weighed—it'd usually be well over one hundred kilograms—and then the bidding would start. At the end of the day we'd usually pocket five hundred dollars, which was a good sum of money in those days. After petrol and bait expenses, we'd split it straight down the middle. We went out as often as the weather would allow. It evolved into a hobby that we thoroughly enjoyed. It sure beat packing boxes of fruit and vegetables.

Lyn and I kept our financial struggles hidden from the children, but Lyn used to cry a lot when times were so tough. We had gone from earning a decent living in the plumbing business to struggling to make ends meet, living in a shed, then later in a caravan, with three kids. We also had the added responsibility of caring for so many animals without being able to make an income from our new venture until we had more visitors. But thanks to these after-hours endeavours, we were finally able to build a family home in the park. That made life a lot easier for everyone.

I built the house myself in a private area of the park which we called The Compound. It had a big fence running around the perimeter for privacy. It was a very comfortable double-brick house. And almost as soon as we moved in, we wasted no time in filling in every available space with all kinds of critters.

While Lyn really enjoyed getting involved with the reptiles on display, her forte was the rehabilitation of orphaned and injured wildlife. With this in mind, when I built the house I tiled the entire kitchen and dining area and made a little gate so that all the little animals we were nursing could be confined to that area. But the sugar gliders didn't get the memo: they'd flit anywhere they liked around the house. If you couldn't find them straightaway, then sure as anything they'd be making a nest in a tissue box in the bathroom.

Our lounge room was a hive of activity. There was rarely a time when Lyn wasn't caring for orphaned kangaroos, gliders, tawny frogmouths and possums of some variety or another. It wasn't uncommon to walk into the house to see twelve pouches set up on the backs of chairs, koalas hanging off curtains with gum-tree branches entwined in the curtain rods, or Lyn wandering around wearing a beanie with a possum sitting on top. Possums like being up high—so much so that one minute you'd be walking through the house, minding your own business, and the next a juvenile brushtail possum would be clambering up your bare back, digging into your skin with its razor-sharp claws.

Lyn's training as a nurse came into its own during this time; she just loved nursing little things. She started inventing her own milk formulas using powdered milk and yoghurt, because tins of powdered food concentrate weren't even thought of back then. She was always tweaking mixtures and trying out new things and became really successful with it, eventually passing on her knowledge to many carers in the local area.

But caring for little animals was a full-time job that required around-the-clock attention. She juggled regular bottle feeds with running the front ticket office, taking the kids off to school and doing the daily rounds of the park. She was a powerhouse, and rarely got a full night's sleep.

As the park became known in the local area, people began bringing all kinds of animals to us. We'd take them into our care and look after them until they were fit for release back into the wild, or we'd give them a full-time home with us if their injury was permanent. If the kids showed an interest in a particular animal and wanted to raise it themselves, Lyn and I always encouraged them. Mandy, in particular, was right into that, especially with the furry little critters. One of the first animals she raised was a flying fox named Wolfie. Lyn and I were always adamant that the kids had full responsibility for any animal they took on. 'That animal is your concern. You have to learn everything you can about how to care for him,' I said to Mandy as she was handed Wolfie.

And she cared for him very well indeed. He slept in her bedroom by night and went to the park by day. She used to hang him on a coathanger up at the park entrance, but as soon as he heard her voice he would fly over to her. It was a good education for Mandy. She learnt everything an animal needs in order to survive, including the most valuable lesson of all: to send them back to the wild when it was time for them to go home, knowing you'd given them the best opportunity at a second chance.

With so many new animals around the house, there was never a dull moment. In the very early days, a particular trio—Egg Head the emu, Curley Bird the bush-stone curlew and Brolly the brolga—became just like an extension of the family. It was exactly like having another three kids around, because they sure acted like children. We had to parent those animals almost as much as our own kids.

Egg Head was a typical emu: he wasn't all that intelligent. A carer had raised him from a small chick, but when he got too big we were asked to take him on. Egg Head lived with us in The Compound. One day I was painting one side of the house in mission-brown paint, a very popular colour at the time. I was kneeling down on the concrete, concentrating. I wasn't taking too much notice of Egg Head; he used to quietly wander around behind people, just part of the furniture. But the next minute he'd dunked his whole head into the bucket of paint, like a sausage roll into a bowl of tomato sauce.

'You stupid bird brain!' I shouted, but it was too late: he lifted his head out of the paint tin and sprayed wet paint absolutely everywhere. There was mission-brown paint strewn from one end of The Compound to the other, all over the windows, the bricks and the concrete, not to mention Egg Head and me. I had to hang onto him to wash all the paint from his beak, eyes and nose before it dried; it was a race against time.

He loved the water so he'd go mental whenever you put the hose near him, and this day was no different: he kicked his legs, jumped up and down, rolled over on his back, and did all sorts of other crazy emu things while I was trying to hold onto him. Once I'd finished cleaning him off, I set about cleaning the rest of the dried paint off everything else.

Egg Head used to regularly escape from the park. He and his emu friend would somehow scale the eight-foot-high fence, complete with three strands of barbed wire at the top. I wouldn't know about it until I got a phone call from someone in the local area, saying, 'I just saw your emus wandering along the railway line again.' I'd roll my eyes and start up the truck. Sure enough, there would be Egg Head and his offsider, just going for a walk.

Luckily, he wasn't difficult to catch. He'd come up to me and I'd push him down towards the ground so that he'd fold his long legs beneath him, and then I'd get my arms underneath him to pick him up and carry him home. It must have been an unusual sight. But even with all of the headaches he caused, I had quite a soft spot for old Egg Head.

Steve wasn't a huge fan of Brolly, on the other hand, because she'd always pinch his marbles. He'd have his game set up in the yard and the next thing Brolly would wander over and casually swallow them all. He'd have to wait till she'd excreted them before he could collect them, wash them off and play again. In the wild, brolgas live in large family flocks of up to one hundred birds, so the sibling rivalry between Steve and Brolly was the natural extension of her need to claim her territory, which happened to be in all the places he liked to play. But Brolly had a bit of an advantage over Steve: her extremely long and sharp beak. One day she pecked a massive hole in his head, knocking him unconscious, because he hadn't respected her space.

But he used to love dancing with Brolly. It was quite a sight to see the pair of them dancing out in the yard. The brolgas' dance is very graceful; they usually do it in pairs as a mating ritual. She'd jump almost a metre into the air, stretching her wings and extending her neck up, then bow to him and start strutting around. Steve would get Brolly started: he would dance, and then she'd join in. I wouldn't exactly call Steve's dancing graceful but I never got tired of watching Brolly.

Brolgas are monogamous in the wild, choosing a mate for life. I never knew for sure if Brolly considered Steve her boyfriend, or just her dance recital partner. If it was a romantic crush for Brolly, some of their set-tos could certainly be explained as lovers' tiffs.

***

If you took Steve out in the bush, the hardest job for the whole trip would be to keep an eye on him. The only truly successful way, which I never tried, would have been to tie him to the truck or to put a leash on him.

'Can I catch it, Dad?' Steve asked me hopefully on a day trip to some bush near Kenilworth. Steve had spied a lace monitor, more commonly known as a goanna. They're a pretty impressive sight. The second largest of the Australian monitors, they can grow to just over two metres in length. This fella was wandering around in the dry scrub, flicking out his forked tongue to detect traces of prey nearby. Lace monitors are the only lizards equipped with a forked tongue like a snake. I knew it wouldn't have been much use to refuse Steve an opportunity like that; he was like a bull at a gate as soon as he caught sight of him.

'Yeah, sure!' I said, and he raced off after this goanna, which in turn ran effortlessly up a really tall tree. Goannas' exceptionally long claws are perfectly designed for their tree-dwelling lifestyle.

Steve, of course, was right behind it, up the tree like a rocket. That kid could climb like a monkey. He disappeared up into the boughs and I waited at the base of the tree, pretty sure how things would pan out. The next thing I knew, droplets of blood came dripping down the tree, right in front of where I was standing.

'At least you've got him!' I called out to Steve, knowing full well that it was in fact the goanna who had Steve.

'I can't get it off,' Steve yelled, in pain. It had his hand in its razor-sharp teeth. Goannas' teeth curve backwards, making it very hard for their prey to escape.

'Well, you're going to have to bring it down. I'll get it off you when you get back down here. But don't pull away, 'cause those teeth'll cut like razor blades and you'll need a lot of stitches.' Privately, I wondered how he was going to manage climbing back down the tree with a whole goanna still attached.

I wasn't too worried, but I knew what he was going through because I'd been bitten by quite a few goannas over the years, through no fault but my own, and it's reasonably painful. If he could get back down and convince the goanna to let go, he'd finish up with quite a few painful holes in his hand and a bit of swelling from bacteria in its saliva, but otherwise none the worse.

He finally managed to climb down one-handed, but this goanna had a really good hold of his hand and wouldn't let up easily. I finally managed to get its jaws apart and Steve's hand out. I cleaned up the wound a bit; the goanna had made quite a mess. I was surprised and impressed that the entire way down the tree, with this thing attached to him, he'd never complained once. It would have been hurting like hell.

But he'd listened to what I'd told him and done the right thing. It was a good lesson for him: when it comes to working with animals, you have to learn what you can do, and what you can't do, and that if you make a mistake then you're going to have to suffer the consequences.

Some of those trips with him were a nightmare because I'd only have to stop the truck somewhere and he'd be gone, disappearing outta sight. And so I made a point of sitting him down and making him learn how to survive in the bush, how to orienteer by himself—all of those things the Indigenous people of this land knew by instinct. These were vital life skills to have in the bush. 'If you ever get lost out there and you come across a gully or a creek, follow that body of water downstream and you'll always come out somewhere accessible,' I said to him one day, knowing that sooner or later his wandering would mean he'd have to put this advice into practice.

On one of our family holidays, Lyn, Steve and I were touring the rainforest-scattered Atherton Tablelands in Far North Queensland. It's an elevated region of the Great Dividing Range with many wildlife species endemic to the area, including the elusive Lumholtz tree-kangaroo and the golden bower bird. We pulled up at this stunning little spot with a creek running through it. No sooner had we arrived when Steve wandered off, as he always did. But when we decided it was time to go, we couldn't find him anywhere.

'Steve, we're leaving!' I called out. No response. For hours I walked the length of the creek searching for him, calling his name. The thick canopy made it almost impossible to make out the position of the sun. The further we walked, the denser the rainforest became and it was beginning to get dark. Then Lyn and I became really concerned.

'We should find access to the creek further downstream and wait for him there,' I suggested to Lyn, trying to reassure her despite my own trepidation.

We walked back out to the road until we found another little bush track that wound back to the creek downstream. Then we waited. And waited. And after a disconcertingly long time, a very panicked Steve emerged from the rainforest. He was an absolute mess. Not from crying, but he had been ripped to pieces by the prickly hooks of the wait-a-while vine as he'd struggled through the undergrowth.

'You did really well,' I said, patting him on the back as Lyn fussed about tending to his scratches.

He didn't get into trouble for that. In fact, I spent a fair amount of time telling him what a good job he'd done, because he'd listened to the advice I'd given him about following the creek and working his way out of the situation all by himself.

At this time I thanked God that I was still young and fit enough to keep up with him. Otherwise I'm sure he would have been left out there, wandering around, on any one of our field trips. But, still, it was just marvellous that my son wanted to go out on field trips with me. I was finally one of those fortunate fathers who could take him with me wherever I went, because our new life afforded me all the time in the world.

* * *

When Steve was nine years old, I was asked by Queensland Parks and Wildlife Services to relocate a small colony of freshwater crocodiles on the Leichhardt River in the Gulf of Carpentaria in Far North Queensland. I decided to take him along with me.

That was a fairly intrepid adventure; roads weren't even built into some of those areas and we often made our own tracks into the places we wanted to go. The crocodiles were living in an isolated waterhole that was about to be drained and filled. Freshwater crocodiles, colloquially known as freshies, are exclusive to the far northern parts of Australia, and it was to be our first experience catching wild ones.

I'd long had an interest in crocodiles, and soon after the park opened, I got in touch with the owner of Hartley's Creek Zoo, north of Cairns, and asked if I could purchase some of his crocodiles. I'd already built the enclosure, so thankfully he said yes and I made the long journey up north to bring them home. My enclosure turned out to be a terrible design, because I hadn't known that freshwater crocodiles are exceptionally good climbers; eventually I had to build the whole thing again from scratch. But that was ahead of me; for now, I just sat admiring them for hours, fascinated. I couldn't believe these animals had remained unchanged for nearly eighty million years. *They must be doing something right*, I thought. The modern human has only been here some 200,000 years. I couldn't wait for the opportunity to see them in the wild.

On this freshie catching trip, Steve and I camped in a magical little spot on the banks of the Leichhardt River. The water was so clear we could see straight to the bottom of the creek bed. During the day we'd go snorkelling and watch the freshwater fish, and the little crocodiles motoring around with their powerful, muscly tails.

Although freshwater crocodiles can grow to more than three metres long, they're shy in comparison to their saltwater counterparts and reasonably harmless if left alone. We camped pretty rough; we didn't have tents or anything like that, we just laid a big tarpaulin on the ground at night with a mattress on top. This set-up wasn't always ideal. It didn't work out too well the night a massive colony of fruit bats decided to set up camp in the tree above us. Without any cover, the bat poo pelted down on us like it was raining. The next morning the splodges of metallic-grey droppings made us look as though we'd been targeted by an army of paint-ball enthusiasts. Observing how they did it made it seem all the more intentional too. Although they hung upside down for most of the day, we were fascinated to watch them swap from hanging by their feet to turning themselves the right way up to hang by their wings in order to excrete. We'd learnt our lesson: we washed everything and found ourselves a new spot to camp the following evening.

As night fell, we set to work to catch these crocs, pushing out into the river in our small aluminium dinghy. I controlled the outboard motor with one hand, and with the other used a spotlight to pick up their red eye-shines reflected on the surface of the water.

'There's one,' I whispered to Steve. 'Take the motor for a second.' I kneeled at the front of the boat and, as we pulled up beside him, I leaned over the side, grabbing the croc around the neck and at the top of his tail and pulling him into the boat.

I'll never forget that first croc I caught. I wanted to keep cuddling it, albeit with a very firm grip, as I marvelled at it. It was fifty centimetres long, a small juvenile, and one of the cutest things I had ever laid eyes on. As I held it, it cried out in fear.

After that the hardest thing was trying to keep Steve in the boat. Over the next few nights, he watched me catch croc after croc as he piloted the boat in the direction of my spotlight. I put the little freshies into bags for their relocation. After a couple of nights observing my technique, I knew he was chomping at the bit so I eventually let him have a go. 'Get up here then,' I said, handing him the spotlight. He was overwrought with excitement as he picked out his first set of croc eyes, and I navigated in the direction of his torch beam. 'Just wait until I tell you to jump!' I said. But he could barely wait; I could see by his already bent knees that he was itching to get out there.

We idled up beside the jaws of a crocodile resting stealthily on the surface of the water. I had checked out the croc and knew it was small enough for Steve to safely handle himself. 'All right, go!' I shouted. He was in mid air before I'd even got the words out, and thrashing about in the water hanging on to this crocodile. But then he disappeared below the surface. It's safe to say that I didn't practise a lot of workplace health and safety back in those days. I just reached over the side of the boat and grabbed him by the back of the shirt, pulling him and the crocodile into the dinghy. He was still hanging on to it, arms wrapped tightly around it and grinning up at me, as I pinned both him and the crocodile to the bottom of the boat. I just shook my head in disbelief, not able to fathom the confidence of that kid. But I was as proud as a father could be, and watched him master his technique over the next couple of days, spearing himself into the water off the front of the boat like a little champion.

We'd get back to camp at some ungodly hour of the night for a cup of tea and a bite to eat, and then I'll be buggered if he didn't want to set right out and do the whole thing again. All I'd want to do was hit the hay, but it was impossible to refuse him because he got such a kick out of the whole thing.

That trip wasn't only memorable for me, it was formative for Steve as well; it was the start of his croc-catching career. We knew then that his interest and passion would only grow, and it sure did. The crocodile thing was in my blood, and it got in Steve's too. It was a continual thirst for more knowledge.

After that trip to the Leichhardt River, crocs became an obsession. I wanted to catch more and more crocodiles for the park and make them a centrepiece of our reptile collection. Our family's passion for crocs must have been fated, because the logo for our very first advertisement for the reptile park was a silhouette of a crocodile, long before we'd ever dreamed of displaying one.

***

The Queensland state government introduced the *Fauna Conservation Act* one year after we opened the park, in 1974. This formed the foundations for the start of the protection of our precious native wildlife. Before that there'd been no limit on the animals anyone could kill or capture. But as this Act came into effect and time passed, I found better ways of doing things and I became ashamed that I'd made such basic mistakes in the beginning.

Before the Conservation Act, anyone could pay a local contractor to catch whatever animal they wanted. I admit that I had been just as guilty of this as anybody else—up until then I'd just gone out and caught whatever I wanted to display. If I wanted a more uncommon native species like a green python or a scrub python, I'd go out into remote areas to find them, and at the same time see where the animal lived and the kind of environment it came from, so that I could better understand the conditions I needed to provide for it back at the park.

Of course, with hindsight, such a free-for-all was completely unsustainable. But in those times, this laissez-faire attitude towards wildlife was the norm. Reptiles, in particular, had no protection in Queensland under the legislation up until this point. Once the Act came into effect, there was a huge learning curve, not just for me, but for the zoological industry across the board, and for the authorities themselves, as we all adjusted to a new way of operating.

Under the new system, I eventually got a permit to catch five freshies to display at the reptile park. Lyn was happy to get rid of me, I think, and her parents, Nanna and Pa, would help her run the park while I was gone. Peter and I headed off with Lyn's brother Graeme, who was also visiting from Melbourne. It was the sort of road trip that wasn't for the faint-hearted.

We first went up to Mount Isa to try to find some. As we studied the banks for crocodile slides, we were disappointed to find only shotgun cartridges lining the rivers and no crocs whatsoever. Where once the crocodiles had been kings of the river, hunters had systematically emptied the area clean of them. I decided to travel further up to the Leichhardt River, to the same place I had taken Steve. I knew there was an abundance of crocodiles in a particular location on the Leichhardt Falls, and so we set up camp there. The river was very low and the falls were dry, so we had a large, shallow area to explore, this time teeming with crocodiles.

The first freshie Peter caught was a tiny little one, a small juvenile, perfect for his first ever catch. But Peter had grabbed it incorrectly and it spun around and bit him, drawing blood with its needle-sharp teeth. Still, Peter had a smile spread from ear to ear like a little kid. 'How good is this!' he exclaimed. 'Now I can go home and say I've been mauled by a crocodile!'

We continued to catch these tiny little freshies while we honed our technique. We'd keep them in the boat and if we caught a bigger one, we'd let the original one go. Landing the bigger ones was a little bit trickier. At that size, we couldn't just reach over the side of the boat and pluck them from the water, because they were too hard to hold. So we had to virtually harpoon ourselves off the boat straight onto the crocodile and push him down to the bottom of the river. The crocodile-catching wound up being quite a playfully competitive exercise, each of us wanting to outdo the other in grabbing the biggest one.

After finally agreeing on the largest five to take—crocs about five feet long—we broke camp and began the long, hot journey home with our freshly caught wild crocodiles. The crocodiles were riding on the back of the ute in purpose-built wooden crates that I had made.

I was getting really concerned about how the crocs would fare on the road. I knew crocodiles were extremely susceptible to stress, and temperatures in the Far North Queensland summer were thirty degrees Celsius and higher. So I decided to stop at Winton, a small town in central west Queensland and the last place to stop for a few hundred kilometres. We pulled into the caravan park, where I asked the owners if we could hire out their laundry for the day. They were immediately intrigued. I realised it was a bit of a strange request—why would three grown men want sole use of a laundry?—but I was hesitant to tell them the reason: I wanted to give a handful of wild crocodiles a bath.

But I needn't have worried: the owners agreed, and actually had quite a laugh about it. In fact, once word got out around town a bit of a crowd formed. I suppose not many people would stop to give a couple of gnarly crocodiles some leisure time in the bath.

So the crocodiles cooled down in their laundry tubs. We spent the entire day rotating the crocs in and out of the water, and watching them closely to make sure they didn't wander off. Their mouths weren't tied up, and these five-foot crocodiles were capable of doing a fair bit of damage to our vulnerable hands beneath the water. Crocodiles are basically one big muscle, incredibly strong. But I didn't like the idea of tying their jaws closed for such long distances. If they'd just eaten when they were caught they may have wanted to vomit, and with their jaws tied I was concerned they might have choked. But I was also worried because I'd learnt my lesson before.

Some time previously, I'd been driving home from Cooktown when I became stranded between some flooded creeks. I was relocating animals needing a new home after a small zoo had closed down. On the back of my trailer were some agile wallabies, a brolga and a fair few big freshwater crocodiles, all in timber boxes I had made for their transport back to Beerwah. For my benefit, the crocodiles had their mouths taped closed to make it easier to manoeuvre them in and out of their crates.

I had been stuck for five long days on the other side of the river and was desperate to get these animals to their new home when another driver offered to tow me through the flooded river. But his engine stalled as we crossed, with me attached by a cable behind him and stuck in the floodwaters too. That was a nail-biting situation, but I finally got the truck out with the help of a couple of other people and headed for home.

It wasn't until I was partway there that I realised I had lost one of the crocodiles out of the crate while the trailer was in the water. I immediately felt sickened as I realised the crocodile's mouth was still tied up. I just hoped like hell that the tape would eventually come loose, and he'd be able to survive that.

That sort of guilt never leaves your memory, and probably for good reason: so you never ever make that same mistake again. I vowed never again to travel with crocodiles with their jaws taped up, no matter how difficult that made matters for me. I'd prefer to be bitten than know that they'd come to any harm because of my interference.

But this time, our freshies all got back to the park, cool and safe and sound. They went straight into their enclosure, where I fussed over them for days, proud as punch.

With these new freshies, all the other animals we'd sourced, and all the injured wildlife locals had brought to us, the park had quickly grown far too big for us to manage on our own. And with money still very tight we couldn't afford to employ any staff. But help soon came as Lyn's parents relocated to the Sunshine Coast from Melbourne. It was a wonderful time: we all got along like a house on fire and they loved their new Queensland lifestyle. And they became a huge help to us around the park.

Nanna was able to help Lyn with everything from raising the creatures she had in her care to looking after the kids. Pa was an exceptionally kind man with a vigorous work ethic, despite his war injury. He started working with me a few days a week, assisting with many of the maintenance jobs. And after already saving my bacon once before, he soon saved my life again.

On that particular morning, I had been doing the rounds, feeding the crocs, when all of a sudden I was looking at a large freshwater crocodile clamped onto my bloody arm; I could see the croc's bottom teeth coming up through the skin from below.

The croc in question was Old Man Freshie—a resident of our reptile park—who was clearly keen to defy the reputation freshwater crocs have for even-tempered dispositions. To be fair, this fellow had every reason for holding a grudge: he had two bullets lodged beneath his skin from an encounter with hunters and it was clear that he'd never forgotten.

I had been cleaning out Old Man Freshie's pond, which he shared with a couple of females. Old Man Freshie was the largest of them, over three metres in length. Freshwater crocodiles don't get much bigger than that. He was aggressive whenever I had to go into his enclosure—to mow the lawn around his waterhole, for example. But on this particular day he had succeeded at something he had long wanted to do—try and eat me.

I must have taken my eyes off him just long enough for him to get too close. Suddenly, out of the corner of my eye I saw him launching out of the water, aiming for my head. I raised my arm to block him and he took hold of that instead. Then he tried to pull me into a death roll. All I could do to stop that from happening was to hold him between my thighs, with my legs like scissors. But I was now stuck: I had no available limbs left to do anything else with. If he'd managed that death roll, it would have cost me my hand. And I was quite attached to my hand.

Thankfully Pa was close by, and I could see him run to my aid. Pa always carried a towel on hot days to wipe away sweat. As he entered the enclosure, I talked him through how he could free me from the jaws of this crocodile. Pa carefully worked the towel into Old Man Freshie's jaw as I pushed his bottom jaw down with my free hand, and I managed to finally pry my arm free. Pa and I then moved like the clappers to get out of Old Man Freshie's way.

My arm was bleeding profusely from a gaping hole. We bandaged it up to stem the blood loss and made for the hospital, where the surgeon checked me over. 'How'd you get all of those holes in your feet?' he asked me.

'I don't have any holes in my feet!' I replied, puzzled.

Slightly amused, he pointed to my feet and said, 'Well, I'm telling you there are holes all over your feet, and they're going to need repairing too.'

We worked out that while the big guy had me bailed up in the pond, the smaller females in the enclosure had been chewing on my feet and I hadn't even realised because the pain in my arm was so intense.

I was more cautious around Old Man Freshie after that. A lot of people thought I should shoot him. But it wasn't his fault at all, I couldn't blame him. I had clearly lost my concentration, and in that kind of environment you simply can't afford to do that.

Well, I guess I learnt the hard way. I was out of action for a long time after that. It took many months of physiotherapy to get the hand functioning again, because Old Man Freshie had devoured vital working parts. But I was extremely thankful to have had Pa on hand that day—to save my own. Pa had proven yet again that he most certainly was worth his weight in gold.

* * *

Steve was one of those kids who needed to be constantly physically tested. Playing sport was one way of channelling some of that restless energy—he seemed to have far more of it than any person of his age required. So he started playing cricket on the weekends. At one match, while under the supervision of his school sports teacher, he was growing impatient on the sidelines, waiting to be called up to bat. But Steve didn't do waiting all that well. So he decided to wander off instead and catch himself a few red-bellied black snakes. Seven, to be precise.

He pulled out one after another from the knee-high grass clumps in a swampy area in a nearby paddock; they were all between one and two metres long. These stunning serpents are distinctive for the crimson scales on the underside of their shiny jet-black bodies and their short, stubby heads. But they are also renowned for their potent venom. When approached, the red-bellied black snake will often freeze to try to avoid detection, making it an easy target for a silly boy to catch; this day that silly boy was my own son, embarrassingly enough. A fiercely shy snake by nature, it will generally only deliver a serious bite after severe provocation.

As Steve had no catching bag, one of his good friends and partner in crime, improvised, emptying the bus driver's esky onto the grass and handing it to Steve. As their engrossed team-mates looked on, Steve wrangled each annoyed snake into the esky, before replacing the seal-tight lid and proudly carrying it onto the bus. The bus driver was less impressed: when he caught wind of the fact that Steve had not only redeployed his own esky as a catching bag but had also brought venomous snakes onto his bus, he floored it all the way back to the reptile park.

I was surprised to see an irate bus driver standing beside Steve at the front of the park. 'Your foolish son has caught red-bellied black snakes and put them in my esky!' he shouted angrily at me.

I looked at Steve. He was beaming and proudly presented me with the esky, excited to bring me his live gifts. But his smile disappeared when he saw my fury. I'm not afraid to admit that

I kicked him up the backside before leading him by his elbow straight down to the house, where I had very stern words with him about risking his life and that of everyone else on that bus by doing something as senseless as that. 'You're an absolute bloody turkey!' I said, a name that I'd become accustomed to calling him whenever he got into mischief. Needless to say, the name 'Turkey' became a common word in our household. It became his lifelong nickname.

Once again he had got caught up in his less-than-normal upbringing, and had forgotten about the possible consequences when dealing with such dangerous animals. The funny thing was, that kid wasn't scared of the red-bellied black snakes whatsoever. But he was terrified of me, stunned by my furious reaction.

I realised that his adventurous spirit would always draw him towards these dangerous situations. I'd long known that he had tons of curiosity and wanted to experiment, which also got him into continual strife with animals. After the events of that day, and the brown-snake incident, I realised it was inevitable that he'd always be finding and handling snakes, and that I wouldn't be able to watch him every minute. I decided that, even though he was just twelve years old, it was time to teach him proper care and safety out in the field with me where he could learn and maybe expend some of that energy under my watchful supervision. Until now he hadn't had a great deal of experience with large venomous snakes, just his few highly dangerous dabbles. I couldn't just tell him how, I had to show him—he wanted to experience everything for himself. I knew that was the only way a boy like him was going to learn.

So I took him on his first trip out to Windorah, on the black soil plains of central Queensland, together with Peter. It was a long drive from home, almost fifteen hours nonstop, and it was difficult to keep Steve occupied for that length of time. Windorah is spectacular: vast plains dramatically butt up against rocky volcanic escarpments. I'd get this incredible feeling when I was up high on those escarpments: I'd look out towards the north-west and there'd be nothing, just an open expanse, for about forty kilometres. To many people it might've seemed a featureless landscape, but it was like a playground for Peter, Steve and me: a huge sandpit for us to scratch around in.

In the distinctive red sandy hills, you could easily see the snake tracks left in the sand. I knew there were plenty of reptiles here and with a huge diversity of isolated habitats to explore, you never knew what you were going to find. Wandering around one day, we discovered areas in the escarpment country where the Indigenous people had lived in ancient times—we found signs of where they'd made their tools and where they'd camped. It was a fascinating place that never disappointed; all we'd do is walk around during the day, or drive around at night, looking for whatever we could find.

One day, Steve and I were walking through a gully lined with clumps of dry, sparse grasses when we saw a beautiful big eastern brown snake. It was doing its thing, moving about in the tussocks of grass, searching for mice by testing the air with its tongue, flicking it out and getting scents of nearby animals back on its receptors.

'Let's just follow him around for a while,' I whispered to Steve, keeping our distance. I wanted Steve to learn how the snake lived, what he preyed on, and the environment he moved about in. We'd been doing this for quite a while when all of a sudden the snake wheeled around and started coming directly for us. Instead of slowly backing away and getting out of its path, I said to Steve, as softly but urgently as I could, 'Just stand still. No matter what that snake does, don't move at all.'

I was confident that it was time for him to learn more about snakes in the wild, in a situation where I could be there to guide him and step in if anything went wrong. I knew firsthand that if he could experience something profound then it would never leave him. Steve was similar to me in that he was a better student out in the field than sitting in a classroom. But still my heart was in my mouth as the snake, unpredictably, slithered right up to Steve's feet. I watched on, immobile, as it flicked its tongue on his bare legs, testing if he was edible.

I realised we had passed the point at which I could have stepped in. I suddenly thought I might have made a terrible mistake; if Steve had become spooked by the snake or made a shift in any direction, that snake would have bitten him. And I was also all too aware that Steve found it hard to keep still for any period of time. I just hoped like hell that he wouldn't move a muscle.

In the end, that snake merely enquired about him and then, realising that Steve didn't smell like a mouse or a lizard, went back to doing his own thing, completely unfazed. Meanwhile Steve's eyes were nearly popping out of their sockets. He was in absolute wonderment at how close that snake had been to him. I looked at Steve's face and I thought to myself, *How good was that?* I knew he had felt something powerful. He had been so confident, just exactly as he needed to be, because in the animal kingdom there's no grey area when it comes to fight or flight: you either run at the speed of light, or you don't move at all.

As he bounded around the campfire that night, he was thrilled. He just wouldn't shut up about that experience. It was unbelievable, the spectrum of emotions that went through that little kid's head. To be able to show him how I felt—for him to now be old enough to digest that kind of information—made me feel really delighted. It was a key moment for him. He viscerally learnt that under normal circumstances, when they're not provoked, reptiles pose absolutely no threat to humans.

I felt really proud of him. It was remarkable how a young boy like him had handled that whole situation. He wasn't afraid or worried, and he had had every reason to be, finding himself being licked by one of the most venomous creatures in the world. He was just so excited to have gained such an insight into the workings of such an animal.

To anyone else, there might not have appeared to be anything in that encounter apart from a few hair-raising seconds. But to me, it revealed that Steve had something really unique, an understanding that went well beyond his years. A force-field. A gift. I believe that children are inherently kind but that as we grow up we repress that, in order to survive. But that kindness just never seemed to leave Steve. The fact that he understood, even at that age, that animals are individual living beings that want their life just as much as we want ours was quite remarkable.

If you don't intuitively understand an animal you're more likely to fear it, especially if it has big teeth or it's venomous or able to do some physical damage. I could always sympathise with people who feared snakes, but to me it simply boiled down to a lack of understanding of how that animal works, nothing more, nothing less.

If only everybody *did* understand. And not just about snakes, but about all animals. If only everyone understood that their motivation isn't to kill us; that in fact every animal out there, including snakes, sharks or crocs, would prefer not to have an interaction with a human at all. If we all had this basic understanding, and understood what animals need to survive, maybe we wouldn't destroy their habitats by felling forests, polluting oceans or poisoning rivers. Maybe, if we all understood, just maybe we'd find a better balance.

Steve never forgot that experience; he talked about it for years afterwards. In fact, when it came to Steve's understanding of animals on their own level, it was just the beginning of something far bigger.

***

In 1977, Mum came up from Melbourne to visit us. The kids loved showing her around and telling her all about the animals, giving her a running commentary on everything at the reptile park. She fell in love with the orphaned sugar gliders living in our house, even as they used our faces as landing pads as they flitted from person to person. I was really glad she saw firsthand our labour of love and knew that it had all worked out for us after leaving Melbourne behind.

Mum fell ill with stomach cancer a short time later, so I went back to Melbourne to spend a couple of weeks with her and Dad, who was still battling with the debilitating effects of emphysema. I knew they didn't have all that long. I wanted to spend time with them on my own, to thank them for the opportunities they had both given me. Everybody has their own ideas about funerals, but I decided that I wanted to spend time with them now, while they were still alive, rather than afterwards.

I wanted to remember them exactly as they were: the strong, hardworking people who raised me.

Shortly after I returned to Queensland, Mum passed away at the young age of fifty-nine. A year later, Dad, now aged seventy-six, succumbed to his own long battle, and joined Mum. I had known that Dad wouldn't last very long without her because he loved her so dearly. They were an inseparable pair and it was comforting knowing he didn't have to withstand a broken heart for too long.

Mum and Dad had both always been so enormously supportive of our ambitions. Lyn would send them newspaper articles about the park when they appeared in the local paper. Mum kept them in a little scrapbook to show off to her friends. Because of their backing, I really felt as though Dad had given me one final tick of approval for the new road we had paved as a family. Although I was sad to say goodbye, I couldn't have been more thankful to have had a dad like him. It's a funny thing: no matter how old you get, you still set out to seek the approval of those you look up to. I knew in his absence I'd still strive for all of those important things he'd taught me: hard work. Passion. Family. Now I'd focus on inspiring my own son in the same way he had affected me.

That felt like the end of my childhood family. It was a very long time before I returned to Melbourne: our southern chapter had well and truly come to a close, and our future was deeply planted in Queensland. Just like trees, nothing can remain standing if its roots aren't deep. There was no more looking back; we were here to stay.

3

Queensland Reptile and Fauna Park

By 1980, Beerwah Reptile Park was steadily trucking along. Every single cent that came through the front gate in takings went straight back into the running of the park. Day by day, week by week, year by year, the park continued to progress and, finally, began to turn a profit. As we became one of the Sunshine Coast's premier tourist attractions, we reached a point where we had even outgrown our name. We decided it was time to rebrand the business to better represent what our little family park had evolved into. As a family, we settled on the name Queensland Reptile and Fauna Park. Beerwah was suddenly too limiting, and we had established more than just a collection of reptiles, having expanded to house all kinds of furry, scaly and feathered fauna. Bursting at the seams on our three-and-a-half-acre block, we also purchased an adjoining five acres next door, allowing us to finally expand the park.

As we got on our feet financially, we could afford to employ staff for the first time. Now that the park had quite literally doubled in size it had become a lot for our small family to manage. But in the early days I struggled to find appropriate people to fill those positions. After the social liberation movement swept across Australia at the tail end of the 1970s, a large majority of applicants openly smoked marijuana and they weren't backwards in coming forwards about mentioning it in the job interview. I'd have to explain that because of the kind of work they'd be doing—dealing with venomous reptiles, crocodiles and large birds of prey—I couldn't risk employing someone with reduced faculties. I don't know how many people I must have interviewed before I finally found a handful of dependable people who shared our vision. It was a small team to begin with, but they were of enormous assistance to the park.

Our eldest daughter, Joy, eventually joined us in Queensland and enrolled in an environmental studies degree at university. Mandy was getting involved in horse-riding on weekends, and both of the girls did a wonderful job running their own business serving food and drinks from a kiosk that I had built at the front of the park. I had made it a point to teach them very early in the piece that with a small family business, whether you were running a reptile park or a kiosk, you needed to be able to do just about anything yourself. Because a lot of the time you'd be the only one around to do it.

When Mandy's involvement in horse-riding competitions became serious, I used to take her to all of her shows, hitching the horse float to the back of my car. She absolutely loved her horses, and I loved going out with her and seeing her immerse herself in something she was really passionate about. Eventually she got her own vehicle. Then one day she called me out to help her with a flat tyre. 'One thing you've got to learn, Mandy, is that if you get a flat tyre you've got to be able to fix it yourself. You've got to learn. So we'll start right here, right now,' I said to her as I arrived at the scene. My advice was always the same. 'Don't use force, get a bigger hammer,' I concluded.

She listened carefully as I talked her through changing the tyre and then repeated the steps over and over until she eventually got the hang of it. I knew then that whenever she went out, she'd be able to look after herself. I was very insistent that both of the girls were independent like that, because I knew that as they got older I wasn't necessarily always going to be around to help them or to be there to do it for them. All of the children wound up being very capable in that way as time went along; you only ever had to show something to them once. Steve, on the other hand—well, he was another story. At fourteen years old he was still escaping out of his bedroom window. I think it takes boys a lot longer to get themselves sorted.

***

Around this time, my mentor and most treasured friend on the wildlife scene, David Fleay, became gravely unwell. In the face of his declining health, David parted ways with his thirty-seven-acre sanctuary to the Queensland government, after which it became a conservation park only displaying native wildlife in their natural environment. As David found homes for his exotic animals, he offered to give me some of his prized animals, including Alistair, an American alligator; his magnificent boa constrictor; and Harriet the Galápagos tortoise, at a staggering one hundred and fifty plus years of age the most esteemed animal I had ever known and a living antique. I was temporarily overwhelmed and then over the moon, delighted to have been entrusted with such special creatures. To receive that from the man I considered one of the best in the business was the greatest privilege I could ever imagine.

Her Majesty Harriet was a much-loved elderly lady with a long history thought to go back to the 1830s, when colonial Australia was just forty-two years old. David had first sighted Harriet at the Brisbane Botanical Gardens in 1939. Back then she was thought to be male, and was one of a trio of tortoises named Tom, Dick and Harry. Upon learning in the 1950s that she had been put up for sale, he purchased her to live out her days in peace at his sanctuary, and subsequently discovered that Harry was in fact a Harriet.

It was plausible that Harriet had arrived in Australia on a sailing ship in the nineteenth century. Tortoises were often stowed as food for the sailors; up to forty at a time would be flipped on their backs in the hold of the ship, where they could survive for up to a year without any food or water. It was a possibility that Harriet was brought to Australia on the HMS *Beagle* after being collected as a specimen by the great naturalist Charles Darwin himself, and later gifted to the Brisbane Botanical Gardens by the retired captain of the ship.

Harriet made her final, not-so-grand voyage in the back of my humble Toyota Landcruiser wagon, nicknamed the Poo Mobile. It came to have that name because the first three letters of the number plate were P-O-O, which the kids found painfully comical. But Harriet cemented the car's nickname that day, as, far from genteel, she smeared poo throughout the back of that wagon. It stank to high heaven and she made an astonishing mess which took many days of airing out to get rid of the stench.

We had a lot of trouble getting her through the front entrance of the park because she was so impressively large, weighing more than two hundred kilograms. In the end we removed an entire panel of the fence and chaperoned her in the Poo Mobile right up to her new enclosure. She was greeted by a throng of journalists and visitors who had gathered in excitement to welcome such a highly esteemed creature. I had made her a beautiful enclosure, complete with a heated house to retreat to in the cooler winter months. We were determined to give Harriet a home fit for the grand old queen that she was; it really did feel like we were receiving a member of the royal family, we were just that thrilled to welcome such a special creature into our care.

Harriet fast became an adored addition to our family, as well as a favourite of visitors and staff. If we were ever under any stress we would just go and sit quietly with Harriet. We could confide all of our woes to her, and she'd barely bat an eyelid. In fact, because Galápagos tortoises rely more on their eyesight than their hearing, she could probably barely hear us anyway. But she absolutely relished fresh fruit and her favourite treat of all, hibiscus flowers. It was like taking flowers to our grandmother: we'd arrive at her gate with a bunch of pink and red hibiscus and she'd slowly make her way over to us. She'd slowly devour them all, eyes closed in pleasure. We'd sit beside her and she'd stretch her neck out like a periscope for us to scratch her creased, leathery skin. She had a face like E.T., feet like an elephant and a domed shell the size of a mansion.

It was hard to get my head around all the years she'd been on the planet. I wished that Harriet could somehow share her knowledge of our world, from the perspective of one of the longest-lived vertebrates on the planet. I'd think about her long journey, which had begun with her infancy as a tiny little tortoise hatching somewhere off the west coast of South America that finally brought her to us at a ripe old age. And I'd always reflect on what a privilege it was to have Harriet as part of our family. And I think she was pretty damn pleased with her retirement too.

Despite the fact that I'd installed a comprehensive drainage system when we'd first established the park, it was prone to flooding. With the arrival of the summer storms, it seemingly only took a sprinkle for the park to be inundated with water. At times we even had to close the park while we waited for the floodwaters to recede. Late one evening as the water began to rise, Mandy, Steve and I headed out to check on the animals. I was particularly worried about a little pen housing injured birds that were unable to fly—a curlew and some baby kookaburras and tawny frogmouths. After taking care of them, we checked the rest of the park and found Harriet's enclosure completely underwater.

'She'll sink like a rock! We need to keep her above the water,' I called out to the kids as we all waded out to Harriet, who was sitting in the middle of a growing pond like a giant boulder. We set about trying to move her to higher ground. We knew we couldn't lift her, so we resolved to take turns to hold her afloat in the now waist-deep water to make sure she wouldn't drown. At the time, you just do whatever is necessary for the survival of the animals in your care. We must have held her for hours before the water eventually began receding. Finally we collapsed in bed, knowing she was out of harm's way.

So imagine our surprise when the next morning we saw our damsel in distress swimming from one end of her enclosure to the other. She'd become buoyant, extending her neck out like a snorkel in the water and breathing perfectly. All two hundred kilograms of her was effortlessly doing a tortoise's version of doggy paddle. Here we were thinking that Harriet was going to drown because our assumption was that Galápagos land tortoises can't swim, and there she was, getting about in her new water feature like she was taking a few leisurely laps of her local swimming pool in a flowery bathing cap. That was such a laugh. Eventually we all witnessed Harriet swimming on many more occasions throughout the wet seasons at the park. Needless to say, we didn't worry too much about her the next time it rained. She was always one step ahead of us, our grand old lady.

On receiving another of David's estimable animals, Alistair the alligator, I could hardly wait to introduce him to Daisy, a beautiful female alligator I already had. I had fond hopes that they'd fall in love. Daisy had always enjoyed making nests in her pen. As she was kept alone, her eggs were never fertile, of course, but she'd tirelessly fuss over her nests regardless. But once I put Alistair into Daisy's enclosure, her attitude changed from big black pussycat to being flat-out aggressive. Those alligators fought like cats and dogs; I couldn't understand it. It all came to a head when Daisy broke Alistair's jaw. It was a bad break: she virtually snapped poor old Alistair's jaw in half.

In those early years of the park, finding any sound veterinary advice was difficult, and I certainly wasn't anywhere near experienced enough in that field. Not a lot was known then about what drugs would work on reptiles, and at times it became exasperating trying to find anyone at all, especially on the Sunshine Coast, who had the knowledge to care for our large collection of exotic and native species.

We eventually stumbled across a local vet named Angus Young, whom we saw for our dog, Trinni. He was working out of a clinic that specialised in normal, garden-variety animals like dogs and cats. But I was immediately struck by his compassion and willingness to get involved when nobody else was prepared to even try. He was such a big-hearted bloke; we could always be sure that no matter the time of day or night, if we called he'd provide his input and give his professional advice. No matter how unfamiliar a species they were to him, he'd only be too happy to try his best. We came to rely on him, and as the years wore on we most certainly would have been up that proverbial creek without a paddle without him.

When Alistair's jaw was broken, Angus agreed on the spot to help and started making enquiries around the world about anaesthetic protocol for alligators. He also tracked down a portable anaesthetic machine. We were finally able to begin the painstaking operation to reconstruct Alistair's jaw. After many hours, Angus had successfully pinned together Alistair's top jaw, drilling a hole through the bone and fixing it in place with a steel pin, all while the kids excitedly handed him his instruments through the fence. It was an exciting procedure for everyone to watch; pinning the jaw of an alligator doesn't happen every day. Everything went exceptionally well—that was until Alistair wouldn't wake up from the anaesthetic.

The anaesthetic had been too much; there just wasn't enough information around. And Angus did an exceptional job then in making enquiries about how to wake a heavily anaesthetised alligator. While Alistair was unconscious, the whole family took it in turns to sit in a lounge chair inside his enclosure, keeping an around-the-clock vigil. Of an evening, I rolled out my swag and slept beside him in his pond, one of the rare times Lyn was upset about the attention I was giving to the animals. It was Christmas and I'd even spent Christmas Day out there in that pond.

'You devote more time to that alligator than to me. When are you spending a night in the house?' she shouted, before taking off in the car after one of the very few arguments we ever had.

But I was so concerned about Alistair drowning. We had to keep him submerged so that he could excrete the excess medication. Alligators will only excrete in the water, so someone had to be there with him to keep him afloat at all times. I decided to take on the job of making sure he didn't drown, keeping my hand under his head to keep him out of the water when he slipped back down. After school, the kids would join me and we'd camp out in the enclosure in our swags by the light of the torch.

Finally, after almost two very long weeks, Alistair opened his eyes. He was a modern-day Sleeping Beauty with a reptilian twist. After his jaw recovered, he returned to normal, as strong as the steel pin holding him together, and now in his very own enclosure. I never paired him with Daisy again, because I had also discovered, during this whole ordeal, that Alistair was in fact Alison. He was not a male alligator at all. Those two females, it seemed, had become territorial.

Lyn eventually forgave me, and I was allowed to sleep in the house again. Angus became one of the most knowledgeable veterinarians in the area, able to treat a variety of ailments across a broad spectrum of exotic wildlife. He certainly stood out for his dedication to always finding out the best practice, despite being unfamiliar at times with the kind of weird and wonderful animals that we often presented him with.

I had a good laugh with David about our escapades with the animals he had entrusted to me. I considered them tests from David, generating some of my greatest lessons yet in animal observation: I learnt that Galápagos tortoises can in fact swim exceptionally well, and that you should never assume the sex of an alligator despite a rather masculine name.

***

Ultimately David's ill health meant he was confined to bed. I found those visits incredibly difficult. I'd still sit by his bedside and have a cup of tea with him, and despite how unwell he became he'd still answer all my questions. When his days were numbered and the end was in sight, I hurried to ask him everything I could possibly think of. When David finally passed, a vast wealth of knowledge was lost with him. That was an awfully sad day for the animals.

He had been a trailblazer: from his work to help develop the first taipan antivenom to pioneering captive breeding of endangered wildlife, he expanded our knowledge of the natural world. His life was dedicated to the betterment of animals and their environment. David was the first person in the world to breed platypuses, emus, koalas, powerful owls, wedge-tailed eagles and countless other native Australian wildlife in captivity. So much of what's known today about our Australian wildlife is thanks to my dear friend David.

***

Monty was my very first saltwater crocodile. I got him in exchange for a monitor lizard that I bred. He was only two and a half feet long when he was welcomed into our park. Almost as soon as I got him, I fell under his spell and for that reason I used to spoil Monty rotten. As soon as I'd closed the gates to tourists for the day, I'd go and sit with him. I thought he was just the absolute king of the park and I'd give him extra food as a special treat. Before long he was over three metres long.

Monty had his own pen complete with a tiled swimming pool, but as he grew he needed more space, so I constructed a spacious new enclosure for him. I was so impatient to show it to him that instead of sensibly restraining him and lifting him into his new home, I thought I could do it without catching him, just let him walk proudly in himself. Monty was a good-natured boy, despite his size; I'd never had any problems with him. I had built a metre-wide alleyway between the pens. I opened the gates of Monty's old pen and of the new enclosure at the far end, and let him into the alleyway. I naively thought I would be able to encourage him to walk there all by himself as if taking my pet dog for a stroll off the leash.

At first everything went to plan. Curious about all the activity, he climbed out of his pond and slowly walked, high up on his legs, halfway to his new home. Salties instinctively tail walk—where their belly and most of their tail are off the ground. In the wild, this is a skill they learn as a hatchling to catch small prey up on the banks. But now, excited that my plan was working, I made the mistake of walking directly beside him, level with his head. A lightbulb went on at that moment. In the instant I realised it I thought, *Well, you're an absolute dummy, Bob*. But it was far too late. I knew very well that the last place for me to be standing was beside his head. Whammo, he got me. You should never stand next to a salty, because they can move sideways so quickly that you won't even see it coming. And I didn't.

The next thing I knew, I was airborne. Monty had picked me up by the hand—the same limb Old Man Freshie had got a few years before—and swung me sideways with such force that I somersaulted in the air and landed on my feet on the other side of the pond. It was all over in an instant; it was just that quick.

I looked at my hand, and said aloud, 'Here we go again.' It was a right mess: he'd peeled the skin of my thumb back. In some ways, I was relieved that he'd grabbed my right hand, because it had never fully recovered, and it meant I still had one perfectly functioning arm. Amazingly, after tossing me across the enclosure, Monty had sauntered into his new pen, so when I had stopped the bleeding we secured all of the fences again. So at least that was done.

But he was obviously annoyed. I'd simply got too close to him for comfort. He thought he'd teach me a little lesson in respecting his space. He clearly had no intention of doing me any great harm, because he'd had the opportunity to come after me again, and he hadn't. He'd just sat there looking at me, like the king of the castle he was, as I staggered around pathetically. He had conveyed his message loud and clear: 'I'm the crocodile. You're the human. *Capiche*?'

When I arrived at the hospital, the same surgeon from last time greeted me in the emergency room. He took one look at my hand and said, 'Have you ever thought about changing your career?'

'You did such a good job last time, I thought I'd come and see you again,' I said.

He stitched me back together and sent me home. But he'd been unable to do anything about the split fingers, which were now even more crooked than they had been before. They were here to stay. But it was, again, just down to pure complacency and stupidity on my part. *One of these days, Bob, you'll learn your lesson*, I thought.

I never held a grudge against Monty; in fact, I appreciated the fact that he hadn't eaten me. He was my first salty, and had given me such an amazing insight into the way they operate, and he wound up being one of those special animals that you never forget. And he'd made sure I'd never forget him: I will have a decent-sized scar on my hand as a reminder for the rest of my days. Yes, Monty, crocodiles do rule.

Not everyone shared our ideas about animals. Our conservation message, in particular, often fell on deaf ears. 'I'd cut off his head with a shovel if that thing came into my yard,' visitors would say of the snakes, or of Monty they'd remark, 'Gee, he'd make a nice pair of boots.' It really used to irk me when I overheard comments like that, but it remained an all too common attitude towards snakes, crocodiles and other gravely misunderstood animals in the '70s.

One afternoon, a group of men lined up to buy entry tickets from Lyn. They'd brought a hefty supply of beer, and when Lyn pointed out that no alcohol was allowed, they proceeded to skol the lot, throwing the empty tins on the ground. They were rough-looking blokes, seemingly as wide across the shoulders as I was tall, and they towered over us as they made their way through the gate.

They wandered around the park for a while until they gravitated towards the snake pit. Here lived our beautiful copperhead snakes, incredibly shy reptiles that will do anything to avoid encountering people. As they leaned on the four-foot besser-block fence at the front of the enclosure, Lyn saw one of the men pull out a tin of beer he'd snuck into the park. She couldn't believe her eyes when he poured the contents onto one of our beautiful copperhead snakes. The snake was soaked in beer and highly agitated.

That was it—I could practically see the smoke coming out of Lyn's ears and I thought to myself, *Oh no, what's Stumpy going to do here?* (Stumpy was my nickname for Lyn because she was such a tiny little thing.)

'How dare you do that to my snakes!' she yelled, as she marched over to him. Lyn had a funny way of walking like that when she was on a mission. Then she ripped the tin of beer out of his hand and, all five feet of her stretched up on her tiptoes, she poured the remainder of the beer onto his head. He just stood there looking dumbfounded. Then she handed the empty tin back to him and with hands on hips shouted, 'Get out!'

I thought she was amazing, as I hid off to one side behind a tree. Those men were twice my size; I certainly wasn't going to provide any assistance. Lyn fought this battle on her own and won decisively, as the men sheepishly retreated. She never tolerated cruelty of any kind towards the animals.

You can't force people to think the same way about the animals as you do, you can only hope they will. It's got to be something they want to accept. You can't teach people, or give them advice, if they're not willing to accept it and embrace the whole message.

***

Noel Peck:

> In 1973, I fatefully noticed a reptile park at Beerwah when my wife Jill had wound up rearing a couple of wallaby joeys. Information on their care was difficult to come by. When one wallaby joey fell ill, I called in to the park to see if they could offer any advice. Advice we did get, marking the beginning of a lifelong friendship with the Irwins.
>
> That day changed Jill's life, giving her the inspiration to care for wildlife. As a result of how far that went, Jill and Lyn becoming the best of friends, and they became so sought after for their knowledge on animal husbandry that together they established the Wildlife Volunteers Association (WILVOS), a successful wildlife rehabilitation organisation that still exists today.
>
> A few years on Bob said to me, 'You drive, let's go', as he encouraged our family to take on a rundown wildlife park of our own in Airlie Beach in the early '80s. Being uncertain about what to do, I asked Bob his opinion and he heartily replied with, 'You can do this'. His expertise was always at the ready, his support unwavering whenever we asked anything of him at all. Those years were the happiest, saddest and most rewarding years of our lives.

A few years later, Jill and Noel sought advice about a gorgeous little grey and mauve female joey named Jedda. To all intents and purposes, Jedda appeared to be a regular rock-wallaby from the local area. But as Jill fed Jedda in a pouch at a Wildlife Preservation Society meeting, a member noticed that Jedda was no ordinary rock-wallaby at all. In fact, Jedda was a highly endangered species: a Proserpine rock-wallaby, or *Petrogale persephone*. This species was thought to have gone extinct, and was listed as that in many marsupial books. Jill quickly discovered that Jedda was the only one of her kind in captivity in the world.

Noel Peck:

> On one of our many visits to the park, Bob was excited to show me some of his new lizards. 'Hi guys!' I said as he held up one to greet me. Straightaway Bob replied on the lizard's behalf, 'Say hello to Dickhead.' The name stuck, and from that moment on we were forevermore known to each other as Dickhead.

***

One of the greatest joys you can have in working with wildlife is to be involved in breeding an endangered species. What better legacy is there than knowing you've contributed not only to important research, but to the very survival of an entire species? If every zoological facility, sanctuary or aquarium took it upon itself to breed just one endangered species native to our country, what a difference that could make out there in our precious environment. It was always in the back of our minds that Lyn and I would get into the breeding side of things, in order to eventually assist in the recovery of wild populations.

Macquarie University in Sydney soon got in touch after Jedda's story made headlines in newspapers. They hoped to come and take samples from Jedda in order to take a closer look at her DNA. It turned out that the university had been carrying out a lengthy thirteen-year study into the genetics of the Proserpine rock-wallaby but it had all ground to a halt with the supposed extinction. With their research they hoped to prove that all sixteen species of rock wallaby in Australia were in fact the one, and that, because of this, different species could mate and reproduce.

Jedda's genetic composition painted a very interesting picture indeed. Their findings showed that out of the nineteen rows of chromosomes, only one differed from that of the close cousin of the species, the endangered yellow-footed rock-wallaby. The scientists focused their research on the most critically endangered of the rock-wallaby species, which they thought needed their attention first. While the Proserpine rock-wallaby is endemic to north-eastern coastal Queensland, the yellow-footed rock-wallaby is endemic to semi-arid areas of New South Wales and South Australia. Up until now, after 6000 years of separation, they had been considered to be two distinct species, but it was looking more and more as though the two could in fact be the same genetic species, despite their different colouration.

To test this theory, the suggestion was made to breed Jedda with a yellow-footed rock-wallaby. As part of the project, Lyn and I got permission to receive a yellow-footed rock-wallaby from Adelaide Zoo, a male named Rocky who hated people with a vengeance. The Macquarie University research team wanted to see if these two different species, separated for six thousand years, would mate and produce a joey together, and if they did, whether that joey would be fertile. If you mate two different species, you get sterile offspring. Just as a mule is the sterile offspring of a horse and a donkey, if a Proserpine rock-wallaby and a yellow-footed rock-wallaby were in fact two different species, then it was almost guaranteed that they too would produce an infertile joey.

After some turbulent first dates, thanks to the very hostile Rocky, the pair eventually had a successful mating and produced a gorgeous little joey named Bindi. To everyone's surprise, the joey turned out to be fertile. That proved that the two rock-wallabies were the same species, and suggested that perhaps their original habitat had been continuous from South Australia right up into Queensland. But then widespread urbanisation, the introduction of feral predators and the change in climate had interrupted their traditional habitats, causing the group to split and become two isolated groups, evolving physically to adapt to their new environments.

Jedda eventually came to live at the park with us, and Bindi went on to live at a sanctuary in Charleville in south-western Queensland, where research continued as she was mated with a colony of yellow-footed rock-wallabies. All of Bindi's offspring were fertile and so the experiment was doubly proven.

When Jedda passed away, the university requested her body for scientific research but we made the collective decision to decline. We felt Jedda had given enough to science, and buried her in the park. In her short existence she had made an incredible contribution to science, resurrecting her species. It was a case of one little hop from Jedda, the day she arrived in Jill's care, and one incredible leap for wallaby kind.

That was a remarkably exciting project to have been involved in, even more so to have undertaken it with some of our very best friends. By turning up when she did, Jedda not only saved both the Proserpine and yellow-footed rock-wallabies, but the Proserpine rock wallaby was then added to the threatened species list, and the Queensland Parks and Wildlife Services commenced a national recovery plan for them.

But fate had other plans for Noel and Jill's park. 'The animals are yours, Bob,' Noel said to me grimly over the phone. In 1983, they had to foreclose on their Airlie Beach wildlife park due to the economic downturn. It was a tough pill to swallow for both of them. They'd put so much work into the unkempt park they'd taken over, bringing it up to scratch in just three short years by working many an eighteen-hour day. Closing down was not a decision that came easily.

Winding down a wildlife park can be particularly difficult: while it is still a business and you need to make ends meet, closing isn't just a matter of downing tools. The animals still need to be fed, housed and cared for with the same attention and expense as when the business was solvent. Noel and Jill were trying to do the right thing by all the animals in finding them the best possible homes.

'When do you want us?' I asked Noel. We were making arrangements to drive up to firstly collect their cassowary. He knew I had a soft spot for cassowaries, a prehistoric bird native to the rainforests of Far North Queensland. Apart from zoos, they didn't live anywhere in the south of the country. Noel and Jill had taken such amazing care of that animal, bringing it back to health after it was rumoured to have been fed only mouldy bread for years.

So Peter and I hitched a horse float to my car to go and bring this magnificent bird back. On arrival, our excitement turned to apprehension when we realised we'd have to get the cassowary out of the enclosure without tranquillising it first. Cassowaries are a flightless bird standing 1.8 metres tall. They're capable of jumping up to two metres. And, most importantly, they're equipped with a five-inch dagger-like claw in the middle of their three-toed feet, which, at the end of their enormously powerful legs, can cause serious damage to human flesh.

'Be careful, or he'll kick you to bits!' Noel said to us with trepidation as we approached the enclosure. But as we got closer, it was clear that, while usually a shy species, this particular bird was well accustomed to people. After cautiously entering the enclosure, Peter moved to one side of him, and I moved to the other, and then we just picked him up, carefully tucking his legs beneath him.

'Where's the problem with this bird?' we teased as we carried him past Noel to the truck. 'He's a dream!'

We loaded the cassowary into a specially prepared horse float, where he was nice and secure. There was just a small eight-inch gap around the top to allow cool air in on the journey home. Noel and Jill had formed such close bonds with all of their animals and it wasn't easy for them to see the first of them driven away. I imagined how this would feel for our own family in the same situation. I felt a deep sense of sadness for them as we drove off with their prized bird. They knew, of course, that they could visit him as often as they liked back at the reptile park.

But we hadn't driven more than fifty kilometres down the highway when I slammed on the brakes. I could see the cassowary in the rear-view mirror, lying dead in the middle of the road. How it had escaped is beyond me, even now. We thought we had considered every possible escape route and secured against them. I was devastated. We moved the body off the road and then the two of us just sat in the car and cried. The guilt that overcame me was unlike anything I had ever experienced before. That it had happened on our watch simply ripped my heart in two. Peter and I didn't speak for the rest of the ten-hour drive home.

When we got back I had to break the news to Noel in a phone call that I had dreaded making.

'Bob, accidents happen with animals. You know that,' Noel said. He was understanding, but I couldn't accept it and I don't think I ever have.

Out in the wild, animals die constantly. And we can understand it: there are predators and prey, and that's just how nature works. But when you take an animal into captivity, then it becomes your responsibility. I think the hardest thing to accept in our line of work is when you've made a mistake that results in the death or injury of any creature. The death of that cassowary was one of the saddest days I can recall in my time working on the wildlife scene. That image never left me. But when you live in a wildlife park and work with animals on a daily basis, they have plenty of opportunities to get their own back.

***

'Yeah, I'm not feeling so good. Did you want to drive?' I managed to say to Peter before slumping in my seat. I was starting to feel the effects of the highly potent venom of a western brown snake, one of the world's deadliest snakes.

Earlier that evening I had been feeding a large western brown snake as part of my rounds. While brown snakes are by nature cautious and shy, preferring to flee before attacking, they will defend themselves assertively when cornered. But as far as brown snakes go, this fellow was a pretty relaxed customer and I'd had him for years. I had put my hand into his enclosure to feed him a mouse and obviously wasn't concentrating because the next thing I knew he had hold of my finger instead of the mouse. *Well, that was pretty dumb*, I thought to myself. And then I planned my next move.

He hadn't displayed any irritated behaviour; it had clearly been a mistake on his part as well as mine that he'd grasped my finger instead of that mouse. It's up to the snake whether he puts venom in his bite or not, and snakes won't waste their venom when it's unwarranted. Most people don't realise that the majority of snakebites are dry bites, just puncture wounds with no venom injected. These days there are testing kits which you can use to swab the wound to check for venom. But back then there was no way to judge—until you started to feel life-threatening effects, that is. And the western brown snake has the same type of venom as the eastern brown snake; that is, pretty much as toxic as it gets.

So I considered all the possibilities as I looked down at the two puncture marks on my finger, now oozing blood. Finally, I said to Lyn, 'That'll be a dry bite for sure. He's not angry or anything. It'll be okay.' I was so sure, I didn't even bother putting a constricting bandage on it to minimise the spread of any venom.

Shortly afterwards Peter arrived at the park and we set out in the truck to catch cane toads by the bucketful for his biological supply business. But now things had taken a turn for the worse. Peter took one look at me and raced us back to the house, as my condition deteriorated rapidly. When we got to the driveway I said to Peter, 'Just drop me off here, I'll walk in . . .' before realising that I couldn't see a thing—I was completely blind. Peter carried me into the house and Lyn immediately called an ambulance.

I was delirious and in and out of consciousness by the time I was rushed into Nambour Hospital, a twenty-minute drive up the highway. Nursing staff and doctors sprang into action. Lyn had called the hospital, even before the ambulance arrived, to let them know what type of snake it was, because it was still early days as far as the antivenom went. They used eastern brown snake antivenom because it would also work on western brown venom. I could hear Lyn's panicked voice as she ran beside my trolley, but I couldn't see her—I was still completely blind. I was also freezing cold—I felt as though I was in the Antarctic without a coat on, when it was actually a typically scorching Queensland summer's night.

'We have to give him the antivenom now or he's not going to make it,' I heard the doctor say, and Lyn hastily agreed. Without wasting another second, he administered a jab. And then, mere seconds later, the lights came back on and I could see again. My faculties rapidly returned. That's how powerful that antivenom is.

It was a very different experience to a black snake bite I'd received a few years earlier in Melbourne, and it surprised me how dissimilar the effects were.

On that occasion I had been feeding the snakes in our Snake Room at our home in Essendon when a substantial black snake, well over two metres long, got hold of my thumb. He wouldn't let go, chewing my thumb as he tried to digest it. After a painful few minutes, I finally managed to work my thumb free. But I quickly realised that, being the nice bloke he was, he had gifted me all of the venom at his disposal. I instantly threw up, and then spent days in hospital, ultimately getting gangrene at the bite site. I came very close to losing my thumb. The rotten flesh had to be cut out again and again over many months before it eventually came good. At that time, there wasn't an antivenom for black snake bites, just a polyvalent, which was a broad-spectrum antivenom.

So in comparing the venom of the black snake and the brown snake, you've got to consider which is worse: thinking you're going to die, or wishing you were dead. The pain of a black snake bite is so long-lasting because it contains necrotoxins that break down body tissue. At least with a brown snake the venom kills you reasonably fast. You might not be able to breathe and things like that, but it'll be over quickly.

Thankfully I recovered completely from the western brown snake bite in no time. But the lesson had been driven home: I shouldn't have considered for a second not getting checked out at the hospital, because it's impossible to tell if a snakebite is dry simply by looking at it. You should always assume the worst. That day could have turned out very differently; I was just incredibly lucky.

But we would be returning to Nambour Hospital all too soon, when, in precisely the same circumstances, Lyn was bitten by another of our park's scaly residents: a death adder. Death adders are also one of the top ten most venomous land snakes in Australia, needing just ten milligrams of venom to kill a grown human. As before, the snake struck Lyn's finger instead of the mouse. And like me, Lyn was so sure that it was a dry bite that she refused to go to the hospital, giving me a dose of my own stubborn medicine. Well, we had been there and done that once before and learnt a very valuable lesson.

'You are, and that's the end of the discussion,' I said quickly, hoping I'd won that round. I rang the hospital to notify them of the type of snake and that we were on our way, and then I wound a constricting bandage around her finger where the snake had bitten her, and up around the whole arm, to constrain the spread of the venom. I marked the bandage where the bite was.

The wound was awfully red and swollen and bleeding a lot from the puncture wounds. Death adders don't grow to be all that long, rarely over a metre. But what they lack in body length, they make up for in fangs: the death adder possesses the longest fangs of any Australian snake.

The hospital staff had once again done everything correctly: they had the antivenom out of the fridge to warm to room temperature in preparation for our arrival, and they had the drips and equipment set up and ready to go. They got Lyn into the intensive care unit, and then the doctor rapidly ran through all of the normal questions, double-checking that the type of snake that had bitten her was in fact a death adder. I showed him the puncture marks on her finger. As they began her treatment I gathered my thoughts and checked my watch. It had been over an hour since Lyn had been bitten. As the doctor was about to give her a dose of life-saving antivenom, I suddenly shouted, 'No, don't give it to her!'

The startled doctor replied, 'Sir, we need to give your wife the antivenom urgently.' But if she had done that, she would have killed Lyn. It had in fact been a dry bite. In all the time that had passed since she had been bitten, Lyn had shown no symptoms whatsoever. Her pupils weren't dilated, she wasn't sweating, the area where she'd been bitten wasn't tingling, she didn't have any problems breathing, her eyesight was clear and her eyelids weren't flickering. She was just sitting up in the bed chatting away, perfectly healthy. So I took her back home.

They hadn't waited for signs of envenomation before preparing to administer the antivenom; they evidently hadn't considered that a snake could bite without injecting any venom. If Lyn had been given antivenom without any venom in her system, it would have been as toxic as a death adder snakebite—but with nothing then available to counteract it. Back then there wasn't as much known as there is today about snakebite effects and venom and antivenom.

These two encounters were pretty big wake-up calls for both of us. We needed to concentrate more on the job at hand and take more care. You can't blame the animal for doing what comes quite naturally to them. If Lyn or I had come to harm from either one of those snakes, it would have been through no fault but our own. All we could do from now on was to take more care. And we certainly did, as I'm sure it wouldn't have been a fourth time lucky.

***

Our collection of snakes wasn't complete until I'd acquired the deadliest of them all, one native to our very own state of Queensland. In the early 1970s, a herpetologist friend of mine from Queensland Museum, Jeanette Covacevich, had been mailed the preserved head of a snake for identification. It had come from graziers Herb and Pearl, from a station west of Windorah in the Channel Country. She couldn't readily identify it but suspected it might be part of the remains of a 'fierce snake', or inland taipan, that hadn't been seen by scientists for a hundred years, since the snake was first described back in the 1870s. This resulted in a quest by the Queensland Museum to rediscover the fierce snake. To begin, Jeanette and fellow herpetologist Charlie Tanner travelled to Herb and Pearl's property to catch a live specimen. In the weeks that followed, they located not one but thirteen of these elusive fierce snakes.

In the decade following their rediscovery, the fierce snake became one of the most notorious snakes in the world, after it was found to have the most toxic venom of any land snake. It was a close relative to the coastal taipan but with four times the toxicity of their venom. One bite would be enough to kill almost one hundred grown men. So I became a man on a mission. My plan? To catch one of these by hand.

Over the years I had got to know Jeanette and Charlie fairly well. I'd discuss all things reptiles with them, drawing on their combined wealth of knowledge that they were only too happy to share with me. Knowing that I could assist them with their findings, Jeanette put me in contact with Herb and Pearl on their property out of Windorah, which was of course one of my favourite places in all of Australia. I wasted no time in driving up there, taking Steve with me on the 2600-kilometre round-trip from Beerwah.

The property encompassed a large expanse of grazing land in central western Queensland with a graphic contrast between the volcanic rocky escarpments and the stark black soil plains. I liked Herb immediately. He drew us a map pointing out the best places to explore, such as a very remote inland lagoon only accessible by a concealed dirt track.

He knew his country like the back of his hand, regularly soaring above it in an old biplane that looked like it was made of cardboard. I didn't go up there with him, but he took Steve up, who was beside himself with excitement. From the skies, Steve was able to take in the vastness of those endless plains.

Herb and Pearl had a feral pig called Piggy Wig. She was more guard dog than pig and she'd stalk you everywhere you went. Much as I liked Herb and Pearl, I didn't get along with that pig at all, and Piggy Wig felt the same way: for one reason or another she took a particular dislike to me. One day while I was out helping Herb unload the mail truck, I jumped off the truck, my hands full of some fencing that had been delivered, and there was Piggy Wig, with all of her piggy authority, forcefully ramming one of her tusks into my leg.

In talking about the fierce snake with Herb and Pearl, it was clear that it hadn't, of course, disappeared for all that time. The snakes had always been fairly conspicuous to local graziers, but generally its home areas in the semi-arid regions of central east Australia were so unbelievably remote, and sparsely inhabited, that before the interest of the Queensland Museum, nobody had ventured out in so long to do the necessary research. To the locals they were just another snake in the bush.

I wasted no time in setting out to find myself a fierce snake. But the time I could spend exploring was dictated by the weather. At Windorah you've got to be prepared to withstand extreme temperatures: in winter it can be fiercely cold, and in summer it can reach forty-six degrees Celsius in the shade. And it only becomes more intense the further west you go. In summer, little can survive above the surface in the heat, so you'd only have a chance of seeing the animals at the crack of dawn or as the sun was setting. And those cooler times were still a scorching thirty-two degrees Celsius.

To escape the heat, and because I had no air conditioning in my truck, I followed this schedule too. I'd hang around a water tank or billabong during the hottest parts of the day.

The bush flies were relentless, the worst I've encountered anywhere. The only place to escape them was in the truck with the windows up, but that wasn't an option because of the heat. So I'd just have to endure them, as they were all over me constantly. When the afternoon brought about a cooler change, I'd get back to searching.

Not a lot was known about the fierce snake's habits, and so it was a bit like finding a needle in a haystack. Looking out at the dry black soil plains, I knew why this species had remained unseen for so long. Below the surface were deep cracks, sometimes wide enough to put my truck tyre through, that teemed with small mammals, mainly rats, for these snakes to feast on. And due to the extreme heat, fierce snakes only surface for about thirty minutes a day. They rarely need to expose themselves, because their prey also lives underground, keeping cool beneath the ground. We had arrived in spring, knowing that was the only time of year when these snakes sun themselves outside their underground labyrinth. But that was about as much as we had to go on.

Despite their fearsome name, giving them the stigma of being an aggressive snake, the fierce snake is actually one of the most placid snakes in the world. Driving cattle was the only time the stockmen would come across these highly elusive snakes. As their galloping horses and cattle caused vibrations in the ground, the snakes would rise to the surface in an aggressive display to show their agitation. In actual fact, these snakes are not aggressive whatsoever.

After a few days of searching, without success, I decided to venture out to the black soil plains earlier in the morning, and bingo: at precisely eight o'clock in the morning, I spotted a dark tan-coloured snake, with a round-snouted head that was noticeably dimmer than its body, making its way through some tussocks of grass along the edge of a crevice. The snake wasn't large, less than one metre in length, but it was unquestionably the snake I had come to find. I couldn't contain my excitement, but I didn't move in for fear of driving him into the crevice. I decided to just lie on the ground, keeping as still as I could manage, and observe him moving in and out of the fracture in the earth.

But he was aware I was there, and flicked his forked tongue in my direction to smell me. I now questioned the wisdom of my move, given how little I knew about them. The fierce snake may be generally calm, but if agitated they don't hold back. During attacks on prey, they're known to strike multiple times with extreme accuracy, envenoming in almost every single case.

But this guy didn't display any aggression, he just observed me and curiously approached me a couple of times. Carefully getting to my feet, I picked him up and lowered him into a catching bag. I felt as though I'd found a hidden treasure.

He wound up being the very first fierce snake in captivity. I doted on him, wasting no time in setting up his enclosure, complete with a background I painted depicting the spectacular black soil plains of his home. Because I'd spent time out in his environment, I was able to replicate his conditions in the wild to the best of my ability in his enclosure. I wanted everyone who came to admire him to find out something about where the fierce snake lives, what they prey on, and how important they are to those arid environments of Australia.

My hope was to eventually be able to breed the fierce snake in captivity, and I went on to catch many more of them, assisting the

Queensland Museum in their research. But attempts at breeding never worked out, and it was hard to work out why but so little was known about them in those days.

Our fierce snake took pride of place in the Snake House at the reptile park, one of the most revered snakes in all of Australia. Thanks to our incredible new addition, our Queensland Reptile and Fauna Park housed the largest collection of Australian species of reptiles in the country. That snake lived to be over twenty years old, becoming not just the first but one of the oldest fierce snakes in captivity.

***

After spending so much time out in the semi-arid desert country west of Windorah searching for the fierce snake, I realised that that area was just a few kilometres from the home range of the perentie, the largest monitor lizard in Australia, which can measure up to two and a half metres long. They live on the escarpments neighbouring the black soil plains. I also discovered that very few zoos were working with them. But after receiving a permit to catch one, I spent years trying without any success. For the largest monitor lizard out there, they're certainly hard to find. Like the fierce snake, they're found only in arid areas of Australia, isolated from human habitation. It became Peter's and my avowed mission to finally catch us a perentie.

Prior to our trip, I'd met a filmmaker named Vic, who'd filmed goanna eggs hatching at the park. He was filming a special on monitor lizards for Channel 7's nature show *The World Around Us*, mainly in Australia, which is home to twenty of the world's seventy-plus species of monitor lizards. Vic decided to join Peter and me in our upcoming trip on the trail of the perentie, in the hope that he could film the moment we first captured one. We sure hoped he'd be able to film a capture too.

Lyn was really good at letting me venture off to catch things and she'd keep the park running in my absence. And having new staff made things easier for me to be able to get away. I'm sure Lyn always snuck in a few changes she wanted while I was away, perhaps hoping I wouldn't notice. Guaranteed, there'd be new flyers or souvenirs in the gift shop when I got home. And I had to concede that the ideas worked out in the end; she always had the foresight and plans to make the park bigger and better.

So Peter and I were out wandering in the rocky outcrops of western Queensland when at last we caught sight of a perentie. It was only a small one, about three feet long. 'Down there, down there . . .' Peter whispered, as he pointed his net at a cream-coloured lizard with tawny-brown designs edged in dark brown across its body. It was absolutely stunning, particularly in contrast to the dry, red earth beneath us.

This is our chance, I thought. And then watched, horrified, as Peter put down his net, picked up his camera and started snapping away.

'What are you doing?' I whispered, as emphatically as I could without scaring off the animal. I couldn't believe it: after so long, we had come so close, and yet here was Peter capturing the moment instead of the perentie. He was a mere three metres away from it, the closest I had ever been to capturing one.

Finally, he carefully lowered the camera, picked up the net again and in one leap he had it. I nearly had a heart attack, I was that excited. Perenties are painfully shy and difficult to find. And they're even more difficult to catch, as they can dig a burrow with their powerful front legs and claws and disappear deep below the surface within the blink of an eye. These burrows can be extensive networks that open onto several exits. Perenties have disappearing down to a fine art.

'She's a female,' I said to Peter as I took a closer look at her. We were both grinning from ear to ear. But Vic had missed the whole thing. Our greatest catch of all time and there we were, alone with a perentie in a net, while the cameraman was off in the distance filming an eagle's nest.

When Vic eventually returned and found us sitting there admiring this monitor, he was determined to get some footage regardless. 'Can you release it and recapture it for the camera?' he asked.

My heart was in my mouth at this request. It had taken so many years to get to this point. If we released her, chances were that she'd escape down a burrow and we'd never find her again. It had been our lucky day to find her in the first place. But we finally agreed, after taking her out to a red sandy plain. We hoped that somewhere like that we'd have a chance of outrunning her before she scampered off over the rocky escarpments.

When Vic was set up, he gave us the cue. As soon as we released her, she took off like a bolt of lightning, making for a tree and effortlessly clambering up the trunk to the highest, fragile branches. So Peter climbed after her, to the very top of the tree, and luckily managed to get hold of her again and bring her back down. We relived the excitement all over again, and couldn't believe our luck that she hadn't escaped us.

Peter took great pleasure in placing her into her very own enclosure when we got back to the park. I couldn't wait for her to be on display. Many of our visitors would never have heard of these creatures before, despite their status as the largest monitor in the country.

When I managed to catch a male some time later, my mission became working out how to breed them. If we were successful, I could return them both to the wild, keeping only their offspring. Our project was off to a good start when the female perentie laid some eggs. I couldn't afford to buy a proper incubator for the eggs so I made my own out of an old poultry incubator. It was a ghastly-looking piece of equipment, but it served its purpose and after nine long months, the first tiny perentie split the first egg and emerged magnificently into the world.

There were six tiny little babies in that first clutch, and they were the prettiest little things. Surprisingly they weren't aggressive when they hatched like some of the other monitors. The perentie was a monitor that had it together. Eventually I made good on my word and returned those original perenties to the wilds of Windorah.

As the park grew, we became specialists in breeding perenties, and many other species besides, in that old incubator. There wasn't anybody else out there trying to breed the large monitors, and so my findings became of interest to many others in the herpetological world. But I couldn't write papers about it—I just didn't know how all of that worked. In the end a researcher from Melbourne Zoo offered to publish scientific papers on my behalf, which was great; we could now share with others what we'd learnt about breeding native reptiles. We bred so many perenties in the end that it was embarrassing.

Vic had continued making his documentary, and now planned to film the world's largest monitor lizards, the venerated Komodo dragons in Indonesia. We couldn't believe it when he invited Peter and me to join him. We didn't have to think twice. I had never been overseas and it had always been a dream of mine to see the dragons, the true dinosaurs of this world.

In the 1980s, Komodo Island was a destination for the intrepid, and tourism to the island was in its infancy. We arrived in a small town called Sape on the island of Sambawa. From there we caught a barge across to Komodo Island. But the water I had to wade through to get from the shore to the barge was full of rubbish, as though someone had emptied a garbage truck straight into the sea minutes before we got there. There wasn't an inch of water visible. It was like nothing I had seen before: beaches back in Australia were pristine in comparison, especially in the more remote areas that I frequented. I wanted to get out there with a big scoop and clean it up; I was horrified by the devastation that rubbish would have caused to the marine environment. The boat finally took off for the island, and as the local kids threw rocks after it, I thought that we couldn't get out of Sape quick enough.

Due to the danger the Komodos posed, tourists had to have a guide with them at all times. Although Komodos eat mostly wild deer, they're renowned ambush predators, with a very stealthy approach, and most often go directly for the throat. They grow up to three metres long, and with no natural predators they dominate the island. The locals leave them alone: fortunately for the dragons, their skin is reinforced with armoured shields, making for terrible leather, so they've always been able to thrive.

To see the dragons with our guide, we first had to buy a goat to sacrifice. After this, the guide took us down to a creek bed where he strung up the goat from a large overhanging tree.

Within no time, Komodo dragons came from every corner of the island. Having a fantastic sense of smell, Komodo dragons can locate a dead animal from up to nine kilometres away. It was a highly primitive thing to witness. They were a mighty impressive sight. They didn't disappoint.

But I very quickly lost patience with being escorted around. Every time the dragons got close to us, the guards would chase them away, and if there was a snake on our path, they didn't hesitate to smash it or beat it off with a stick. So I just started sneaking out. Catching Komodo dragons is of course a major no-no; we just wanted to get them on film. I also wanted to explore this new landscape for all kinds of exotic reptiles. I knew the island was alive with venomous cobras, the enormous Tokay geckos and Russell's viper. I also wanted to interact with the Komodos, see how they lived. Our approach became that it was better to ask for forgiveness than permission.

But you can only do that so many times. One night, I had got as far as the beach and found these amazing snakes that I couldn't identify, when a spotlight was shone directly in my face and I was quickly marched back to my cabin by armed guards. The next day I got caught down on the beach again and the island officials were waiting for me when I got back to camp. I was marched up to the commandant's office and sternly warned that if they caught me again, I'd be kicked off the island.

By that stage, I had become so ill that being escorted off the island was starting to sound like a good idea. Almost as soon as I set foot in Indonesia, I had started to feel unwell, and it had worsened as the trip went on. My stomach wasn't used to the cuisine, and that, combined with my usual fussiness about food, meant that I was pretty much surviving on white rice.

I became so sick that I couldn't keep anything down. Peter was so concerned that he made his own spear gun by fixing a nail to the end of a broomstick and in the middle of the night speared a beautiful reef fish for me to eat. He thought that if I could just get a bit of food into my system I'd turn the corner. But I was too sick to eat anything by that stage.

In the process of catching that fish for me, Peter had planted his hand right on top of a venomous sea urchin, getting toxic spines deep into his hand. His hand was painful for days and he couldn't remove the spines until he turned his knowledge of biology to the problem: he knew the spines were made of calcium, and that calcium dissolves in acid, so he used acidic seeds from the tamarind fruit on the island to extract the spines. That's what I loved about Peter: there was always something for me to learn. It made him one of my favourite people. He was endlessly interesting and made those adventures that much more fascinating when he was around. It doesn't get much better than being in that kind of company.

'We have to get you home,' Peter eventually said. By that stage, I was so weak that I completely caved in. But I had no money left to get back home, and neither did Vic, so Peter gave me fifty dollars, which would get me most of the way home. He offered to come with me, but I didn't want him to miss out on the journey ahead, which would be the experience of a lifetime.

I caught a boat ride from the island which left in the middle of the night. The journey was horrendous, the rough seas throwing our tiny fishing boat around like the inside of a washing machine. I was just so ill on that voyage home. Then the engine failed in the middle of our passage and we got caught in a whirlpool.

There was nothing on board to paddle with and so we had to pull timber boards off the cabin to paddle out of it, and then all the way to shore. There was another tourist on the boat, who told me that eggs would set me right, so when we arrived in Labuan Bajo, a fishing village on the island of Flores, he kindly bought me some from a local market stall. I got them down, but vomited them back up almost instantly. I was as sick as you could get while still being able to walk.

From Labuan Bajo I flew to Denpasar, and then on to Sydney, and finally Brisbane. I was skin and bone by the time I stepped off that last plane, and I'd already been pretty slight. Lyn eventually booked me into a health clinic, I was that ill, and it took me a fair while to recover.

Peter went on to have the most wonderful wildlife adventure, filming all kinds of exotic species, including a close encounter with a Komodo dragon, the bats and swallows' nests in the caves of Kuching, the orangutans of Borneo, slow lorises, tarsiers and giant jungle pythons. I was thrilled to hear all about it and of course I wished I could have been there to finish the expedition, but I couldn't have been happier to be home.

***

In his late teens, Steve wanted to go off and be an independent young bloke for a while. I knew he had a gift for wildlife, but I also knew he had to get the normal teenage thing out of his system first and give himself the chance to find his feet. Although Lyn and I knew he'd had a really unique childhood, growing up in a reptile park and travelling to remote parts of Australia, Steve had yet to realise that. He just wanted to be more normal for a while, more like the kids at school. You know, the grass is always greener on the other side.

He decided to head off to Bali on a surfing expedition with a couple of mates from school. He'd played all kinds of sports—rugby, cricket and soccer—but as a young adult, surfing had really become his outlet. Out on the ocean he could push himself to the point of exhaustion. With surfing, no two waves are ever the same, your improvement is slow, and it's a lot of physical exertion for the chance at riding a wave that lasts only seconds of elation, so he found it a great way to challenge himself to get better and better. But being out on the ocean could also be very calming—a place to quiet his endlessly busy mind.

Lyn was quite concerned about him travelling in a foreign country, far from home, with no way to communicate with us apart from a telephone. But I wasn't worried. That boy could jump on crocodiles. I was confident that he could look after himself.

I also knew that if we didn't let him go, he'd always be wondering what might have been. I believe that if you really feel you need to do something, then you should get it out of your system. Many people never do and I think it chips away at them. I was really confident that a break would give him that time to refocus, and realise what he really wanted to do, whether that was wildlife or working in another industry altogether.

He was gone for many months on that trip. But when he came back, he was a transformed young man—he knew what he wanted to do. Steve never did anything by halves, and now he was absolutely certain. Being away from the familiarity of the park, the unique world in which he lived, had shaken him up, smacked him awake and made him realise his true direction. It was almost as though he had followed the herd to 'normal-ville' but eventually reached a fork in the road and decided to take the sign leading him exactly back to the road he'd already been paving for himself. You have to find your own niche. That's the best reward you could ever hope for: taking the road less travelled, not the well-trodden path.

'Dad, I really want to work for you in the park,' he said. 'I've got so many ideas about what we can do together. I want to help you to build the Crocodile Environmental Park.' And that was that. I don't think he ever took off that khaki uniform again. Steve was never going to shake the wildlife factor. It was in his blood.

Travel log: Bob and Amanda on the road

CAPE YORK, QUEENSLAND, AUGUST 2015

AMANDA

We were out on the river in pitch darkness, with just a few torches to light our way. Bob had assigned me the task of looking for crocodiles. I was nervous, not knowing what to look for and if I would be observant enough. At first, to my untrained eye, there was no difference between the reflection of spiders' eyes on the bank and crocodiles' eyes on the surface of the water. Bob didn't hesitate to show me the ropes. 'No! Crocs' eyes reflect red, spiders' reflect white.'

It was my first time in croc country. With Bob at the helm of the aluminium dinghy, my job was to find a croc's red-eye shine on the water's surface with the powerful spotlight he'd handed to me. Then, instead of calling out to Bob and frightening them off, I was to silently point him in the right direction with an up-and-down motion of the torch beam.

Bob was taking our group of young wildlife enthusiasts for an evening of spotlighting on the water to allow us our first glimpse of a wild crocodile. We'd each driven for days, from different parts of southern Queensland, to experience this. When you see Bob out in a place like this, he suddenly makes sense. You understand why he bypasses the cities and tourist traps in favour of such remote settings. Bob is the bush, and the bush is Bob. There's no other way to describe him. You get to really see him in his element out in the wilds of Far North Queensland.

I finally caught a glimpse of some eerie red eye-shines illuminated by my torch. *It doesn't help the reputation of crocs any that their eyes glow demon-red*, I thought. I won't lie, I also worried briefly that we might be approaching a crocodile bigger than our boat and I realised how much trust we'd put in Bob at this point. But then our boat pulled up beside a tiny freshwater crocodile on the surface of the water, just thirty centimetres long and well camouflaged among sticks and other floating debris. The little guy was floating in the water, completely still, with his legs splayed out like a frog. We three novices on board were ecstatic to lay eyes on our first wild crocodile. It may have been the smallest in the river, but I suspect our animated reaction would have been the same whether it had been twenty centimetres long or two metres. Bob killed the outboard motor and reached over the side of the boat to pick it up.

'Do you want to hold it?' Bob asked me, as if he were about to let me in on a little secret. I knew he was full of knowledge about what I was about to experience, but he wasn't going to tell me—I had to experience it for myself.

I nodded excitedly. I nodded so hard, in fact, that I nearly sent my head torch flying off my skull. I held out my hands and he carefully placed the crocodile into my upturned palms. As I sat frozen, not knowing the etiquette for handling baby crocodiles, Bob busily repositioned my fingers so that I had one hand around the neck of the crocodile and the other tightly around the top of its tail. Once he was confident that the animal was relaxed, and that I had it comfortably in my grip, he sat beside me on the seat of the boat and together we admired its exceptional evolutionary design.

Bob talked me through all the amazing features this crocodile was equipped with in order to survive in the water-world beneath our dinghy. This was the closest I had come to holding a dinosaur, and I couldn't wipe the smile off my face. Microbats flew directly at us as they feasted on the swarm of insects attracted to the light from our head torches; whichever way I turned, life was just teeming around me. I kept saying, 'Wow.' I'm not sure exactly what I had been expecting to feel as I held a crocodile in my hands, but I'm sure it wouldn't have been the affection I was feeling now. The croc's skin was exceptionally smooth on the underside of his body. He had a strong, streamlined tail. And his exterior was well designed for battle, equipped with armour-plated shields across his back. Then within seconds he revealed his fear about this abduction and cried like the little baby crocodile he was, a sound so endearing that my heart just melted. He sounded like a human baby crying for his mum. In an instant, my perception of crocodiles evolved from fear to absolute amazement. A surprising thought emerged: a croc could actually be considered cute!

Bob looked on affectionately at the crocodile in my hands and laughed along with me at my childlike excitement. 'I love him, Bob. I absolutely love him.'

It was as clear as day, despite the darkness that engulfed us, that Bob got a real thrill out of sharing that kind of experience with us. The fact that I had been able to feel a tiny iota of his passion for crocodiles seemed to really electrify him. Bob spoke to the rest of us, beaming. 'And that's exactly my point. If you can touch it, you will love it. These little guys are just so misunderstood. They're an animal just like any other animal. They feel pain, experience stress and they've got a right to survive like any other animal on the planet. The more you get to know about them, the more you understand them.'

He let me hold the crocodile for a moment longer before becoming concerned about stressing him out. 'Come on, little guy, let's put you back. You've got to go and catch yourself some tucker.' Bob took him gently from my hands, gave him one last lookover and then bent over the side of the boat to place him back in the water. Like a flash the little croc was off.

Bob then set off again with a new spotter, ready for another encounter. His excitement was unwavering as he allowed each person on board the opportunity to experience what I just had. We weren't going home until we'd all had a taste of it.

As the boat eventually motored home to camp and the warm tropical breeze blew across my face, I was buzzing along with the thousands of moths attracted to my torch beam. What a kick! I knew how raw and personal encounters with nature could be contagious. I could see why it was important for Bob to break down the barriers we seem to have built up, where the animals are over there and we're over here. Bob was right: people will fear what they don't understand; conversely, once they can understand something they'll ultimately want to protect it. That was certainly now true of me and the other passengers in our vessel. We were the newest crocodile fans in Cape York.

Later, as we sat around the fire in our camp chairs talking excitedly about that hour on the river, Bob explained how his first experience with wild crocodiles was exactly like ours, on that trip to the Leichhardt River with a nine-year-old Steve to relocate crocs. 'Steve was jumping off the front of the boat, on little freshies about that size, over and over, until he started to get in with bigger and bigger crocs as he grew more confident in what he was doing. That was it. We were hooked.'

In my opinion, there is no better storyteller to have beside a campfire than a man who has spent a lifetime capturing some of this country's largest crocs. Over the next few hours we all sat wide-eyed, enthralled by his stories from the early days, of a father and son with no previous experience, equipped with just a net trap, a contract to catch crocodiles and a passion to save them at a time when they were loathed and feared. That had been the beginning of something really quite impressive: the making of the Crocodile Hunter himself.

4

The crocodile hunters

When Steve said that he wanted to work for me in the reptile park, he clearly hadn't thought that it might involve some sort of apprenticeship first. In 1984, Lyn and I took our first holiday together in fifteen years, reluctantly handing our kids the keys to the park. To our horror, but not surprise, we'd only been gone some fifteen minutes when Steve decided to handfeed Anvil, a large resident salty, in front of a thrilled group of patrons. These live crocodile demonstrations continued until we returned six weeks later, horrified to find that not only was he doing this outrageously dangerous thing, but he was also charging people extra for the privilege of witnessing it.

But although Lyn and I were initially not on board, I couldn't help but notice that the entire dynamic of the park had shifted. People were excitedly making their way around the crocodile ponds. This level of audience participation was something we hadn't seen before in the park. Nobody had lined up for anything except for buying a can of Coca-Cola from the kiosk.

Patrons went from vaguely interested at seeing a large stationary reptile, to captivated and awestruck, witnessing firsthand the latent power of a prehistoric animal exhibiting its array of natural behaviours you would only otherwise see in the wild. And, I could see that Steve's unorthodox approach was actually a really effective way of getting across our message about the importance of these colossally misunderstood apex predators.

So I had to suck eggs and admit that to Steve. Those demonstrations were useful in showing why we needed to respect crocodiles. We wanted to show what crocodiles were capable of out in the wild, and this was the perfect way to do it. Mind you, there were no doubt people watching who were just there in case things went wrong. They always had their cameras poised, ready for disaster. But that was human nature. You had to start by getting people interested, and I always liked to be optimistic that we could eventually win those people over too.

* * *

Meanwhile, away from the park and out in the wild, the odds were increasingly stacked against the crocs. I was only just starting to figure out that despite being the ultimate survivors, it had taken humans just thirty short years to decimate these ancient animals, the largest reptile left on earth, with commercial hunting. While Aboriginal people had long hunted crocodiles for their meat using traditional methods, the impact of hunting on crocodile populations had been minimal until the advent of .303 rifles in the 1940s, in the wake of World War II.

Prior to this, crocodiles had been respected for their supremacy—humans simply couldn't contend with the sheer power of a crocodile. But with the introduction of these weapons there was now a reliable method to gutlessly shoot our apex predators. With the pull of a trigger, crocodiles were now targeted for their skin. Cairns became an international hub for this lucrative new trade in hides, which attracted commercial and professional hunters and other recreational enthusiasts from far and wide.

It's a sobering fact that by the time our family opened our reptile park, a mere thirty or so years later, saltwater crocodiles had been nearly hunted out of existence. And when they became scarce, we humans couldn't help ourselves: hunters moved on to target the smaller freshwater species of crocodile. As a result, the freshwater crocodile species numbers then declined dramatically too.

In 1974, the slaughter was halted when both freshwater and saltwater crocodiles were declared protected fauna in Queensland. But it was almost a case of too little, too late, as crocodile populations had dropped to critical levels when Queensland finally became the last of the Australian states to implement this legislation.

Fortunately the thing about Mother Nature is that if you give her a chance she's incredibly efficient at healing herself. Crocodiles were testament to this, as their numbers slowly began to recover when they were finally left alone. Like earthworms, crocodiles don't overpopulate their environment; they have a distinct hierarchy and manage their own populations accordingly.

Of course in dealing only with captive crocodiles, I wasn't privy to most of this until around 1985, when the Queensland Parks and Wildlife Services implemented the East Coast

Crocodile Management Program in response to the rising number of crocodiles in inhabited areas. In my view, it wasn't so much a case of crocodiles encroaching on populated areas as it was humans encroaching on the crocodile's territory. The east coast of Queensland was one of the fastest growing urbanised areas in Australia. These areas weren't remote locations where people were few and far between; these were areas tourists frequented, and where fishermen and farmers worked.

The department didn't have the manpower to monitor the vast areas crocodiles inhabited, nor the expertise to remove them. As a result they decided that crocodile farms and zoological facilities were best equipped to handle the animals that were deemed to pose a risk to humans.

While crocodiles now had greater protection in the wild, our state's crocodile protection service was now legislating and managing the commercial side of the industry. Crocodile farms had started popping up all over the far north. Crocodile meat was introduced onto the market as a by-product after their skin had been turned into wallets, bags, shoes or belts.

I have always been vehemently against this industry, because I believe we shouldn't farm and destroy any native wildlife for profit. To me, the term 'sustainable use' seems to give people an excuse to impose our will on native animals that we have a responsibility to safeguard. I don't care whether it's crocodiles, kangaroos or emus, I don't think we have the moral right. I have many friends in the crocodile farming industry, and they know my views. I think it's very un-Australian to eat our own special, endemic, native wildlife.

And while my opinion was formed long before I ever visited a crocodile farm, when I did I was disturbed by the conditions.

In those days, large numbers of animals were crammed into small pens, competing for space. Crocodiles simply don't live like that in the wild; they're a highly territorial species that competes for its domain and has a well-defined social ladder. The welfare of those crocodiles didn't seem important to those people running the farms. There was a total lack of care about how the animals were kept, and how they may have felt.

But for now the Queensland Parks and Wildlife Services was focusing on trouble spots where humans and crocs were coming into close contact. My brother-in-law Graeme and I decided to venture up to the Gulf of Carpentaria to help the Queensland Parks and Wildlife Service rangers capture a particular saltwater crocodile, which had been demonstrating a lack of fear towards humans. It was frequenting a boat ramp; thereby causing concern about a potential attack, so it had been marked for removal. If we could trap the crocodile, I had approval to give him a home back at the reptile park. So Graeme and I set out on the thirty-hour drive north, towing a tandem trailer full of materials so I could build a transport crate for the crocodile on-site.

In my naivety, I had also arranged in advance a place for the croc aboard a Douglas DC-3, a fixed-wing propeller aircraft, to transport him back to Brisbane. With its large double cargo doors, it was the only way to transport something so large that far. But unfortunately the croc wasn't interested in my flight schedule. After a week we still hadn't trapped the animal.

We knew we were in the right place because we could see the very large slide marks where it was coming in and out of the water. I'll admit the size of those marks made me a little apprehensive. And I was right to be, because when we finally caught sight of him he was the biggest crocodile I had ever seen in my life. It was immediately obvious to me that my equipment and methods weren't adequate to lure and trap an animal of that size. The crocodile was the better part of five metres long.

But the most alarming aspect of the whole expedition was meeting the person who was the catalyst for the department's relocation of the animal. I was astounded when we arrived to find the very fisherman who had lobbied the department for the croc's removal standing waist-deep in murky, croc-infested water, casually casting out his fishing line and reeling in catfish.

'Aren't you concerned about getting eaten?' I asked him.

'I'm concerned about him all right—concerned about him destroying any more of my flamin' fishing nets, that is! That crocodile is costing me a bloody fortune,' he replied. 'But no, I'm not worried about that old bugger bothering me personally. He's been around here for years.'

It all started to piece together in my head: this river was a smorgasbord for that crocodile. There was such an abundance of food around for him, he wasn't interested in interfering with something that might pose a threat to him, like a human. Crocodiles in these parts are incredibly wary of people, having survived the bullet of many a hunter—the bullet casings lining the banks wherever we went were evidence of that. And I couldn't lure him into my little old net trap because there were hordes of thirsty agile wallabies wandering down to the water's edge for a drink every day, an easy feed for a lazy old crocodile. That, coupled with the tempting freshly caught fish in fishermen's nets, meant the bait in my trap was not an attractive option.

It was also clear to me that this croc was being persecuted because that fisherman had unintentionally habituated him by setting his traps in the same place every day over many years. He'd worked out that he didn't have to do much but turn up every day. But just as that crocodile had learnt where that fisherman put out his bait, there would likely also come a time when he'd work out that the fisherman himself would make for an easy target. The crocodile would know what time he put in his boat, where he cleaned his fish, and exactly where he fished, waist-deep in water. That's what crocodiles do; they're a highly skilled, calculating ambush predator.

While Peter and I returned to the reptile park empty-handed, it wasn't long before I got my first hands-on experience with a wild saltwater crocodile. I had again been asked to assist the department by removing a rogue animal from Ninds Creek near Innisfail in Far North Queensland. It had been bothering a cattle farmer, pinching his livestock as they came down to drink from the river. So we went up to have a look at the spot. We could see the slides showing where the crocodile was coming in and out of the water. And we realised that the riverbanks were so muddy that any livestock drinking there would be getting stuck in the mud, making them sitting ducks for the crocodiles.

It was again a case of man encroaching on the crocodile's natural environment. The livestock had access to the creek because it hadn't been properly fenced. Farmers were clearing land, cattle were grazing on riverbanks, and crocodiles were interacting with people because we were moving into their territory. That farmer might have paid his money to the government to own this particular patch of grass, but deed titles don't mean a thing to crocodiles. That old territorial croc had probably fought tooth and nail over decades to claim his patch of that river. We spent a great deal of time on that trip pulling cows that had wandered down to the water's edge out of the mud.

We spent the remainder of our time carefully setting my net trap. This time I had made sure it was a lot larger and lined it with fresh bait, both in the trap and near the entrance to entice the croc in. Then we sat back and waited for time and tide to deliver us a croc. I checked it every morning and after a few days the crocodile was finally in the trap. But there I was stuck: I had a three-metre saltwater crocodile in my trap but no clue how to get him out.

I called the ranger, and when he came down we all worked together to untangle the crocodile from the trap as it thrashed and death-rolled. Every part of my body surged with adrenaline whenever I got close. There's nothing that can quite prepare you for the force of a prehistoric predator in its own environment. There was no particular best way to get it done; we had to work it out for ourselves. While the department ranger knew a little bit more than I did, it wasn't much; we were both learning together.

It was a bit of a procedure, firstly to secure its jaws, and then to secure it with ropes to get it into a ready-made crate I had built for transportation. As the crocodile lay there on the ground, I put my hands on its head and tried to imagine my way inside its mind; to visualise how a species could survive close to one hundred million years with very few physical changes, and also how it'd coped with everything humankind had thrown at it just in the last decades. I sat there thinking how we'd nearly brought this species to the brink of extinction. If we'd managed to kill them all—and let's face it, we came pretty close—then that would have been the end of it. There's no going back when that happens; nature simply isn't an unending resource. Extinction is forever.

It isn't until you put your hands on such a large predatory animal that you feel the underlying power they possess, that you can grasp their sheer muscle, energy and supremacy. Sitting on the back of one when you start to feel it tense and shake, well, there's nothing you'll ever do in your life like that again. It's like sitting on a volcano that's about to erupt.

What stood out to me was that these two crocodiles had been targeted for removal through no fault of their own. Like many wild animals, generally speaking crocodiles don't want to have an interaction with a human. Nine times out of ten, at waterholes tourists and fishermen frequent you'll hardly see a crocodile, because they don't want to be observed. They just want to stay out of the way and not have anything to do with humans at all.

And yet people get complacent, lulled into a false sense of security once the biggest, baddest croc is removed. But he was just the one you could see. Below the surface of the water, with their exceptional underwater vision, in their own aquatic world, there are more crocodiles just waiting for the chance of an opportunistic feed. They know about you, but you don't know about them. That dominant croc we removed, he kept the balance. So, really, even though he was now gone, would you really want to get back in the water?

In 1987, the East Coast Crocodile Management Plan asked for expressions of interest from external subcontractors to remove from certain river systems crocodiles deemed to pose a threat to people, dogs or livestock. Steve and I signed up almost immediately. These crocodiles labelled as a problem were those most likely to have had some kind of negative interaction with a human. In my opinion they were wrongfully accused, but whether we agreed or not, removing them was what we were contracted to do. Steve and I felt our participation in the program was a way to make the best of a bad situation. Our aim became to catch and relocate the crocs before people took matters into their own hands. Saving these magnificent crocs from this hatred and slaughter became our motivation. I had always wanted to display more saltwater crocodiles in the reptile park but I didn't want to buy them from crocodile farms.

I started up my faithful backhoe and began digging crocodile ponds almost immediately, turning our undeveloped five acres into a home for the crocodiles we were likely to catch; it became a new section in our park that we named the Crocodile Environmental Park. I built a series of enclosures with clay bottoms and nice murky water for them to hide away in and grass pens in which they could bask out in the sun. It was basic to begin with, but I knew the crocodiles would be comfortable enough.

I started to visualise making crocodiles the centrepiece of our facility. It wasn't about stocking the park so people could be intimidated by their size or menacing looks: our objective became to bring these crocodiles into the heart of every visitor and help them appreciate the importance of our most significant apex predators. We strongly felt that our participation in the crocodile management program was the best way to protect crocs from humans.

We knew that out in the wild the unjustified hatred for crocs by humans could be reduced by instilling common sense in people, and getting them to exercise greater caution in croc territory. There's no point sugar-coating the predatory nature of a saltwater crocodile: if you get in the water, you run the risk.

Les, Mum and Aunty Kath and the two little horrors in the front, Ron and me. I admired my stepfather, Les.

Mum, Grandma, Ron and me down at Point Lonsdale, out fishing. I used to make those fishing poles out of rangoon cane.

At the church on our wedding day in Essendon. Lyn was about to have Joy at the time this photo was taken. I had a suit and a tie too; I don't think I owned it.

With Joy on a surf ski I made. I made my own surf skis to get further out to sea to fish. Photo taken at Port Lonsdale. It was certainly a favourite spot.

The whole family down in Essendon, Victoria.

Steve at kindy.

Primary school photo of Steve. He was actually pretty good for a boy at school. He was a little bit like me; he liked sports days better than any other days.

Steve hanging up in a tree like an orangutan.

Joy and Steve with Santa. Melbourne days.

A chip off the block. Steve loved it when I'd take him fishing as a kid.

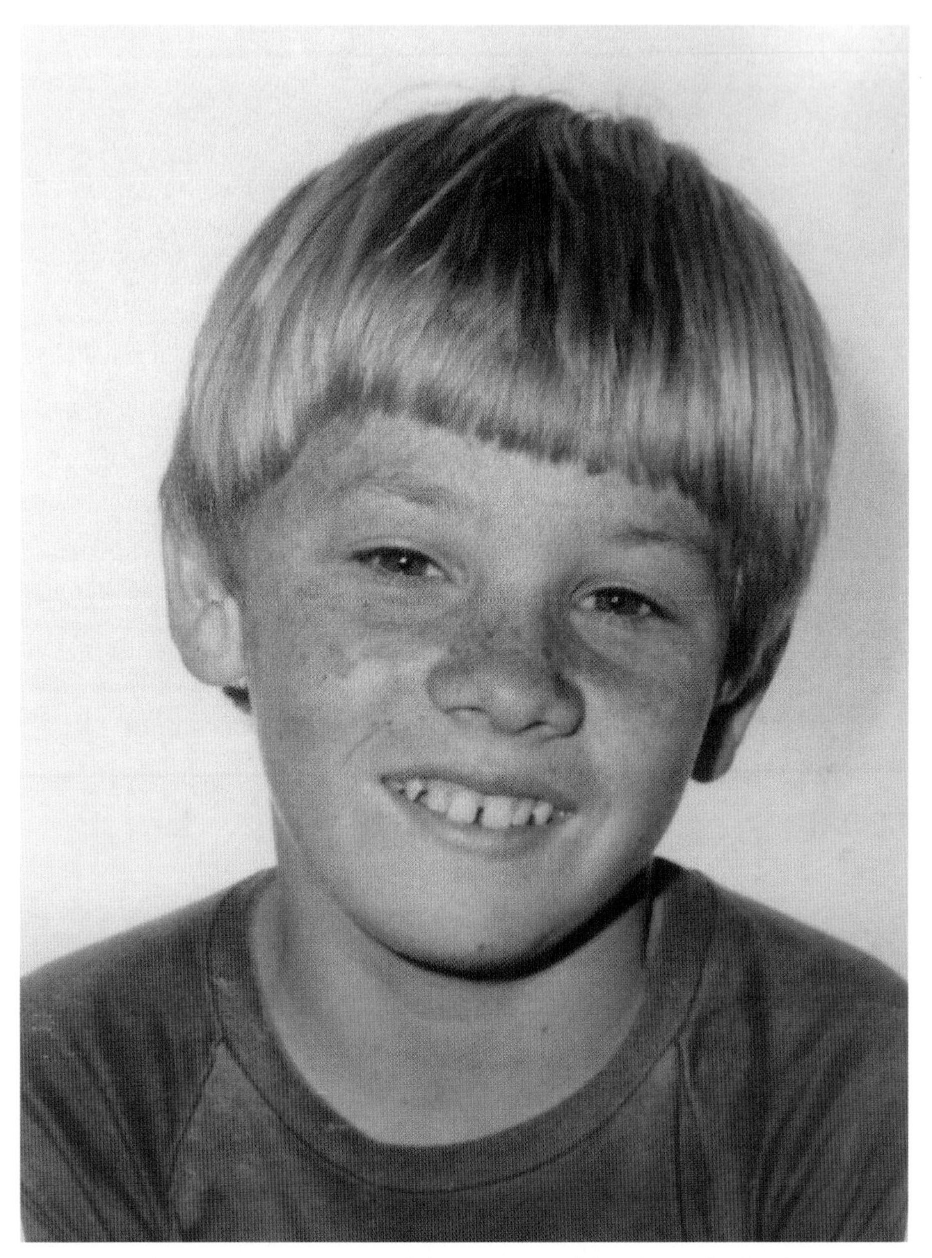

Here's trouble. Steve as a young fella. You wouldn't know by looking at this photo how much energy that kid had.

Steve, Joy, Lyn, Mandy and me out the front of our Primrose Street home. The whole motley crew.

My beloved FJ Holden. I loved that car and also the chick (Lyn) who's sitting on it.

Some of the first wild freshies I caught on an early field trip to the Leichhardt River with my best friend, Peter Haskins. PHOTO COURTESY OF PETER HASKINS

Steve, Mandy, Lyn, Joy and me outside the brick veneer house I built for the family inside the reptile park.

A rare photo of Lyn and me out of khaki.

Steve with a rescued platypus that came in from Beerwah—a local farmer was cleaning the mud out of his dam and came across this little guy. We kept it for a while and then found a nice area to release him. IRWIN FAMILY PHOTO

Steve navigating the rainforests of Far North Queensland as a young man. IRWIN FAMILY PHOTO

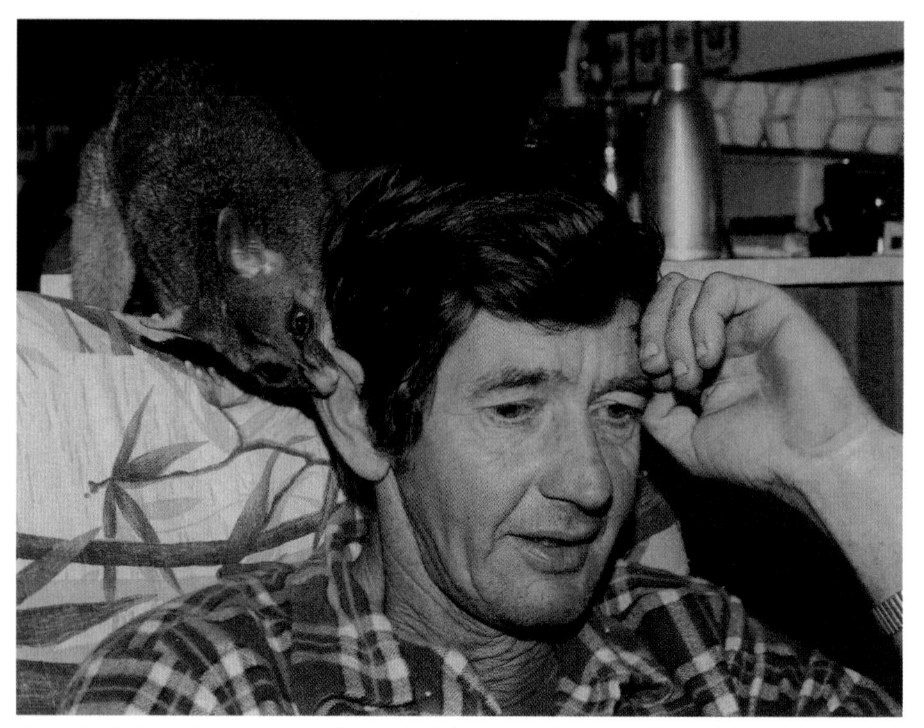

A typical sight in the Irwin household. One of our orphaned brushtail possums chewing on my ear, having the run of the place. PHOTO COURTESY OF PETER HASKINS

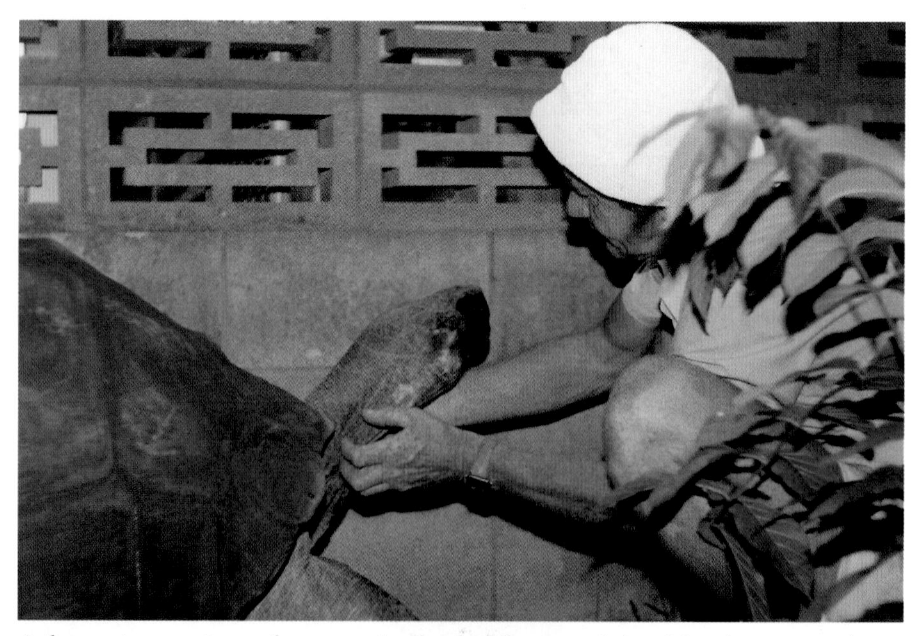

A favourite pastime of anyone in the family was giving Harriet a scratch. What a special animal she was. IRWIN FAMILY PHOTO

Me and Lyn with Fred the python. The first snake that we purchased for Steve, for his sixth birthday. IRWIN FAMILY PHOTO

Lyn, Mandy and me at home in the reptile park. IRWIN FAMILY PHOTO

Steve with his two sisters, Mandy and Joy. IRWIN FAMILY PHOTO

Lyn, Harriet and me. She was just a part of the family. IRWIN FAMILY PHOTO

Me with a green python, a species from the tropics Steve and I had a fascination with. PHOTO COURTESY OF NOEL AND JILL PECK

Bringing our first wild caught Perentie back to the reptile park. We became very successful in breeding these monitors. PHOTO COURTESY OF PETER HASKINS.

Lyn and me at Steve and Terri's wedding in America in 1992.
IRWIN FAMILY PHOTO

Steve and me feeding the crocs for the public, back at the reptile park.
IRWIN FAMILY PHOTO

It wasn't crocodiles that had put us in danger, it was in fact our own species that had put the crocodiles in danger. The Crocodile Environmental Park would be a place where creatures that were feared and wronged because of basic misunderstanding would be respected and valued.

For ten dollars, we purchased from the department a permit to remove fauna under the Fauna Conservation Act. This was one of five permits allocated at that time. All but one of the other contractors were from crocodile farms, where the crocs they removed would go into their facilities as breeding stock, and their young would be raised and slaughtered for their skin.

We all had to supply our own equipment and manpower and there was no financial compensation whatsoever. In fact, we had to pay a royalty to the state government for every crocodile we took out of the water. Thankfully the park was earning enough money that I could afford to pay Steve a wage and he enthusiastically signed on to be my apprentice.

Although it actually became an apprenticeship for both of us; we learnt as we went along. There was no crocodile-handling course we could take, no *Crocodiles for Dummies* handbook. We would learn at the hands of the crocodile itself.

The first permit we were assigned was to remove every crocodile from Cattle Creek, just on the outskirts of Ingham in Far North Queensland, a sixteen-hour drive from our reptile park. Cattle Creek was a vast tidal system popular with locals for fishing and boating. Queensland Parks and Wildlife Services gave us a map of the creek showing the private properties that accessed it. From there on, it was our responsibility to build relationships with the owners so we could access their properties and base ourselves where the crocodiles lived.

So we did our research, loaded up the truck, donned our best khaki shirts and went door-knocking around Ingham.

Stephen Accornero, Cattle Creek:

Dad, Mum and I were having our regular 3 p.m. 'smoko' break on our family sugarcane farm when we noticed a mysterious vehicle approaching the back of our house, loaded up with camping gear, nets, tarpaulins, large wooden crates and an upturned dinghy. In our small town of Ingham, we knew pretty much every local farmer and sugar-mill worker by name as well as their work truck. The two fellas got out of the truck and made their way up to us and extended out a hand to shake. 'I'm Bob Irwin and this is my son, Steve. We'd like to catch crocodiles on your property, with your permission,' the older bloke said. From the looks of these two men, this was not at all what we were expecting to hear. The father wasn't built like any crocodile hunter we'd ever known and his son was just as slight, and only in his early twenties, the same age as me.

Bob did all of the talking, Steve didn't say much. He seemed reserved, although in hindsight we now know this was mostly out of respect for his father, because generally Steve only had one setting and that was full noise.

Bob told us that they wanted not to hunt crocodiles but to save them by catching them as part of a government scheme to remove nuisance crocodiles from our creek. But what intrigued us most of all was their planned method: they were planning to catch the crocs with slightly adapted fishing nets and by hanging homemade weights in trees.

It was certainly an oddity. Nobody relocated crocodiles. When there was a rogue crocodile lurking around, people generally took matters into their own hands. In our part of the world, people either shot them or took them to croc farms. And yet these blokes had driven sixteen hours from the Sunshine Coast in order to catch monstrous crocodiles with their bare hands and then drive sixteen hours back to their park each and every time they caught one, and all to save crocs' lives?

'So, you're experienced at this?' Dad asked. 'I imagine you've caught a lot of salties before.'

'We've only caught one wild salty before, but we'll manage. It's a bit of an apprenticeship. We've got room for fifty or so crocodiles back at the park,' Bob said alarmingly.

Irrespective of their unusual idea, we wanted to help them out. 'Do you know where you need to go?' Dad asked, interested, getting down to business.

They knew precisely where they wanted to access the creek, right down to where they wanted to set up camp on our property; it was an uninhabited area that we used solely for running cattle.

'Okay, then, you can set up your camp here. We'll come and see you in the morning and see how you're getting on,' Dad said, granting them permission.

'We'll be completely self-sufficient. You won't even know we are there,' Bob said. Those famous last words still ring in my head to this day.

The pair of them then set off excitedly to get their camp established. As they disappeared down our driveway, we all just looked at each other, slightly amused.

'They're going to get eaten for sure,' Dad said, and we all burst out laughing.

The subsequent years spent listening to Bob and Steve talk about wildlife had a deep and profound effect on our family and our way of farming. When our land went from cattle grazing to cane farming, we left wildlife corridors along our creeks. We've left a couple of hundred acres to the environment and waterholes along the way to provide natural water sources for the animals. And that wasn't because of a government department regulation; that was all because of the Irwins. Dad and I immediately felt a connection with Bob and Steve. As a father and son who also worked together in our family business, it was apparent that they shared a real closeness, working away and bouncing off each other without having to give each other instructions most of the time. I knew that a bond like that only comes through working with someone over many years. That stood out like a sore thumb.

These days, when I come across the authorities putting a trap out for a croc in Cattle Creek, I have to force myself to stand back. I listen to them talking, 'Don't come close', Don't do this and that'. And I just stand there listening and looking and thinking to myself, 'Yeah you were in nappies when this was all being designed.' But I don't tell them, of course. Understandably they haven't got a clue who I am or the years that I've spent on this creek with the people that I've had the pleasure of having here. They think I have no idea what I'm talking about or how those animals operate. But I know exactly what they're talking about. You know why? Because I was taught by the fella himself—Steve Irwin. I was with Bob and Steve back when it all began.

I'm a bit wiser now, and a bit sorer. But I still remember vividly what it was like thirty years ago. With Bob and Steve we were gifted some of the best times of our lives.

The Accorneros became our closest friends in Ingham over the next few years and ever since, though when we first knocked on their door they thought we were a bit different, that we weren't the full quid. But I think you've obviously got to be a little bit different to do what we were doing.

Park rangers had initially surveyed Cattle Creek by sight and used the number of crocodiles they observed to calculate the total number of crocodiles we were required to remove for the duration of our permit. But we very quickly realised that there were nearly triple the number of crocodiles than the permit outlined.

From the very first moment we set foot in that environment we fell in love with Cattle Creek. It was an impressive tidal system, adorned with rich mangrove and wetland ecosystems fed by the luscious ancient rainforests of the Great Dividing Range. Cattle Creek was such a large expanse that it was more like a river than a creek. This picturesque waterway nourished a wealth of wildlife, from the top of the food chain, the saltwater crocodile, to the smallest members of that intricate web of life, the agile wallabies, the fruit bats, and all of the microscopic marine life below the water's surface. Every animal we encountered, gigantic or minute, was just as vital to the balance of that environment as the next. Nothing was insignificant. The mangroves—plants that specialise in growing in excess salt and moist airless soil—provided shelter and food, operating as a crèche for every organism to breed.

It felt like a playground for Steve and me, this uninhabited landscape teeming with wildlife. We started scanning the riverbanks on the low tides, by day and by night, hoping to glimpse slides left by the crocs we'd come to find. We were entering Cattle Creek via a smaller, winding tributary that hugged the bush; our camp was right at the end of it. But getting our boat in and out proved difficult at times. If the tide was out, we would be dragging our boat across sinking mud that was more like quicksand. You'd be walking along when suddenly you'd sink down to your waist. And the sandflies and mosquitos were a constant hindrance; we welcomed the gusty nights when the sandflies took a night off work.

But as much as we disliked everything that nipped, stung, pricked or prodded at us, they became part of our daily life. If the creepy crawlies got really bad during the day, we'd go down to the creek and cover ourselves head to toe in mangrove mud, which offered some relief. But then we'd have to consider how we were going to remove that thick dark grey muck, now dried and binding to our skin, when we wanted to climb into our swags at night. There were no showers, and we couldn't exactly get into the creek when the crocodiles were out hunting under the veil of darkness. Although I admit that occasionally we did.

Steve and I made all of our own traps out of trawler mesh. Embarrassingly, the first ones I made were too small, so I chucked them away and began again, fine-tuning them as we went along. We also had to consider the tide as we set the traps: if we got it wrong, we risked having a crocodile drown if it got tangled in a trap below the water.

But the most significant thing we learnt was just to think like a crocodile in everything we did. *If I live in this river system, do I really want to go up there and get a piece of pig? Does that trap look too intimidating?* We had to camouflage our traps meticulously, making them look like just another part of the riverbank.

Sometimes it took an entire day to set up a trap correctly, and then we'd wait for low tide to trudge through the oozing mud and position it on the bank, tying it to overhanging branches to keep it in place. When we were happy with how it was assembled, we'd always go back out on the river to take a look at it from a distance. If it didn't look right, we'd get back to work. We weren't satisfied until our traps looked just like another part of the river.

The time spent perfecting the traps paid off. One sign of this was when we caught the same undersized crocodile again: he was too small so we released him, but there was real satisfaction in outsmarting a crocodile that knew the creek better than we did, even more so when we caught him for a second time.

Mary was one of the first really memorable crocodiles Steve and I caught at Cattle Creek. She was special because she was a really big girl, just over three metres long, and we didn't think females even grew that big. She was also a grand old dame: you can tell a croc's age in part from the darkness of its skin, and she was completely black.

We had first seen Mary as we scoped out her territory in our little dinghies. We were thoroughly exploring the entire river system to see what might be around in the way of crocs. We'd just idle along each bank, looking for claw marks, head indentations or slide marks from their heavy bodies. It's easy to track crocodiles in tidal areas like Cattle Creek because you can see their imprints better in the mangrove mud than on a sandy bank. I'd mark the signs we'd find on a hand-drawn mud map and then at night-time we'd return to those spots we found with torches, looking for the red-eye shines of the saltwater crocodile.

We observed Mary for quite a while, working out how we'd catch her. As she sunbaked on the bank, I watched from the boat hidden in the mangroves opposite. Belly slides showed where she'd come in and out of the water; she'd obviously been doing this for years, judging by how much undergrowth she'd flattened over time. As I had to return to the park, I marked all this on a map for Steve, as well as everything I'd witnessed about her behaviour and the areas she frequented. Steve then set the trap and caught her just days later.

That became our way of working: when I was there I would observe the crocs, and then Steve would often hunt them down and trap them. Setting traps became Steve's thing. We worked together as a team, not talking a lot, both knowing what needed to be done. He would always climb the trees to set the weight bags for the traps, because his arms were strong like an orangutan's. And I'd do the preparatory work on the ground, filling the bags with mud and tying them up, throwing the ropes up to him.

After Steve caught Mary, I drove straight up to collect her and bring her back to the park, stopping to have her processed before leaving the far north. When you caught a crocodile, you had to take it to the nearest place to be processed, which in this case was the Queensland Parks and Wildlife Services office in Ingham. Every crocodile we caught had to be measured, sexed and tagged, and issued with a permit to transport it back to the park. It was quite a process: we'd catch a very large crocodile, get it out of the trap, get it back to camp, restrain it, get it in a crate, and then get it out of the crate all over again for the department's records.

Mary continued to breed for us every year thereafter. I'd provide her with all the material she needed to build a nest, and she'd rake it all up and construct it. Then she'd lay a clutch of fertile eggs. The amazing thing is that a female saltwater crocodile builds a slightly different nest depending on whether she wants to have baby male or female crocs. A difference of just one to two degrees Celsius changes the sex of the baby crocs, and she can regulate the temperature of that nest to suit. It's up to her, and she decides what to do in tune with the requirements of her river system.

I always really regretted taking Mary's eggs away from her, but I couldn't leave the hatchlings in that enclosure. They would have just walked out through the fence, out into the park, and no doubt ended up somewhere in the wilds of the Sunshine Coast. It was always really hard on Mary when we'd come to collect her eggs; females are fiercely protective of their nests in the wild. I'd apologise each time as I collected them all, undoing all her hard work.

Saltwater crocodile babies are nurtured by their mum. In the wild, as the eggs hatch, the mother listens for their cries and then digs them out of the nest with her claws. Then she'll carry the hatchlings ever so gently in her mouth to the water. There, she'll continue to watch over them, creating a protected crèche amid floating debris in the shallows in which to hide them until they're old enough to fend for themselves. I was sad to know that Mary, once queen of Cattle Creek, couldn't live as she had in the wild, but I suppose she still had her life.

Of course, when you think like a crocodile might, then you have to wonder if life in a zoo, where you're safe and nurtured, is truly better than being in the wild and taking your chances. We can't ever know, of course, but it was always in the back of my mind with every crocodile we removed.

***

Steve enjoyed taking photographs at Cattle Creek. He was having the time of his life and he desperately wanted to share it all, so he'd take photos of everything: the captures, where he'd found the crocodiles and the new methods he'd designed to process them. He'd hurry to have the rolls of film developed, impatient to show family and friends when he got home. But he was always dissatisfied with the uninterested reaction. You could almost see yawns as he showed them photo after photo, with a lengthy story attached to each. But the animation was missing: you couldn't hear his thrilled voice as the trap was sprung, the roar of the crocodile as it growled in protest, the clunk in the hull of the aluminium boat as it thrashed about. Photos simply didn't do it justice.

Lyn and I eventually decided to buy him his own video camera. It was one of the first that came onto the market in Australia—a big Panasonic National M7 that was a nuisance to lug around. We weren't sure how long it would last in the rugged terrain, but it surprised us all; that robust camera survived the mud, the boat, the sun and the salt water, not to mention Steve's famously heavy hand.

That camera changed everything for him: he'd stick it in the boat or hang it in a tree or sit it in the mangroves and just let it roll. He shot hours upon hours of footage, of just whatever he was up to. It never ceased to amaze me that he'd be in the middle of getting a crocodile out of a boat all by himself and he'd remember to jump out to pause the tape while he moved on to the next location. Then he'd hang it up in the tree to record the next instalment, and so on until he captured the entire process of catching a crocodile from trapping to transportation. He didn't miss a beat.

Now when he brought those movies home, he got a very different reaction. He could finally show his wild life at Cattle

Creek: every hilarious, outrageous, gory or simply unbelievable occurrence of a day in the life of a young crocodile hunter. Suddenly, everyone's interest grew and they wanted to hear more about Cattle Creek.

Although those recordings nearly gave his mother a heart attack, they became a help to him too. He'd watch everything he'd recorded back in Stephen and Danny Accorneros' lounge room and learn from it, meticulously noting how he could improve on every capture. His goal was to make the whole process less stressful for the crocodiles. And as time went on, he got it down to a very fine art.

That was really important to both of us, because whatever we did, we were always thinking about the welfare of the animal. Most people think of crocodiles as robust, bloodthirsty animals. And physically they are. But they're also supremely sensitive creatures. When crocodiles are under stress, lactic acid builds in their bodies, and if the level climbs too high the crocodile will die from exhaustion.

It's a delicate balance, because you're also dealing with such a physically powerful animal. The big ones are so incredibly strong that they can even do themselves a lot of damage without realising it. The kinds of things we were doing—sitting on top of them to hold them down, using ropes to restrain them, and just fundamentally taking them out of their familiar environment and moving them into captivity—were all so foreign to the crocodiles. It certainly wasn't pleasant for them. If you muck up, you cost that crocodile its life.

On occasion, we didn't do as well as we would have liked. What happened when we caught one of the very first crocodiles at Cattle Creek showed our inexperience, and afterwards it was never far from our thoughts, always a reminder to us of what not to do.

We had caught a seven-foot crocodile, small enough for one of us to handle alone if we needed to. In the trap we had tied its jaw tightly closed with a piece of tape and were ready to get it into a crate and back to the park, when it suddenly escaped back into the river.

Steve and I were beside ourselves with concern that it would die out there in the wild. So we spent hour after hour diving into the water in the middle of the night, trying to find it, to no avail. When you consider that there were a lot of big crocodiles in that river system, it was a crazy thing to do, but we were just so frustrated with ourselves for allowing it to happen. Not only would that crocodile be unable to catch food, it would be unable to regulate its temperature. To avoid overheating, crocodiles lie with their jaws agape, allowing cool air to circulate over the skin in their mouths. Finally we admitted defeat, and went back to camp. Neither of us went to bed, we just sat by the fire and cried, stricken with guilt.

We hoped that the tape might have loosened and come undone, or the croc might have rubbed it off on a log somewhere and survived. In the weeks that followed we never saw a body, so we hoped that it had been a happy ending for that crocodile but still, it didn't make us feel any better.

We never spoke about it after that, and we didn't tell anybody else what had happened either. We just felt so stupid that we'd made this kind of basic mistake. It showed us just how easy it was to do irreparable damage any time we interfered with nature in this line of work. It took us a long while to get over it. And of course it made me question what we were doing, and if we'd ever become experienced at it, or if we should just pack up and call it a day. But your best teacher in this life is always your last mistake. So Steve and I constantly strived to get better and faster and to minimise stress as much as possible. Every catch was a chance to make improvements.

During this time, Stephen and Danny Accornero, the property owners, had quickly become our friends. They'd regularly come down to see what we were up to and join us by the campfire, telling all kinds of lies the way blokes do whenever they have a chance. And they'd also muck in and help out. We could always rely on them. When catching a crocodile, there's nothing worse than giving a bunch of people directions, saying, 'I'm going to jump on the head of this crocodile and I want you guys to jump on right behind me,' and then thirty seconds later finding out you're the only one sitting there. That's just embarrassing. So after a while I could count on just one hand the people I would ask to help with crocodile wrangling—and Stephen and Danny were among them.

Of course, when we'd told Stephen and Danny the day we met that we'd be self-sufficient, we hadn't meant it. There was no way known to man that we were going to be able to do that kind of physical work without occasional help from local people, particularly when it came to capturing some of the larger crocodiles. When Steve was up there by himself, he relied on Stephen and Danny's help with the larger crocs. And the largest of them all was the mighty king of Cattle Creek.

The day Steve called me at the park to say he'd finally captured the grand old fourteen-foot crocodile, he was both elated to have finally outsmarted such a wise old crocodile, and also devastated to remove what he knew was the king of the river. After Steve relayed all the details of the adrenaline-filled capture we made arrangements to transport the croc back to the park by rail.

But first Steve would need help. 'I need a lot of people and I need them fast,' Steve said, and then hung up to call Stephen and Danny, and to rally help from other farmers in the area.

We'd been trying to catch this particular crocodile from day one. This big black crocodile was notorious for attacking and killing cattle. The four-metre giant was known to surface next to small three-metre dinghies and frighten the life out of fishermen. Many of those fishermen of Cattle Creek carried high-powered rifles in their boats specifically in case they encountered him. So there was a fairly high chance that this crocodile was going to get shot at some point.

In fact, this particular croc was the very reason for our permit. Local farmers had complained about him to Queensland Parks and Wildlife Services for years. But he remained elusive. Then one day while out scanning the banks, I caught sight of a belly slide that simply had to belong to this crocodile; it was almost as wide as my dinghy itself. Just from that, I knew Steve would have his work cut out for him the day he eventually caught this enormous croc.

After I had returned to the park, Steve set two traps just upstream from this belly slide. It was an area teeming with all kinds of easy prey for the croc: wallabies, fish and feral pigs. When, after a few days of checking the traps, he saw that his lead-in bait was gone, Steve knew he was in the right vicinity. Four days later, he was lured out in the early hours of the morning by the sound of the mangroves erupting with the thrashing of a large crocodile. When he approached, he realised that the crocodile was bigger than the trap itself, with his tail and back legs hanging out of it.

He also realised he didn't have a lot of time; the tide was coming in and he was worried the croc was going to drown.

'We've got to do this. We've got to get it safely out of the trap,' he said to Stephen and Danny in a panic, asking them to gather up farmers in the local area who'd help.

People came from all over, despite having no previous experience with a crocodile. Steve directed all the activity with a series of rapid-fire instructions: 'Get in here,' 'Tie that up' and 'Put your hands here.' He suggested that they tie dinghies together to create a makeshift barge.

Once there, with its jaw tied, they managed to collectively manhandle the crocodile onto the makeshift raft—which immediately sank. So they rebalanced it, running ropes around the crocodile and two other boats. The dinghies were only an inch or so above the water. The dinghy the crocodile was actually on was twelve feet long, the crocodile was fourteen feet long. There were legs and tail all over the place.

Stephen and Danny were standing chest-deep in water on either side of the crocodile, which was tied into the boat, and Steve stood in the middle of the boat with the croc, holding a knife. This wasn't for his or anybody else's protection. If the boat went down, Steve would cut the crocodile loose to make sure it didn't drown. They were so low in the water that if the croc had started thrashing about, they would have sunk. It was a slow trip back. He really cared about the well-being of that crocodile. He already felt guilty about removing the king from his domain and his number one priority was that crocodile's safety.

Meanwhile, the farmers wondered how they would get back now that the croc was taking up all of the room in their dinghies.

'You can all swim. He's tied up!' Steve joked.

'But we've just manhandled him for two hours. If he gets free he'll be well pissed off with us!'

'Well, then, you'll just have to swim faster,' came the reply.

Eventually, they managed to get the crocodile back to land and load it into a custom-made crate. They used a tractor to get the crate onto the back of a truck and then drove it to a train for the trip back to the park by rail, which was our only option for such a big fella.

Steve gave Stephen and Danny naming rights in gratitude for the incredible help they gave that day.

'Let's call it Acco, after the Accornero family,' they replied. And they always kept in touch with Acco and all of the Cattle Creek crocodiles whenever they visited the park thereafter.

Once Acco's train arrived at Beerwah, there was one drama after another. His crate was just so monstrous and weighed a tonne. The challenge was to get the crate from the train wagon onto the platform and from there onto my truck. A lot of people gathered around to watch, because it was a really interesting sight to see in the middle of Beerwah. But that raised the stakes because now people were getting in the way left, right and centre.

I thought it would be smooth sailing once I got him back to the park. All I'd have to do was open the front of the crate and release him into his enclosure and let him settle in. But then I realised he had a rope around his jaw. I'll admit that at the time I was slightly pissed off with Steve for sending the croc down to the Sunshine Coast with the rope on but I also knew that he had his reasons. I couldn't let him out of that crate without getting the rope off. So I cut a hole in the crate itself near Acco's head so I could use a little knife to saw the rope off. The entire time Acco was looking at me and I was looking at him. And I just thought that at any moment I was going to wear it through the side of that crate. But thankfully it all worked out okay in the end, and he was finally in his new enclosure.

But like Steve I felt it was a shame to have to pull the king out of his kingdom. Acco had undoubtedly been the largest, strongest and most dominant male in the area. The CEO of Cattle Creek. He would have decided who was allowed into the area he controlled. If another male crocodile had come along, they would have fought fiercely, to the point of pulling legs off each other, and whichever croc had won would have claimed that territory. Smaller males seeking a territory may well have seen Acco's size and decided to just quietly move on.

So Acco would actually have been doing a very good job of keeping that whole system in check. With him gone, younger crocodiles would come in and run riot. And another system in balance would now be out of whack, because humans had got involved. We'd decided at some point that we couldn't all live together.

The ideal, of course, would be to educate people living in close proximity with crocodiles about crocodile safety. But that'll never be perfect either: there'll always be that minority who won't learn, who'll still clean their fish around boat ramps and swim with their dogs. And sooner or later one of those people will pay the ultimate price for their stupidity, and then so will the crocodile. It was certainly heartbreaking to take such a dominant animal out of his home. That never made us feel any good.

***

As we realised that there were more crocs in Cattle Creek than anyone had imagined, and our short croc-catching contract turned into an ongoing project, we bunkered down for the long haul. Steve and I built a temporary lean-to, mainly for Steve to live in when I had to travel back to the park. Stephen and Danny let me use some scrap materials lying around to build Steve a shelter. It was pretty basic—no walls, just four wooden posts and a flimsy roof to keep out the famous far north rain. We slept in swags and washed in the creek. Most of the campsite was taken up with crocodile-catching equipment, ropes, nets and crocodile crates strewn all over the place next to Steve's canary-yellow Toyota Landcruiser. Tidiness was not Steve's forte. He had seven saucepans, which he named for every night of the week. He didn't wash them, he'd just let his dog Chilli lick them all clean.

The Accorneros looked after Steve, giving him a good feed every now and then. They certainly weren't game enough to eat at his campsite. Covered in mangrove mud, he'd jump straight in his vehicle with Chilli and drive up to their house. He wasn't precious about the interior of his truck. But Mrs Accornero was certainly precious about her house. Before he was allowed anywhere near her clean carpet, she'd send him to the bathroom for a shower.

And in the Accorneros, Steve found a keen audience for his videos. Once a week, he'd go up to charge the battery for his video camera and share the videos of the greatest captures. There wasn't one they watched without being shocked or in fits of laughter at his one-of-a-kind antics. His sense of humour was certainly unique.

Lyn worried a lot about Steve in those days of contract catching. Of course, it was only natural for a mother to worry about her son spending so many months at a time living primitively and alone in the bush. Added to that was the very sobering risk of challenging himself against a predatory amimal in its own environment. Most parents worry when their children reach young adulthood and travel overseas, and here was our son spending months at a time away from home in an isolated environment catching some of the biggest apex predators out there all alone.

But I knew he'd be all right, because this was what Steve was good at. I had had the chance to see that firsthand, having worked so closely with him. That's not to say I didn't worry: I worried most of all while he was out on the water, because that was where the real danger was, where you had to play the crocodile's game. But I knew that once Steve had a crocodile in the trap, he had the upper hand, and although he'd still need to exercise great caution, he could carefully work things out.

Steve was very practical like that. He would sit down, with Chilli, his dog, there beside him, talking her through the whole thing until he'd worked out exactly how he would do something. It might take him an hour to figure it out, but I was always confident that in the end he could.

But the most worrying time came when a few days had passed without Steve making any contact with Lyn or me back at the park. Although he had no phone of his own, he'd often drive up to Stephen and Danny's house or to other friends' places to phone home. This silence told me something was up. I decided to make a trip to Cattle Creek to check everything was okay. I also had a feeling that I might need to drive Steve's truck home and so although I hated catching public transport, I had to cave in and catch the damn bus. Lyn hurriedly packed a first-aid kit, and I booked a ticket and was on my way.

After almost twenty gruelling hours confined to a seat, I persuaded the bus driver to stop on the main highway in front of the dirt track that led into Cattle Creek. Just as I started the three-kilometre walk up to Steve's campsite, I ran into Stephen and Danny, who told me that Steve had been seriously injured and that they'd tried to get him to hospital, to no avail. I just rolled my eyes.

'I'll take it from here, fellas,' I said, as they dropped me at Steve's camp. I could see him staggering up to me with a dirty, rotten piece of rag around his ankle. It was completely soaked with blood and mud, and covered with all kinds of things he'd collected in his barefoot travels. He was surprised to see me there. And as he told me what had happened, I shook my head in disapproval.

He had been in a hurry to get a nine-foot female called Cookie into the transport crate, ready to call me to come up and take her back to the park. A nine-foot female weighs upwards of two hundred kilograms, and that's about the upper limit for a bloke attempting anything on his own. It was the largest crocodile he had ever caught by himself, and I was buggered if I knew how he'd managed to do that.

But he got it sorted without any assistance whatsoever. He'd tied both ends of the boat to the trees along the riverbank so it was stable, and then worked with ropes to restrain the crocodile until he could grab hold of her safely, dipping the boat on its side and lifting the croc over the side of the boat. He motored her back to camp in his dinghy with Chilli, unloaded her from the dinghy to the truck, and then drove to the camp just a little way up from the creek.

His next task was to get her out of the truck and into her transport crate, a rectangular box made of strong marine ply. I knew he was as strong as an ox, but I never really figured out how he managed some of those tasks. What I did know for certain was that he was absolutely nuts for even attempting it by himself. The crate's two ends could be removed so he could pull the crocodile through one open end with a rope and then secure the rear end so she couldn't slide backwards. But as soon as Steve had Cookie on the ground, he realised that the crate was too long for him to reach the end of the rope. Instead of walking around to feed the rope through, which was the sensible thing to do, he decided to wriggle three-quarters of the way inside the box himself, to reach the rope and pull it back out.

Prior to doing that, he'd taken the rope off Cookie's jaws. She was half-wrapped in a big tarpaulin and had a calico bag over her head acting as a blindfold to keep her calm. She had nothing at all restraining her incredibly powerful jaws and she was positioned right at the bottom of the crate. As he propelled himself into the box, legs flicking from side to side, he inadvertently clubbed Cookie on the side of the head with his foot.

Crunch! She grabbed him. The most powerful jaws of any animal—beating even great white sharks—crushed down into his bone. She had him by the ankle and gave him a shake before fortunately releasing him and wandering off, still covered in all of the gear. He reversed out of the box quick smart. A glance at his foot told him she'd done some pretty serious damage, but first he had to catch the crocodile all over again and secure her in the crate, and then manoeuvre the crate into the shade, before he could finally tend to his injuries. For Steve, tending to his injuries just meant wrapping his foot up in a calico bag and getting on with things. He told me the whole story with great gusto, but I was distinctly unimpressed. 'Steve, do you realise that this could have gone really, really badly for you? That croc could have taken your leg clean off!' I said, pointing out to him that if the crocodile had done a death-roll while he was caught in the wooden crate, she'd have taken his foot back to the water as a souvenir without much effort at all. 'Obviously you're not going to go to the hospital to get stitches?' I continued, already knowing the answer.

'Nah. She'll be right,' he said stubbornly. But the real reason was that he was concerned about leaving the traps he'd already set out on the creek. He'd obviously weighed it all up. He knew that if he'd left a crocodile in a trap exposed to the sun, chances are it'd kill the croc. And we both knew that there was nobody to relieve him. It's not like you can say to the neighbour up the road, 'Hey, I've got to get to hospital, do you mind checking my crocodile traps when I'm gone? If there's a ten-foot crocodile in one, just drag it into the boat by hand and I'll deal with it when I'm back. Thanks, I really appreciate it.'

'Well, that foot of yours won't come good in this environment,' I said, looking around at the mud and mangroves, just about the worst kind of bacterial cocktail you could ask for with open wounds. 'The way that's looking, you'll be coming home in one of those wooden crates yourself. Dead. I'm going to get the first-aid kit, and I don't care what you say, I'm going to patch it up.'

He didn't argue, just replied, 'That'd be great, Dad.'

I sat him down, boiled some water in the billy on the campfire and set about cleaning his wounds. They were nasty. Really, really nasty. His foot was covered in deep, purple holes that were pits of rotting flesh. It didn't take a doctor to work out that he'd need more than a few stitches. So I got all of the equipment ready from the first-aid kit and explained exactly what

I planned to do. 'This is going to hurt you a lot more than it hurts me.'

'Get on with it then,' he said, and after that he didn't utter another sound. Not one, as I poked and prodded at these holes, digging out all of the embedded dirt and bits of gravel that had settled into them and washing out the whole thing with effervescing disinfectant. I cut out putrefied flesh with a scalpel, all the while thinking what a state he had let himself get in without doing anything about it.

I don't have an iron stomach for the sight of blood and guts. And I could see what he was going through, but he was prepared to do whatever it took to allow him back out on the water to keep catching crocodiles. Finally I latched on plastic staples that pulled the skin taut to close the freshly cleaned wounds and wrapped up the bottom half of his leg to keep the whole foot uncontaminated. I made it as watertight as I could manage and then I hoped like hell it'd be enough, because that's all I could do.

'It's no good me telling you to stay out of the water, is it?'

He shook his head. I'm convinced he thought he was part crocodile, because crocodiles heal pretty well even after serious injury. They're known to be able to shut off their own blood supply to injured areas in order to stop bleeding and have an incredibly sophisticated immune system, able to fight off the most serious infections. I'd seen many crocodiles minus a leg or with part of their tail missing. In fact, you'll seldom see a fifteen-foot crocodile that's whole. Nine times out of ten an old crocodile will have sustained some pretty substantial injuries. They are remarkable survivors.

But I had to remind Steve that he wasn't a crocodile, that he was a lot more mortal than that, and it wasn't the last time I had to say it either. That bloke certainly put Lyn and me through our paces.

I spent the next day out on the water with him dismantling the traps, and then we loaded Cookie onto the back of his truck and drove her home to the reptile park. Thankfully, that foot healed up magically. And I say magically because that's the only term I can use to describe an injury of that severity healing itself without any intervention but rudimentary first aid.

***

I'm all for laws to protect our rapidly diminishing wildlife, but when that expands to protecting animals that are already dead as a doornail, I start to question the people who wrote the rulebook. Up at Cattle Creek, Steve and I had realised that the best bait for our traps was either feral pigs or roadkill wallabies that we'd collect from the side of the highway. Feral pigs were not always a sure thing, but the roadkill was sadly a plentiful resource.

There was a particularly long stretch of the Bruce Highway near our camp on which agile wallabies, a species native to Far North Queensland, were struck by vehicles throughout the night. By morning the roadside would be carnage: every couple of metres there'd be another obliterated carcass strewn across the bitumen. So Steve and I decided to make the best of a bad situation. We figured that the more we could clean off the side of the road, the less chance there'd be of large birds of prey coming down to feast on the remains and also becoming roadkill. We'd travel along the highway early in the morning and retrieve what we needed to line our traps.

But we found out very quickly that we were in fact breaking the law by using these dead animals. It didn't even cross my mind that that'd be the case. The only thing that interested me was whether I was doing the right thing by the animals themselves. And they were dead. In fact, they were barely recognisable and most had not a skerrick of hair remaining.

But the authority's beef was that they couldn't prove whether we were collecting them off the side of the road, or whether we were in fact killing these animals for our traps. We'd already explained our approach to the Ingham-based officers from the Queensland Parks and Wildlife Services. Their take was that they preferred we didn't do it but they weren't going to prosecute us for it, and offered a few alternatives: 'Can we suggest instead that you use chickens from the local chicken farm, or you can take as many fruit bats as you want.'

I was dumbfounded. White-feathered chickens are of course foreign food to wild crocodiles, and neither Steve nor I could fathom the idea of going to a roost of our beautiful native fruit bats and shooting them out of the trees. They weren't protected at this time, but there was just no chance we were going to kill any native wildlife.

So we kept collecting the roadkill, and somehow the Department of Agriculture and Fisheries got word of it. Two notoriously efficient officers were on the job and keen to prosecute, as they made clear when they paid us a visit at our campsite one morning.

I was fined for using protected fauna in our traps. They weren't interested if those wallabies were dead or alive when we found them. The officers handed me a notice to appear at a court hearing in Ingham. I wrote a letter to the magistrate explaining that we were in fact using dead wallabies found on the side of the road, and even offered to take the magistrate to the very road we collected them from to prove it. In the end, the magistrate was as lenient as he could be under the legislation. I was fined just four hundred dollars, one hundred dollars for each wallaby they had observed in the traps. The upper limit of the fine was closer to four thousand dollars per animal, so I got off reasonably lightly.

I paid the four hundred dollars, but Steve and I had to come up with an alternative for bait, as the fisheries officers were constantly on our backs after that, visiting our camp and launching a boat into the river to check our traps. But the locals were on our side.

Over the years of exploring this environment, Steve had met nearly everyone in the area. They'd be minding their own business, working on their paddocks fronting the creek, and get the fright of their lives when Steve would appear out of nowhere, just walk right out of the creek and ask, 'Where am I?' They'd tell him where he was, and then get to talking, and he'd get a lift back to camp having made a new friend. After so many years of doing that, there wasn't a farmer or fisherman on that creek who didn't recognise Steve—the crocodile hunter from Cattle Creek.

When word got around that the fisheries department was giving us grief, the locals, unbeknown to us, took it upon themselves to pay these particular officers a lesson. We found out many months later that the next time the officers launched their boat at one of the local boat ramps to come and monitor our traps, they returned to find their vehicle and boat trailer at the bottom of the river. Someone had released the handbrake and the car had reversed off the boat ramp and sunk to the bottom of Cattle Creek, trailer and all. The officers were transferred out of Ingham after that.

In the end, I wasn't upset at having to pay the four hundred dollars, as poultry would have cost a lot more than that. I was angered by the stupidity of the whole thing. We were advised to shoot native wildlife rather than use a carcass already rotting by the side of the road; it just made no sense. I was more interested in saving the native animals that were still alive. But it wasn't just in the far north that we had to contend with the authorities. Back at the reptile park, we also had to comply with rules and regulations that were constantly changing in those early days of native wildlife protection.

Two officers from Queensland Parks and Wildlife Services visited me one day to do a stocktake of our animals, to make sure I was complying with my permit. One of them was a really good bloke I'd worked with over many years. We got along like a house on fire and from time to time he'd helped me deal with frustrating situations when the department was being inflexible. The other was a young rookie who was clearly just learning the ropes.

We went through the entire park together, with no stone left unturned. They went through the bother of counting every single one of the big crocs, from the safety of behind the fences. They also wanted to see a behind-the-scenes enclosure full of juvenile saltwater crocodiles I'd bred at the park and raised from hatchlings. As they grew to be over two feet long, I'd built an outdoor enclosure for them. They had a natural earth pond, which they could use to regulate their temperature. Crocodiles are highly sensitive to cold, and they don't naturally occur as far south as the Sunshine Coast. Their preferred body temperature is between thirty and thirty-three degrees Celsius. My hope was that if I could raise these little guys from hatchlings and they could adjust to the temperatures then they'd hopefully cope better when the winter months rolled around.

'How many crocs have you got in there?' the younger guy asked in an authoritative tone. I showed him my records confirming that there were twenty-five, and listing the number I'd bred, and any losses I had suffered after incubating that clutch.

'I'd like to count those ones too,' he said.

Well, I just looked at him. I knew exactly what was going to happen next. These were confident little crocodiles, despite their smaller size. 'Well, how are you gonna do it? How do you plan on counting them?' I asked. It was quite clear he didn't really have a plan.

'We're going to have to catch them all by hand,' he decided.

I just looked at my friend and we both shook our heads. I was tempted to explain how I got my scars, but I kept my hand in my pocket instead. 'If you want to catch them, go ahead and catch them. But I'm telling you right now there's no way to do it and I'm sure as hell not going to do it for you. You're going to either have to accept what I've got on paper, or get in there and count them yourself.'

'Oh no, we've got to do this properly. We've got to get these numbers accurate,' he insisted.

In the end I grudgingly brought over some large plastic tubs to hold the salties as this young fella caught them. I couldn't believe it when he began by removing his socks and shoes. In the clay-bottomed pond, the water was so muddy that you couldn't see a thing below the surface. Crocodiles are equipped for these conditions with a transparent lid that closes over their eyes, allowing them to see very well underwater.

He waded out into the pond, feeling for the invisible crocs by putting his hands in the water. And of course one bit him almost straightaway. It was just a little salty, about a metre long, but they've got needle-sharp teeth and it drew a fair amount of blood. And furthermore, it wouldn't let go.

'It's not going all that well so far,' I observed from the safety of the water's edge.

'I think I'll just take your word for it. Twenty-five crocs, you said?'

'Twenty-five, indeed.' But I couldn't control my smirk and the next thing me and the other guy were in hysterics.

When it comes to crocodiles, there are some things you can do and some you can't. And getting into a murky pond with twenty-five sets of needle-sharp teeth is definitely one of those things you can't do.

***

After our first trip up to Cattle Creek together, Steve and I took it in turns to be up there because we couldn't both leave the reptile park at the same time. But for the duration of our permit, one of us had to be up north catching crocodiles. We weren't there all year round; we were up there at the whims of the weather. In a flood or the wet season it was a lot harder to find the crocodiles. And the crocodiles weren't all that interested in food in winter.

And every time one of us caught a crocodile up there the other would have to drive up from the reptile park to collect it. Sixteen hours is a long drive and you'd have to turn around and drive straight back as that crocodile needed to be settled into its new enclosure with food and access to water as quickly as possible. We'd switch places whenever we got tired, because when you got tired, you got careless, and that was one aspect of workplace health and safety we did pay attention to.

'Dad, I need a pick-up,' Steve would say when a crocodile was ready to go to the park.

'All right, son, I'll be up there soon,' I'd say and make hasty arrangements to drop everything at the park and set out.

On this particular occasion, I was travelling home with a croc with her jaw tied. I'd made a rare exception to my rule because the croc was in the cabin with me in Lyn's small Honda Accord hatchback. I couldn't fit the crate in the back of the car so she was lying diagonally across the folded back seats and the boot. It was a small space for a big old girl.

'You going to be right with her?' Steve asked, as we closed the boot.

'I'll manage,' I said, and I drove off with her wrapped snugly in a tarpaulin, her snout unnervingly close to the back of my head.

I knew that she was struggling with the tarpaulin so I stopped to check her a few times. But when she seemed to calm down I decided to push on. I'd almost reached the Sunshine Coast when I sensed that something wasn't right. I looked out of the corner of my eye and there was this crocodile with her head next to mine, right up at the windscreen, so close that the warm breath from her nostrils had left fog on the glass. She was a matter of inches away from my face, just looking at me as I was looking at her, while doing everything I could to keep from swerving across the road at one hundred kilometres per hour. *Well, this is not good, Bob*, I thought. If she'd clouted me on the side of the head, as crocodiles do in the wild, that'd be the end of me. And I'm not sure that the authorities called out to the crash site would have been equipped to handle a salty trapped inside a small car. They'd probably have left me in there.

Very slowly and carefully, I pulled over on the side of the highway, and got out. The hard part seemingly over, I went around to the boot to pull her back. But she objected and finished up loose out on the road with me. She had escaped her tarpaulin. There we were, just standing on the side of the Bruce Highway, an eight-foot crocodile and me. And then the eight-foot crocodile started walking off.

I had such a job then of trying to wrap her up, hold her down and lift her back up into the car. I'm a little bloke, and she was heavy. I couldn't lift the whole crocodile, so I attempted one limb at a time: I'd get the head in, then go around and lift the back legs, then another bit of her, and then her head would come out again and I'd have to start the process once more.

It would have been quite the sight. You don't see crocodiles as far south as Gympie, and here was a man wrangling a sizeable crocodile while standing on the side of the main state highway. I drove back to the park, hoping to get home without being pulled over. Although I had a permit to remove this croc, I was certain that the Honda Accord wouldn't have been judged an acceptable method of transport in the eyes of the law. The police would also have been shocked to pull over a driver chaperoning a crocodile as his passenger.

I eventually got home at an ungodly hour of the morning and woke Lyn to help me get the crocodile out of the car.

'My car! What on earth happened to my car?' she shouted, pointing at a dent in the front bumper. Lyn was more concerned about some damage from a stone thrown up off the road than the large saltwater crocodile squeezed into the back. That last part didn't even cause her to bat an eyelid. That was just how normal that kind of thing was in our household.

***

When we'd first started heading north to catch crocodiles, Steve had gone on a side mission to collect green pythons and taipans from Australia's largest remnant lowland rainforest in the exquisite Kutini-Payamu (Iron Range) National Park on the east coast of the Cape York Peninsula. He had been camping on the snow-white sands of Chilli Beach when a timid female Staffordshire bull terrier wandered into his camp, searching for a feed. She was skin and bone, and had clearly been mistreated. And that was it: the two became inseparable, sleeping out under the stars together every night afterwards. When Steve left, he decided to take her with him, and from then on Chilli became his shadow, going everywhere with him.

In those isolated years he spent camping up at Cattle Creek, Chilli was his greatest companion and crocodile-catching canine accomplice. Out on the boat, her place was right up the front, head high, with the wind in her fur. You could almost have sworn that she was smiling, her big open-mouthed grin meaning saliva flew everywhere. You had to look out if you were downwind of her or you'd end up wearing it. He'd talk to her constantly as he pulled crocodiles from traps into the boat, a running commentary on what he was going to do and how he wanted her to behave. She was fearless and knew exactly when to get her paws out of the way of the jaws of a big croc.

When it was cold, Chilli would curl up in the sleeping bag with Steve because he didn't want her feeling cold. And Chilli always got the best cuts of his meat and rode in the front passenger seat of his truck while the humans took a back seat. I contested that, of course.

We'd often use feral pigs as bait for the crocodile traps. Wild boars had been brought over from Europe to Australia in the 1700s, and quickly caused havoc to the natural environment, one of the most widespread invasive pest species in Queensland. So Steve was welcome to catch feral pigs on lots of local properties for croc bait, and of a night he and Chilli were regularly out there with a spotlight. Chilli was such an exceptional pig hunter that Steve didn't like to use guns; they had their routine down to a fine art. On his command, she would race ahead of him and grab the biggest boar by the ear, holding it until Steve could catch up with her.

One night Steve's local friends wanted to show him a spot chock-full of pigs. As Chilli had hold of a pig, one of the other shooters impulsively shot at it and the bullet passed right through the pig and hit Chilli, killing her instantly.

Steve was inconsolable. He scooped her up and carried her for kilometres, sobbing, all the way back to his camp. He refused offers of lifts from the others; he didn't want to be around people. He buried Chilli right where she had loyally sat beside his camp chair night after night, and then stayed up all night grieving. He grieved for that little dog as much as he'd grieve for any human because in his eyes she was no less of a companion. In his isolated world out there at Cattle Creek, that little dog became his whole world.

I was already on my way up to Steve when Chilli died, and I arrived the night afterwards. He was an absolute mess. He had lost any motivation to keep doing his work with crocodiles, and given that he had more get-up-and-go than anyone around, that told me the depth of his loss. So we hung around the campsite for a good while, after first dismantling the croc traps. It was troubling to see him in so much pain. So I found a piece of wood lying in the grass, and shaped it, and then heated up a thin piece of metal and etched into it the words *Camp Chilli*. I hung the finished sign at the entrance to our campsite. 'Now Chilli will always be here with you at Cattle Creek,' I said.

Steve cried, but it was more cathartic this time. That night, as we sat under the stars around a campfire, he told me how he'd nearly lost Chilli once before. He had been out bush with her one night when she'd run off after a pig. After searching for her for hours, he'd returned to camp alone, beside himself with worry. He'd then headed straight up to Stephen and Danny's house to ask their advice on how to find her. They told him to go back to where he'd last seen Chilli and leave some of his clothes there. She would find them via his scent and stay there until he returned for her.

They meant for Steve to leave a shirt, but Steve didn't do anything by halves: he took absolutely everything off, including his jocks, and went back to camp stark naked. He barely slept a wink and was back to check the spot at the crack of dawn. And there was Chilli, sitting dutifully beside his dirty clothes.

'How did you get back to the spot without your clothes?' I asked, intrigued.

'I drove the truck,' he said.

'What would have happened if someone had pulled you over?'

'I would have been naked,' he said matter-of-factly before breaking into his first smile in days.

He slowly got his groove back for crocodile catching, but every inch of that creek continued to remind him of Chilli, and it all remained pretty raw for a good while. Our campsite on Cattle Creek became widely known as Camp Chilli and that sign hung on our lean-to for the remainder of his croc-catching days and beyond. Steve eventually found a new love, Sui, another female Staffie. She quickly became his next crocodile-hunting canine and companion. But she sure had big paw-prints to fill.

***

After we'd spent years working at Cattle Creek, Queensland Parks and Wildlife Services was confident that we'd removed the majority of the crocodiles and assigned us a new waterway, the Burdekin River. By water volume this is Australia's largest river, running from Charters Towers out to the east coast of Queensland at Ayr. The Burdekin was different from Cattle Creek, in many ways: the sandy banks make it harder to see the crocodile slides, mud leaves a lot more of an impression. The rough track made us really isolated once we got in there and it was a real hassle to get the crocodiles crated in and out of there on the back of our utes because of the rough terrain. The original permit for the Burdekin stated that there were just six crocodiles in that waterway to catch, just a couple of months' work. Well, we probably caught double that number and they just kept on coming. What was originally a quick trip became much longer.

Our camp on the Burdekin was much more isolated, on a vacant property almost one hundred kilometres from the highway. But there were one or two people around. One of the first locals we met was a cattle farmer who lived on the other side of the river. He'd bring his young daughter across the river every morning to catch the school bus. Although he wasn't frightened of crocodiles, he was a bit concerned because he made this trip twice a day with his young daughter in a small boat, and he'd observed a crocodile hanging around the crossing point.

'I'll make a point of catching it, if I can,' Steve told him when they first met out on the water. So we went out searching one night and caught sight of him. He didn't look all that large, so instead of setting a trap we thought we'd try to catch him by hand. I was driving the boat, and Steve, who was a lot bigger and stronger than me, stood up the front searching with the spotlight, ready to spear himself overboard. I started to have reservations as we edged out into the middle of the waterway. If this crocodile was bigger than we thought then all hell was going to break loose. Crocodiles don't give second chances.

Steve suddenly spotted the croc, and wiggled the spotlight in its direction. I slowly idled up to it, keeping my eyes on the red-eye shines, and Steve handed me the spotlight as he got into position. Just as I leaned forward to grab the spotlight, over he went. But the water was only ankle-deep here and he belly-flopped onto a pile of flat rocks.

'You all right?' I asked as I helped him back into the boat, although I could already see he'd sustained a few injuries that he'd probably end up wearing for quite a few years afterwards. But as always, he didn't complain. 'Let's try another night—' I began, but Steve cut me off.

'No, no, let's give it another go.'

So I turned off the motor and we and the crocodile sat in silence for an hour, maybe longer. When you're in an isolated region, you are afforded all the time in the world. You have to just go with the flow.

When Steve eventually turned the spotlight back on, the croc had moved to the other side of the river—what we now knew was the deep side. So I motored closer, and as we approached, Steve jumped on top of it, and of course it was a hell of a lot larger than we had guessed. That crocodile took Steve right to the bottom of the river as he hung on for dear life. And all I could do was sit there in the boat, waiting for him to surface. Waiting, waiting, waiting. Waiting for a lot longer than I was comfortable with. Then suddenly the water around the boat exploded and Steve surfaced with the crocodile in his hands. One hand was around the neck and the other was around the base of the tail. This thing was thrashing around and he just threw it into the boat, nearly capsizing it as he did so. This was all in complete darkness; the spotlight had gone out ages before.

'What the bloody hell are you doing?' I shouted. I was wearing only a pair of shorts, and had bare feet. And this crocodile was flailing about the inside of the boat unrestrained while Steve was hanging on to the side still catching his breath. I finally located the crocodile's head by feeling around, and then sat on it, keeping its jaws closed with my hands. Steve managed to get back into the boat and sat on the bench seat, looking at me as I struggled with the croc, and he laughed, 'He nearly drowned me, it's your problem from here!' But then he came over and secured its jaws.

A person with half a brain wouldn't have done any of that. Of course, jumping on a crocodile of any size in the middle of a river in the middle of the night goes against all common sense.

When we got back to camp that night we just laughed at the stupidity of the whole thing. We didn't go to bed for a long time, we just sat by the campfire and relived it. To a degree we were rejoicing in the fact that we were both still alive. That was one of our really special moments together. There are not too many other people on this planet who I shared those kinds of hair-raising experiences with. And I'm glad about that, because I don't think I'd have been quite so lucky with anyone else.

Steve was able to tell the farmer from across the river that he'd caught that crocodile, which gave the man some peace of mind as he ferried his young daughter across each day. I guess you could say that Steve certainly went to great lengths to make new friends on the Burdekin. But we knew, of course, that it was only a matter of time before another crocodile took its place.

***

'Come on, old man,' Steve said to me, 'let's have a day off to explore this place.'

We were sitting around the campfire of a morning, boiling the billy and shovelling tea-leaves into it. The tea brewed at our camp was so famously strong that nobody else would agree to drink it.

'How long will we be gone?' I asked.

'Not long, just a couple of hours,' he said easily. I looked at him suspiciously. Not trusting him at all, I packed a couple of oranges as sustenance. Because it was a freshwater river, we didn't need to take any drinking water. We threw in the fishing rods and set out in our dinghy along the Burdekin River. The first thing we did was to investigate a couple of croc slides and mark them on our map.

Our work finding crocs never really did stop. It was unusual to have a day off. We worked from waking to bedtime. Normally we'd start by checking the traps early in the morning. If there was a croc, that'd be it: the rest of the day would be spent getting the croc out of the trap and all the way back to camp.

If there were no crocs caught in the traps, we'd hunt for bait or reposition traps we weren't happy with. Steve was an amazing guy to work with; he had boundless amounts of energy. He wore me out at times, but I refused to tell him that I was tired or I'd had enough. I'd just try to keep up with him as best I could.

But our day off was memorable. We cruised along the river, pulling up at places on the banks to explore by foot. We went down turbulent rapids, coming very close to sinking the boat at one stage. Which wouldn't have been good, because we were fast finding out that the Burdekin was home to a lot of very large salties. But that was Steve—his kind of fun wasn't for the fainthearted. If you were concerned about your life, you'd have been best staying back at camp.

We finally pulled up for some fishing close to the junction of the Bowen and Burdekin rivers. I was hoping for barramundi, sooty grunter or mangrove jack. A fresh fish cooked on the campfire would be a real treat. Fishing was my thing; Steve was too impatient to sit and wait.

As my sinker plopped into the water, I noticed a number of turtle heads poking out of the water all around us. I had seen this type of turtle on the Burdekin before, but we'd always been in too much of a hurry to stop and take a better look. They weren't your average freshwater turtle: they had really big heads and were unusually pale in colour. And as we sat there quietly I grew more and more curious about them.

'Let's grab one of these guys and see what they are,' I said to Steve. Just like that, he was over the side, jumping straight onto one of these turtles in the notoriously crocodile-infested Burdekin River, and back into the boat just as fast. As he pulled the turtle on board and we were able to take a closer look, we both concluded we hadn't seen anything like it before.

They were a lot bigger than most freshwater species, with a carapace about forty centimetres wide. We eventually had four of them in the boat. We took photographs of the markings on the head and the shell and then returned them to the water. We headed back to camp well past nightfall, our 'couple of hours' unsurprisingly having stretched into an entire day.

That night we got out the reptile reference books that I always carried with me, but found nothing resembling the turtles we'd seen. When I eventually got back to the reptile park, I phoned around to see if I could find out more. We were referred to an expert in the field, John Cann, as our best bet in helping us to identify this turtle. John's father, George Cann, had been the curator of reptiles at Taronga Park Zoo from the 1930s onwards, and the two of them had been well known for their reptile show at La Perouse in Sydney. John was then known as The Snake Man to many, and luckily for us, he was a legendary herpetologist and specialist on Australian turtles.

Steve drew a mud map indicating where we had found the turtles, and posted it to him together with the photos, addressed to 'the finest turtle man in the world'. We were interested to see if these turtles were anything out of the ordinary.

And it turned out they were. John says:

On the 17 October 1993, I received a photograph from the Queensland Reptile and Fauna Park of a turtle complete with hand-drawn maps of the location in which the turtle was found marked as 'Hidden River'. Almost as soon as I opened the mail that day I knew that I was staring at the face of a previously undescribed species of Australian freshwater turtle.

The turtle was morphologically very distinct from any other turtle I had seen with a primitively white head and yellowish horny sheath on the crown and the shell was marginally different as well. Irrespective of what genetics was saying about its likeness to the DNA of other similar-looking species already identified in the region, I was quick to verify that what we were looking at was in fact a brand new species unknown to science. I hastily made a phone call to Bob and Steve to share with them my findings.

'Would you allow me to describe it?' I asked, hoping for the opportunity to formally publish this exciting discovery bringing it to the attention of the scientific world.

'You're very welcome to it,' Steve replied and I went about naming the species, despite the fact that after word got out about our discovery, a number of other researchers had made contact with the park, eagerly hoping for the chance to identify it first.

I wanted to recognise Bob and Steve for their work in unearthing this turtle, although it was a departure from the Aboriginal names that I traditionally gave to describing new species. I settled on the Latin name '*irwini*', following '*Elseya*', the genus describing large side-necked turtles or Australian snapping turtles. To my surprise, after my findings were eventually published, a fellow researcher made the observation that I'd in fact made an oversight in the naming process because 'i' referred only to one person. The correct terminology was in fact 'irwinorum', 'orum' meaning after two people. I'll blame it on my limited knowledge of Latin grammar at the time, but it was always intended to commemorate Bob and Steve Irwin collectively.

Nevertheless, I officially announced a new species of Freshwater turtle publically in *Monitor Magazine* in the time that followed. From that day forward another species was added to the list of Australian native species becoming known to the world as *Elseya irwini*, or commonly known as, 'The Irwin's Turtle'.

I continued to work with the Irwin family over many more years as I went on to do a significant amount of research on *Elseya irwini*, together sharing our findings. I ventured up on a number of occasions to the Burdekin River myself to study the turtles precisely where Steve had marked on that first hand-drawn topographical map he had posted to me. Admittedly when I initially glanced at that primitive-looking map in the mail, I did think that the turtles would be impossible to locate. But sure enough, they were precisely where he'd outlined. An 'X' perfectly marked on the area of the map which they inhabited. I went on to locate many of the turtles up there as I dived about somewhat uncomfortably in the shallows, knowing that there were a lot of big crocodiles around. But I quickly discovered why Bob and Steve had nicknamed it 'Hidden Valley', a pristine and isolated part of the world complemented by the impressive Mount Wickham in the distance.

> It was apparent that anything could remain unfound in a place like this; the perfect home for the elusive Irwin's turtle that previously stayed unknown to man.
>
> It was certainly an exciting time to be involved in the world of herpetology and I thank Bob and Steve Irwin for that opportunity.

It was all quite a thrill. John Cann was an incredible guy to work with, an exceptionally knowledgeable legend in his field. We couldn't thank him enough for going off our basic observations, to uncover a new species.

So while we might not have caught our dinner that day, what we did find has gone on to be far more significant to the knowledge of our natural world.

***

In the time Steve and I camped up on the Burdekin River for our very last subcontracting permit, one thing never altered: he just never shut up about Cattle Creek. I don't think he talked about anything else as we sat by the campfire at night drinking tea by the bucketful or along the riverbanks setting traps by day. The stories of those days just flowed out of him, and it was clear to me that the experiences he had gained in those years would stay with him forever. Unlike most other young adults, Steve would spend hours of an evening filming a brushtail possum in the fork of a tree, with a commentary on how it lived, what it ate and how important it was. While he didn't have a university education he was wiser than his years, and a self-taught naturalist, with the utmost compassion for all living things.

There was no crocodile-catching textbook then, no manual describing what top jaw rope to attach. Everything Steve and I knew came from the experiences of those years. I guess you could say he was thrown in the deep end, and he did more than swim: he pulled out some of the biggest saltwater crocodiles that a bloke could manage on his own. With the swamps and mangroves of Cattle Creek as his classroom, that twenty-two-year-old boy emerged as one of the most knowledgeable individuals on crocodiles around; it was the making of the Crocodile Hunter himself.

In those years contract-catching for the East Coast Crocodile Management Program, we wound up rehoming close to one hundred saltwater crocodiles to our Crocodile Environmental Park. And during those years, as we removed scores of crocodiles from their natural environment, depleting those river systems of the species that kept those ecosystems in check, there were just three fatal croc attacks in Queensland, averaging one every two years. So to address the very low probability of anyone dying from a crocodile attack, hundreds of crocodiles were removed from their homes. Statistically you're more likely to be killed by falling coconuts or die from a bee sting than you are to be mauled to death by a crocodile. In those same years of our permit, eight hundred or so people in Australia died from accidental drowning. Around fifty people were struck by lightning. Crocodiles were always taking the rap as man-eating monsters but let's face it, not one of those crocodiles stole anyone out of their bedrooms at night.

In most of those fatal attacks by crocodiles, people had willingly entered into the crocodile's domain. It just boils down to the fact that we'd lost respect and wariness around our apex predators out in their natural environment. Steve and

I never personally felt that many of the crocodiles we relocated were nuisance crocodiles. But I guess that depends on your point of view.

Our contract stipulated we were to remove any crocodile over 1.2 metres in size. Well, in my opinion, a 1.2 metre crocodile is no threat to anybody, not even a little child. At that size they're still immature, just little reptilian nomads trying to keep out of the way of anything that could threaten their survival. In my experience, crocodiles aren't a threat until they're around three metres in size, when they've completely lost their fear of humans. Unless, of course, they've been enticed into populated areas by people cleaning fish at boat ramps, for example. Generally speaking, large male crocodiles are the problem. And yet we removed immature females and males, animals that were so wary and elusive. All for peace of mind.

The problem we face, and that our children's children will continue to face, is the lack of harmonious coexistence between humans and large predators. And while it was crocs that people had targeted this time, it's no different the world over, whether it be sharks, lions or grizzly bears. Every single time we hear of the unfortunate event of a human being attacked, the animals also suffered. Yet they were in these places long before we were. Ninety-nine times out of a hundred, it's the humans who have made a mistake.

When our contract expired up on the Burdekin, I didn't sign on for another permit. Our park was full, simply chock-a-block with crocs. It had gone from being a collection of native snakes with a handful of crocodiles to one of the largest wildlife facilities in the state and beyond, with crocodiles as our main attraction. Crocodiles had become our mission.

Our Crocodile Environmental Park was eventually launched with the unveiling of a new addition to the front of the park: a 13.7-metre-long sculpture of a crocodile. It had been carved from a five-ton two-hundred-year-old yellow stringybark tree that had been felled when it got in the way of a new railway line through the local Glasshouse Mountains. But it was put to good use as the symbol of our park. An expert woodchopper, who went by the name of Shane-Saw, spent three weeks carving it into shape with an array of chainsaws. His model was a baby saltwater crocodile we held beside him as he tirelessly chipped away. It was a masterpiece that showed everyone who visited that, in our eyes, crocs ruled.

The Crocodile Environmental Park flourished and before long our carpark was overflowing. Word was spreading about our crocodile demos. But it was all beginning to surpass both my own area of expertise and also my desire to work with tourists. I didn't do people all that well, preferring to toil away in the background with physical work. We had come to a fork in the road. We either had to change to keep up with the demand, or remain as we were and run the risk of going backwards.

And I was leaning towards thinking that the reptile park needed a change. After my twenty years as proprietor we needed young fresh ideas to keep up the momentum. It was all too easy for someone of my vintage to become set in my ways. Steve was ready, full as ever of foresight and enthusiasm. So that was the end of our years of crocodile catching, time with Steve that I'll always cherish, that reinforced our bond. But it was just the beginning of something quite profound for Steve Irwin and crocodiles.

5
Australia Zoo

By the early 1990s, I'd resolved to hand the reptile park over to Steve. It wasn't a hard decision, to be honest. It was a natural next step. I'd always wanted the park to remain a family-run business and I knew that I'd hand it over to him somewhere down the track. At twenty-nine years of age, he couldn't have been keener for the opportunity, and to my mind, he couldn't have been more ready for it either.

'Once you get settled and comfortable in what you're doing, I'll just get out of the way,' I said to him. I initially gave him fifty per cent ownership of the park. It wasn't a legal arrangement, there was no paperwork or documents signed, it was just a gentleman's agreement with a nod and a handshake; a verbal agreement about how we were going to go about a handover and what our responsibilities would be as I started to step to the side. He would pay Lyn and me a wage from the park and he would manage it as he saw fit. There were no finances exchanged, we just handed over the running of the whole thing.

He loved that place; it had become more than just his home. He'd proven beyond any doubt that he had the drive and ambition to take it on. He was so singularly focused on the park that nothing else mattered. He saw his future there, seeking out new ways to use it as a platform for his conservation message about crocodiles.

He built almost every new enclosure and carried out all of the construction work himself, with his bare hands, no contractors or machinery. I'm sure at times his staff questioned whether there would be an easier way to do things, but he always had a need to physically exert himself. His philosophy always was, 'We didn't have any of that when I was younger, so why would we start now?' Like me, he really enjoyed hands-on hard yakka.

He'd often be up and about in the park at four o'clock in the morning, planning for his next project, getting in as much work as he could in the peace and quiet before the gates opened and it became harder to get around the park. He applied the same gusto to absolutely everything he put his mind to, whether it was ramming in a fence post or concreting in a new pathway.

I was really confident that it was in good hands and that it would continue to grow with Steve at the helm. I wanted him to take over the park and run with it while I was still able to be around to provide assistance on the sidelines. It was always my intention to do that rather than Steve wait until I was permanently out of the picture.

Lyn and I really felt like taking a break away from the tourism industry altogether. Although we were really proud of the park, after twenty-six years I had reached the stage where I wanted to go and hide. I didn't want to be dealing with hordes of people anymore. I was quite content to just fade away into the background and let him run the show.

By this time, Steve had married Terri, an American tourist with a background in wildlife management whom he'd met during one of his crocodile demos. At one stage, the thought had crossed our minds that he might not ever settle down. We weren't confident that there was anybody out there who would be able to keep up with him. So when he finally did, we could see that he had found the perfect partner to launch it all off with.

To me, it seemed like a good time for Lyn and I to also make a lifestyle change. As a parent it makes you really happy when your child finds someone they share common interests with, with whom they can take on the world and start building something of their own. I didn't foresee just how far it might go then, but I certainly could imagine that they'd take what I'd started to even bigger and better places.

I didn't want to retire as such, because it was impossible for me to do nothing. They say that idle hands are the devil's workshop and in my case you can pretty much guarantee that tenfold. So Lyn and I moved to a new property four hours' drive away, where we could still be of assistance to the park. As we moved out of our beloved family home in The Compound, it was a chance to reflect on how it had all turned out, and we realised we had achieved more than we had ever dreamed possible.

And to have achieved such great togetherness as a family, well, it doesn't get much better than that. While Steve was looking after the animal side of things with the park, Mandy and Joy were managing the catering side of it, running the food kiosks as their own business alongside him. They grew too and Joy's husband, Frank, and Steve's mate Wes were eventually employed in the park to manage the day-to-day aspects of a bustling tourism facility.

Lyn and I purchased a property at Rosedale on Baffle Creek on the outskirts of Bundaberg, Queensland's sugar town, a four-and-a-half-hour drive from Beerwah. It was a stunning property, sixty-eight acres of rainforest with a crystal-clear stream, Island Creek, running through it. We had a new timber home built with verandahs wrapping around three sides of it, the perfect spot from which to enjoy the rufus bettongs, whiptail wallabies and myriad other wildlife that meandered across our front lawn every day.

It was a dream place to retire to after so many years of hard work, anchored to a park we could rarely leave. We were looking forward to our new chapter in a quieter place, taking a break from caring for wildlife and sharing our home with the public. We'd get back to the things we never had time for when running the park: bushwalking, fishing, and just being more connected with nature itself. For the first time in our lives, we finally had time to ourselves, just Lyn and me.

But our new calm was shortlived. After just two weeks in our new home, with boxes still to be unpacked, the Baffle and Island creeks flooded to record levels. Both creeks broke their banks and joined in a raging torrent right in the middle of our property. The floodwater rose frighteningly fast. Trying to predict how close to the house the water might come, I put a marker on a tree, and then watched in horror as water rapidly swamped it. Island Creek rose from its usual depth of just one foot to an alarming forty-six feet of water in no time at all. Our new purpose-built dream home, containing all our worldly possessions, including precious family photographs, was completely inundated right before our eyes. We couldn't do anything but watch from higher ground as an expanse of brown water engulfed our house.

When the water had started to lap over the verandah, I had decided to close all of the windows and doors to try to prevent the water coming into the house. But I hadn't foreseen that the water would rise as high as the eaves. I was then concerned that when the water levels dropped, there would be so much water inside the house that the pressure would smash the windows out and do even more damage. I decided I needed to try to open them myself. So at the peak of the flood, I launched my boat and motored up to my neighbour, whose property was on higher ground, to ask for his help. He immediately came back with me.

'You stay and hold the boat while I dive in!' I said to him, and I carefully lowered myself over the side of the boat into the water.

While he hung onto the gutter of the house to hold the boat in place, I dived down to the double doors onto the verandah and prised them open. Then I swam through the house, opening every window, resurfacing constantly to breathe. The water inside the house was up to the ceiling and it was pitch black in there. I had to feel my way around the inside of the house underwater, among household debris. Swimming around your lounge room is such a surreal feeling.

As the water receded, we went around in the boat collecting floating lounge chairs, television sets and all sorts of things and tethering them to trees with long ropes so they weren't carried away down the creek. We salvaged anything we could find but the destruction was complete. Everything we owned had been destroyed. The brand-new carpet throughout the house was water-damaged; we cut it into pieces to get it out, and then hosed it down, strung up on long clotheslines tied between trees, trying to save whatever we could. We rewired the house from scratch. It was many weeks before we were able to live there again.

After that I decided we'd have to move the house to higher ground, aware it could happen again the next time Baffle Creek flooded. So I cleared an area of bush closer to the road, and called a friend with heavy machinery that could do the job. We jacked the house up as high as we could and dug two tracks all the way under the house so the low loader could back underneath. Then I got a sawmill to cut some really long beams to lay across the truck that we could lower the house onto.

To get to this point I had to pull all of the verandahs off the house, as well as the roof. I measured and drew diagrams outlining where every single piece of timber went, and every stump and roofing sheet, down to every nail. These big sheets of paper became the instructions to reassemble the house in its new location. The whole process was a nightmare and a test of my very short fuse. We did the entire job ourselves.

Thankfully the property never flooded again but the flood and move cost us a fortune, and it wasn't what you'd call a nice housewarming. Lyn was understandably very upset; it was a pretty traumatic event. The hardest part was that every time it rained after that, we'd wake up and think back to that terrifying day. When we said we wanted to keep busy up there, we had no intention of doing anything quite like that. I suppose you've got to be careful what you wish for.

***

'The kids might have sold their video to America. They could make a million dollars! Can you believe that?' Lyn said, jumping up and down with excitement. She had just spoken to Steve, whose documentary had been sold to an American television network called Animal Planet.

In the late 1980s, Steve had met a television producer called John Stainton through the reptile park. Steve had given John a few of his home videos to review, depicting him catching crocodiles up at Cattle Creek. Those videos showed Steve exactly as he was, no airs or graces, just pure enthusiasm and energy that bounced out of the television and around your lounge room. In the bush Steve came alive; that was where he was able to just be himself. John saw Steve's appeal straightaway. Those tapes were the most intrepid home movies he had ever seen; he was glued to the television all night long. So John suggested to Steve that the two of them get together to film a pilot documentary. Steve and Terri jumped straight on board, spending their honeymoon filming with John, catching snakes and crocs in the wilds of Australia.

Four years later that very documentary—*The Crocodile Hunter*—was a success on Animal Planet, with around seven million people tuning in worldwide. Nobody had put that sort of basic, down-to-earth crocodile-catching on film before, for the average guy in the street to see. And I think that was its charm.

I had nothing but admiration for John and his expertise and the way he operated with Steve. It was great to watch the two of them work in front of and behind the camera. Steve was a natural in front of the lens because he was really determined to get his message out to people. And from day one of shooting, John's advice to Steve was to remain exactly that way: 'Just feel like natural, Steve, be yourself,' he said.

John had wanted Steve to remain exactly as he was in those raw home movies from Cattle Creek. What came across in those videos was effortlessly humorous, action-packed and a true representation of his passion for wildlife. Even after they'd shot what they wanted, Steve would be off doing something unpredictable or chasing another reptile up a tree. I think John understood that simply letting him go and be his natural inquisitive self was the way to go—and just always keep the camera rolling. It was kind of like releasing an animal out into the wild.

I kept out of the way of the cameras as much as possible because I'm not a people person, and Steve used to protect me a fair bit when the media attention grew over the years. Occasionally I'd go out on location with him, helping behind the scenes in catching a fierce snake they wanted to film or helping to set the crocodile traps. It was a good excuse to get back to some of my favourite places and be out there again with Steve.

I'm sure I pissed John off at times with my non-compliance: I'd never shave when I was supposed to and I wouldn't do up the buttons on my shirts. I hated wearing shirts as it was.

But with the increasing popularity of Steve's documentaries came questions about his authenticity. Not everyone, it seemed, was convinced that his high-spirits on screen were genuine. The public, and even friends, didn't hold back from putting in their two bobs' worth. 'That son of yours is crazy!' they said. 'He's not fair dinkum. He's putting it on,' or, 'Nobody can have that much energy, surely.'

Well, we knew better than anyone that unfortunately he did have that much energy. The cameras were now capturing exactly what he'd been like since he was a hyperactive blond-haired boy who'd caused his mum and dad such headaches and near heart attacks. Steve's full-on excitable nature was mistaken by some for overacting, but actually nobody was more genuinely passionate about the state of our planet and the creatures on it than he was.

With his wildlife documentaries, he managed to get the viewer right in the middle of the action. He wanted his audience to be right there with him, just as he did with all those visitors to the park. He was all about getting people to have a personal experience with wildlife, rather than a casual look.

He wanted to undo the disconnection between humankind and animals; he wanted to bring the two together. He had the idea that if you could impart to someone the feeling of a close encounter with an animal, you could also impart the love and respect that came from that close encounter. If he could relay the sensation of that black snake's tongue flicking out or let us hear the crunch of a saltwater crocodile's powerful jaws snapping shut—if he could make his viewer feel it, hear it, see it—then there was a greater chance of engaging people with animals. Because if you can't get people interested, then you've got no hope of conserving that animal. He wanted his encounter to feel like your encounter.

And John enabled Steve to get that across to people. The two of them made an unlikely duo—a raw crocodile hunter and a refined television producer—but somehow it just worked and they made a great team that endured a very long time. It was thanks to John that Steve got to be where he was; he took Steve out into the world and right into people's lounge rooms.

Steve never wanted anyone to try the kinds of things he was doing at home. People saw him work with dangerous snakes and jump on monstrous crocs, handle snakes that swung back to bite him in defence, lie down and let a deadly fierce snake lick his face. But people probably didn't understand that Steve had had a thirty-year apprenticeship, as well as a natural born gift for reading animals.

A lot of money was generated by *The Crocodile Hunter* in the years that followed. It was a fortune in anyone's terms, something we certainly wouldn't have been able to achieve with the reptile park. With it the park was able to grow. It very quickly became a world-class attraction and one of the most well-known zoos in the world. Steve renamed it Australia Zoo in the late 1990s, because he wanted it to mature. He had moved to stocking more exotic animals alongside native ones and a name change made perfect sense. I didn't agree initially, but once again Steve was spot-on.

The zoo went absolutely mental. People were swarming through the gates to see Steve working with the animal he had made famous alongside him, the saltwater crocodile. Things got so busy they had to buy more land for a carpark to accommodate the hordes of people turning up from all over the world to visit the very home of the Crocodile Hunter.

But what was most amazing of all for me to see was that it didn't change him a bit, except he became a hell of a lot busier. His filming took him all over the world doing what he loved—getting close to wildlife. He was able to get out to some other countries and wild regions of the world, which wouldn't have been possible otherwise, and he was able to see with his own eyes what was happening globally for the conservation of wildlife.

Television enabled him to get the conservation message out to the largest possible audience—at one stage he had a viewership of five hundred million people. We could never have even dreamed of that when we started our family reptile park in Beerwah.

And all this meant Steve could put his money where his mouth was. If he wanted to buy conservation land then he could, and he did. He wasn't just able to display an animal in the park, he could also look at securing habitat for that species in the wild. He was able to take our humble local wildlife park and our message of conservation to unbelievable heights through his wildlife documentaries.

From where I stood, it was sometimes hard to believe it had all happened—I could never really digest it, to be honest. It was always quite surreal to see Steve Irwin's name anywhere or his face on a billboard, because behind the scenes we were just doing the same old things: getting our hands dirty, driving the backhoe, catching crocodiles and disappearing for weeks out in the bush with just our swags. To me, he was just the same Steve as he always was, still the same old turkey, only now he was also a household name.

***

Even in our retirement at Baffle Creek we still got involved with wildlife whenever we could. Steve and I ventured up to a property called Escott Station, near Burketown on the Gulf of Carpentaria, to rescue a rogue saltwater crocodile called

Nobby with a jaw blown away by a high-powered rifle. And Steve finally caught himself a pair of elusive canopy goannas. They had first been described as a species in the mid 1980s, when some were shot out of the rainforest canopy. In 1992, after years of climbing trees in the rainforests of the Cape York Peninsula in Far North Queensland, Steve finally got his hands on a pair as Lyn, Terri and I stood on the ground, excitedly directing him on which branches to swing from to catch up with his target. He brought them back to the zoo and began a successful breeding program of this rare species, eventually releasing the original pair back in the same spot, where they could continue to thrive in the wild.

I established a private plant nursery at Rosedale where I grew all the plants for Steve at the zoo. I cultivated thousands of all sorts of palm tree varieties to plant out new pathways, enclosures and landscaped grounds as the park expanded. As always, I got stuck into it, reading as much as I could, seeking information from other people in the horticulture business, and constructing my own greenhouses.

I relocated each tree to Beerwah myself, digging them out of the ground and driving the seven-hundred-kilometre round-trip. It was a chance to check in with the park, to see all the expansions taking place. I had cottoned on that whenever I turned up, Steve had spent the better part of the last few days getting everything in tip-top shape: park staff were prepped, enclosures were extra clean, pathways swept, new constructions finished. He wanted to make a good impression. But he didn't need to; he made it on his own. I was always so proud of him.

In those later years at Rosedale, Lyn and I welcomed a new member of our family, Ailac the Alaskan malamute. He was named after a glacier, because he was so big, it felt as though he was the size of one. When his mother rejected him a day after birth, Mandy raised him until he was five weeks old and then he came to us, where he quickly became part of the family. He was a giant ball of fluff, and shed clouds of fur with every shake of his body.

'Will you get that bloody dog off the bed!' Lyn would shout as Ailac bounded into our bedroom every morning, startling us awake as this thing the size of a rhinoceros tried to wiggle in between us on the bed. I'd make the appropriate noises, but I secretly loved those wake-up calls from him.

He was gentle and playful, and loved to jump into Island Creek on his daily off-leash adventure. He wasn't allowed to go in but he always did, and on the walk back to the house I'd warn him about how we were both going to pay for that, so I'd wash him and dry him and spend an hour brushing his thick fur. When Ailac got into trouble, usually I did too, because whatever we did it always involved a lot of mud.

By the year 2000, Steve had got in our ear about us moving to a new property he and Terri had privately purchased to keep as a wildlife sanctuary. The 1650 acres needed infrastructure built from scratch. Steve wanted to prove that it was possible to run cattle without detrimentally affecting the environment or its wildlife, and also wanted to create a release facility for rehabilitated native wildlife at the same time. The property would also have a plantation of over 33,000 eucalypt trees to feed the koalas back at the zoo. As just one koala needed to feed on around three hundred eucalypts per year across eight different species, that alone would be a full-time job.

By now, Steve and Terri had welcomed their first child into the world, a beautiful daughter called Bindi Sue. She was the apple of Steve's eye, and being a father became the most important job in the world to him. She was the latest addition to our ever-expanding brood of grandkids back down on the Sunshine Coast, who were the catalyst for Lyn wanting to agree to Steve's idea to move. Being a typical doting grandmother, Lyn was convinced almost immediately because it meant we would be closer to the family. But I loved our life at Rosedale, and as usual I took a lot more convincing.

Travel Log: Bob and Amanda on the road

THE ALICE RIVER, CAPE YORK, QUEENSLAND, SEPTEMBER 2015

AMANDA

Enjoyment comes in the form of some of the most basic things when you're out in the bush. Things that I ordinarily take for granted at home. Being covered from head to toe in powdery red bull dust or sweating in forty-degree heat for days on end truly makes me appreciate the very basic necessities of daily life. Like washing my hat-hair for the first time in a week, or shaving my legs, just basic maintenance that feels long overdue since being on the road. Things like this are just a part of my everyday life back in Brisbane, but to be able to take some time out of the hottest part of the day to sit in the shade of a paperbark tree on the banks of a remote waterhole in the middle of Cape York makes the experience a novelty.

On this particular day, an ibis soared gracefully overhead, travelling slowly in my direction. I was enjoying watching him effortlessly glide along, his reflection perfectly mirrored in glassy water below. The moment he realised I was there, he got a fright and awkwardly changed course, almost back-flipping in his panic to get away from me. I could only imagine his thoughts: *What the bloody hell is that thing?* His surprise to see me was the perfect sign of the remoteness of this place. I laughed to imagine city ibis being afraid of people as they raided rubbish bins on our streets. How nice it would be for all wildlife to be unaware of humans in this way, not habituated like the ones having to contend for habitat in suburbia. I felt tiny under the limitless, vivid blue sky of Cape York, reflecting on what an insignificant little dot I was on the vast landscape.

I had an iPad set up beside me playing Jack Johnson songs that resonated with my feelings about this trip, songs about perfect days in a mellow world. Every now and then a little freshwater crocodile would surface in the waterhole beside me and take a good look. I enjoyed playing a little game with him; I'd look away, and then quickly turn back to catch his eye. Every time our eyes met, he'd disappear below the water, leaving ripples in his wake. I found it endearing that he thought he could take a stealthy glimpse at me without me knowing. We were so remote, it was likely he'd never seen a human before. *How good is life?* I thought.

But a familiar voice soon sounded behind me. 'Amanda, what is this disgusting music?'

I turned around to see Bob, beach towel over his shoulder and thongs on his feet, prepared for an afternoon dip. Our swims had become a daily ritual to relieve the heat of the unforgiving late-afternoon sun. When we couldn't stomach another cup of scalding hot tea, and got tired of moving our chairs every five minutes to stay in the constantly moving shade, we'd walk to the river and lie down in ankle-deep water until the sun sank over the sand hills. We'd look forward to being momentarily cool, even though we knew we'd be dripping with sweat again by the time we'd clambered back over the sand dunes to camp. As the sun sank, we'd take a moment to rejoice in the fact that the flies had finally gone to bed. It was always a short-lived celebration, though, because then the other little buggers would come out—the mosquitos.

When swimming alone, I'd be watching my back like a meerkat on duty, but when Bob was with us I'd feel at ease. If Bob was in the water, we were sure to be safe, because Bob can think like a crocodile. I don't know how he does it, but I trust him with my life and I'd sit calmly, my body fully submerged, despite the fact that we'd seen sizeable salties in adjoining waterholes.

'It's Jack Johnson, Bob. And it's not disgusting,' I said, laughing.

'I feel depressed. Even the fish are depressed. Look at them swimming upside down. They're protesting about this awful music.'

It dawned on me that the entire journey north had been devoid of any music. Almost everywhere I travel back home in my car there's a soundtrack to my day. But in all my journeys with Bob, we never once had the radio on or music playing. We would either be talking, or sitting in silence, wrapped up in our own thoughts. More often it'd be silence. For Bob, driving was thinking time.

I'd never thought to ask him about what style of music he even liked. 'Growing up, I really liked Buddy Holly. He was more my vintage, long before your time,' he said.

But he'd gravely underestimated my varied taste in music. We sat listening to 'That'll Be the Day' on my iPad, and I could tell from Bob's toe-tapping that he enjoyed the fifties rock'n'roll echoing across the otherwise still Alice River.

'Look at that. The fish are even mating again!' he cried, with a defiant grin on his face. We sat for hours talking about great bands of the past. He'd seen Roy Orbison live at the Caloundra Civic Centre once with rave reviews, and he didn't mind a bit of Johnny Cash over the wireless too. But it was The Everly Brothers' 'Dream' that brought back his fondest memories, recollections of his early days courting Lyn.

'I find it hard to listen to these songs nowadays and that's why I don't often listen to music. They remind me of the times I had with Lyn, it takes me right back and that's a painful memory. Funny how music has a way of doing that. I try as hard as I can to never let my mind wander there.'

His words saddened me. I went quiet and listened as Bob continued speaking. 'Do you want to know something that sounds silly? I loved her more after forty-six years than the day we first met. That's a feeling that is difficult to explain to anyone who hasn't experienced it.'

As we sat quietly, Bob went on to share with me the story about the day his music died. And while there weren't words to describe his love for Lyn, I wondered if perhaps the Everly Brothers were able to say it for him instead.

A typical photo of Lyn, never without a critter. IRWIN FAMILY PHOTO

Noel trying to teach me how to play the guitar on a six-week camping trip to some fairly remote parts of Cape York. Noel had written a song that night about time on the road with us, called 'Please, Mr Irwin, I Don't Wanna Go . . .' PHOTO COURTESY OF NOEL AND JILL PECK

Steve feeding a large saltwater crocodile for patrons. I was initially hesitant about him getting in with the crocs but, as usual, he was right. The croc demos became a centrepiece of the park. IRWIN FAMILY PHOTO

Peter Haskins on one of our field trips to Windorah where we were filming monitor lizards for a documentary. PHOTO COURTESY OF PETER HASKINS.

Out in the channel country in Windorah holding an inland monitor lizard with filmmaker Vic Martin. PHOTO COURTESY OF PETER HASKINS

Digging out the earth ponds for a new section of our park—the crocodile environmental park. Ready for crocs rescued from Far North Queensland on our contract catching permit. IRWIN FAMILY PHOTO

Peter Haskins, Steve and me exploring the Far North. PHOTO COURTESY OF PETER HASKINS

A day off from crocodile catching at Crystal Creek in Far North Queensland. Steve and his best friend, Chilli. She went everywhere with him.
IRWIN FAMILY PHOTO

On the boat on the way to Komodo Island to see the incredible Komodo dragons. PHOTO COURTESY OF PETER HASKINS

Holding a specimen of the *Elseya irwini* (Irwin's Turtle) on the Burdekin River where it was discovered. IRWIN FAMILY PHOTO

Steve and Chilli getting a croc processed for transport down on Cattle Creek. All in a day's work. IRWIN FAMILY PHOTO

Stephen Accornero with Acco after his capture down on Cattle Creek in the late 1980s. PHOTO COURTESY OF THE ACCORNERO FAMILY

Steve at the helm of his crocodile-catching dinghy on Cattle Creek. Mangrove mud everywhere, as usual. IRWIN FAMILY PHOTO

Mandy loved heading up to spend time with her big brother catching crocodiles on Cattle Creek. Chilli always had right of way in the boat. IRWIN FAMILY PHOTO

The original Camp Chilli at Cattle Creek, with the handmade sign that I made for Steve after he lost his beloved companion Chilli. PHOTO COURTESY OF THE ACCORNERO FAMILY

Steve and me securing top jaw ropes on the crocodile before it comes out of the trap. I'm up on top in case the crocodile runs forward and I need to shut the gate quickly to prevent Steve from sustaining an injury.
IRWIN FAMILY PHOTO

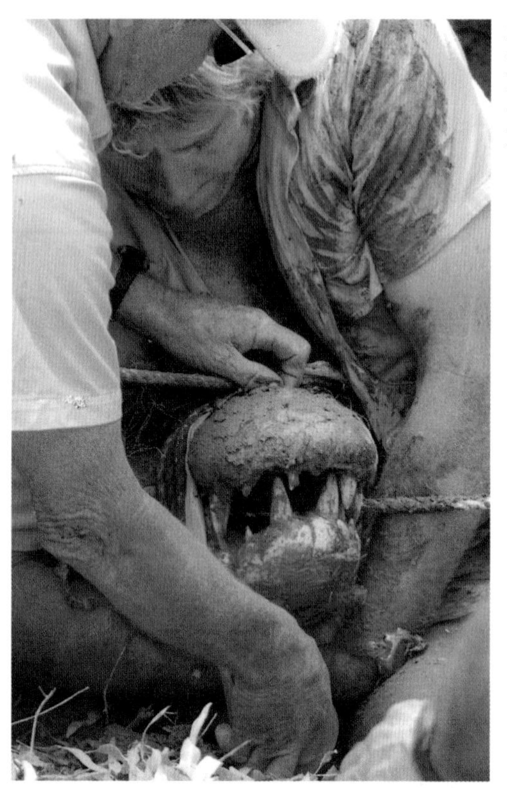

Steve and I often worked at the head of the crocodile together. It was always our favourite job.
IRWIN FAMILY PHOTO

Navigating our crocodile-catching gear into the Nesbit River was a real challenge. The washed-out tracks certainly made it a rough ride in.
IRWIN FAMILY PHOTO

Steve and me when we weren't covered in mud. A sure sign that we weren't catching crocodiles when this photo was taken. IRWIN FAMILY PHOTO

A treasured shot of Steve and me on the job towing a floating trap towards the bank with a crocodile inside ready for processing. Taken in Lakefield National Park. IRWIN FAMILY PHOTO

Lefty and me on the North Kennedy River. This crocodile had just been caught in a soft-mesh bag trap and we're sorting out how to get the top jaw ropes on. This can often take a fair amount of time. IRWIN FAMILY PHOTO

The croc team working in Lakefield National Park on the Bizant River. All hands, or bodies, on deck. IRWIN FAMILY PHOTO

Steve and me at the head of the crocodile, with the rest of the team hanging on for dear life as the crocodile builds up and thrashes everybody around like rag dolls. IRWIN FAMILY PHOTO

Planning our first journey into the remote Nesbit River region. IRWIN FAMILY PHOTO

Steve, Dan and Kyle, using three top jaw ropes in a triangle so as to have better control. Surprisingly, Kyle, at the head of the croc, is in the safest position. Being side on to a crocodile is the most precarious position in this particular situation. IRWIN FAMILY PHOTO

On *Croc One*, on the North Kennedy River.
IRWIN FAMILY PHOTO

Bindi, Steve and me on the North Kennedy River at Lakefield with a little crocodile we've caught ready for processing. Steve loved getting the kids involved as much as possible. His favourite job was being a dad.
IRWIN FAMILY PHOTO

Steve, Judy and a koala joey named Squeaky out at Ironbark Station.
IRWIN FAMILY PHOTO

Judy and baby Burrow, not long after he came to live with us at Ironbark Station. The beginning of Judy's fascination with wombats.
IRWIN FAMILY PHOTO

Judy and me at our wedding in the kangaroo enclosure at Australia Zoo.
IRWIN FAMILY PHOTO

The extended family at our wedding. IRWIN FAMILY PHOTO

6

A sign of life

Convinced I finally was, and in January 2000 I set off for our new home at Ironbark Station, just outside of Blackbutt. Ironbark Station is in the South Burnett region north-west of Brisbane, where the east coast meets the dry west at the Great Dividing Range. I was shadowing the removalists' truck, with my own truck and trailer overflowing with the belongings of our Rosedale life. Towing this much weight was going to make it a long, slow trip, so Lyn stayed behind to do one final tidy and then bring Ailac, who needed a lot of room, and Sandra the bird-eating spider, in her glass aquarium.

The vacant new house I was slowly heading towards was a replica of our beloved Rosedale: everything, inside and out, had been fabricated to be identical to the home we had adored. The wide verandahs skirting the new house were built to the same open-plan style, the bedrooms were laid out in the same configuration, and the kitchen had been duplicated too, with cupboards and benches in exactly the same places. Once our possessions were all in place, it would be a clone of our life in Rosedale—apart from a new outlook onto open eucalypt forest and a much larger expanse of land. We had already weathered one big storm, and reproducing Rosedale would make this uprooting less of a struggle and give us a comforting reminder of our old life. This had been our one condition before finally agreeing to Steve's idea to relocate.

I was sad to be leaving not only our property, but also the deep-sea fishing spots out on the southern end of the Great Barrier Reef that had become favourite haunts for Lyn and me. We'd set out from the quiet seaside town of Seventeen Seventy in our prized fishing boat, in search of red emperor and coral trout to take home and cook on the barbecue. Lyn was a really good fisherwoman. Almost too good, in fact; so much so that it was embarrassing.

But I was ardently looking forward to being closer to our growing brood of grandkids, and also to helping Steve with his plans to buy large expanses of private land to secure as wildlife habitat. Ironbark Station was to be a pilot project, where he hoped to turn private land into regenerated areas for wildlife, similar to the model of our national parks. My role as the property manager would be to build the property infrastructure on the sparse block, the kind of hard work that I enjoyed: building fences, slashing grass, digging out dams, and other general maintenance.

Lyn was looking forward to getting back to wildlife care again too, with plans to develop the property for wildlife rehabilitation in a big way, starting with a large hack-out facility—a soft-release area for injured wallabies and kangaroos. Lyn had been sold on this idea long before I came around to it. I think Steve had got to me through his mum.

But none of it was meant to be. Lyn never called Ironbark Station home. Three hours into her four-hour journey to our much-anticipated new life, Lyn fell asleep at the wheel. Her car hit a tree and she died on impact, together with Ailac. Sandra's glass aquarium shattered beyond recognition. And so did my life.

In an instant, my perfect world was altered forever. All that we'd worked towards in our forty-six years together was ripped away. I had never considered, not even for a second, that we wouldn't grow old together.

I had become increasingly concerned when she didn't turn up when expected; I had called the zoo, Steve, Mandy, Joy, friends and neighbours. But I feared the worst as soon as I saw the police car arrive with flashing lights down our very long driveway. I saw it approaching as if in slow motion. A gentle young policeman named Brett looked downhearted as he knocked on the door of our unfurnished home and introduced himself before breaking the unbelievable news. I could tell from his anguished expression that he hadn't been long in the job. 'I'm sorry, Mr Irwin. I've got some news about your wife, Lyn.'

I don't recall what he said after that because I instantly felt numb. It was incomprehensible. But I was also all too aware that Lyn had a bad habit of getting sleepy when driving long distances. I was instantly consumed with regret that I hadn't made that journey together with her. I thought *if only* every other moment.

The first thing that goes through your head in the days that follow is wishing it was you, and not a person you believe had more reason to live. I would have given anything to have been able to take her place. What a bloody waste of someone who was at the centre of our family. She was a good mother—the best there was—and the Mother Teresa of animals too. But most importantly for me, she was my true soulmate, and my lifelong friend. We had grown up together from young teenagers. I didn't know how this world operated without her in it.

And Lyn, of all people, didn't deserve this. I couldn't help thinking that life was so intensely cruel for having dished this out to us. I couldn't grasp why it had happened. I began searching for answers everywhere. I couldn't comprehend how the lights can just go out on a life like that.

I didn't handle it well. You can't live with someone for all that time and have this happen and just flick a switch and think, *Well, now I'll carry on as usual*. The numbness continued until I couldn't remember feeling otherwise. My formerly carefree world now seemed ghastly and unfamiliar. I didn't recognise anything; everything was tinged with overwhelming sadness.

I couldn't sleep. I couldn't eat. I couldn't stand still. I couldn't be alone of a night in that big empty house. In one way it was full of familiarity, reminding me of our happy times whichever way I turned, but it also couldn't have felt more different to the life we had once made together. The walls were suffocating and so I slept outdoors, messing up the sheets in the bedroom to cover this up from the family who constantly visited to keep an eye on me.

I just shut everybody out. I didn't want to talk, I just wanted to be left alone.

I set up camp outdoors in the sawmill shed, with my swag on the ground. I felt more comfortable outside. The lean-to had just a roof, no walls. It was next to a gully. I'd pace there when I couldn't fall asleep, chewing over my questions. That gully created a sliver of peace and tranquillity among the carnage. Eventually as the night wore on I'd just sit there, under the mass of stars, and quietly try to come to terms with my grief, finding a bit of comfort in the busy night-time goings-on of insects and animals around me.

One moment I'd feel like I might be able to get my head around it a little, and the next the darkness would come on like a stealthy black dog. You can ask it to stay away, you can fight it off with a stick, but eventually you succumb to the grips of despair. I'd slip back down to the bottom of a dark hole that was impossible to climb back out of for another few days.

I would over-exert myself all day with physical work—the busier the better, less time to think. But I'd dread the approach of the dark, knowing that at some stage I'd have to go to bed. In the days, weeks and months that followed, I spent hours just walking through the darkness with absolutely no purpose at all. I didn't achieve anything. I didn't solve any problems. I didn't find any answers.

In the rare instances when I was gifted a night of refreshing sleep, I'd wake in the morning only to remember it all over again, like a punch in the face. It was like losing her anew every morning.

After quite a while, I decided I didn't want to go on. I was so wrapped up in my own grief I wasn't thinking clearly. All I knew was that I didn't want the pain to endure, because it was excruciating. In working with wildlife I'd come to know physical pain; I'd been hospitalised and put back together many a time. But mental suffering is something else. And all you can do is wait it out and hope that it passes, but with each new day that hole just grew into an infinite void. Each day that I didn't see her, I missed her more profoundly. I just wanted to disappear quietly out the back door and be with her again. I didn't know how to live without her and I didn't want to any longer.

So I made preparations. I made sure that all of the kangaroos in the hack-out had plenty of water and food. I told my son-in-law Frank to send somebody out to feed the animals for a few days. I made out that I was going on holidays, but he must have twigged. I had packed enough stuff in my truck for just one day. I knew it would take me twelve hours driving nonstop to get where I was going: the escarpment country on the edge of the desert at Windorah.

I'd left, and could barely see through the tears to drive, when I realised that there was a major glitch in my plan: I'd left the mobile phone inside my truck and it started ringing. It was Steve. I pulled over and answered. I don't know why; perhaps deep down I needed to hear from someone who understood me like no one else did. I didn't speak, just listened to Steve say, gravely, 'I know where you're going and I'll meet you out there.'

He knew because we'd discussed this moment over the years. I had a pact with Steve that if anything ever happened in our deadly line of work to physically incapacitate me, then I was to be the one to decide how it ended. There's no way I wanted to become somebody else's liability, and I wanted any physical pain over quickly. But I had gravely underestimated emotional pain. I hadn't known how it could incapacitate you as much as if not more than physical pain. Steve also knew I loved that part of the country: my favourite part of the wilds of Australia where we'd camped as a family many a time.

'I'm busted up, Dad, just like you,' he said. 'This is real fair-dinkum pain and it's relentless. There's no medication for it.

But I'm not losing my dad too. So if you're going to do it, then I am too. That's the choice you've got right here and now.'

Steve was inconsolable, only able to speak between broken gasps of air. For a bloke with such a hard, robust exterior, he had a real softness on the inside. That was Lyn's gift to him; they were alike in that way. He certainly didn't get it from me.

'No, no, you won't,' I countered. I paused as a truck rushed past, shaking the vehicle violently. 'You can't do that. You've got a child who adores you and you've got a family to look after now. I have nothing left anymore. I've had my time.' We argued for quite some time. Steve was also in a bad way, to the point where the family wasn't sure if he'd carry on with his documentaries.

Grief can be such a selfish emotion; I realised I hadn't been thinking about how other people were feeling. I had been simply trying to cope, to get by, struggling to put one foot in front of the other. But Steve was compassionate beyond words about the things that he loved and he was anguished by the loss of his mum. As a boy he'd grown to share all of her passions, and as an adult, he would have protected her with his life. When Steve's documentaries started to take off, it was Lyn who was his greatest fan.

I guess I found some comfort in knowing that at least she got to see the extent to which Steve had got his name out there, that hyperactive, mischievous kid who had been such a handful for her at times. It would have been beyond tragic if she had not seen how far he got with the lessons she had instilled in him. She had raised him to fight for the preservation of wildlife, and his achievements had made her so proud.

She had been such a steadying influence on all of our kids. She managed to always steer them down the right path. It's not always easy to do, because once your kids get to a certain age, you really can't tell them what they can or can't do. All you can do is guide them and just hope for the best.

Steve, Mandy and Joy were the result of her love, passion and hard work, and she lived on in the legacy she had imparted to them. I realised that I would still have her in our children. As I spoke to Steve, his pain and these thoughts made me turn the truck around. I hung up and began the painstaking journey home to my family.

When I was only halfway there, I did a double-take when I saw Mandy's car on the side of the road. Steve had told Mandy what was happening and she'd decided to meet me on the road to guide me home. She had remembered I always took a particular shortcut and gambled that I'd come that way today.

She got out and eagerly waved me down. I pulled up alongside her, worried I'd upset her further in the middle of her own grief. Up until this point, I had only been thinking of myself.

I was surprised to see her, but also relieved, because right in that moment I longed to feel a part of Lyn and in one of her children I found her. Mandy didn't say a word, just threw her arms around me as I fell out of the truck. I howled, something my children had never seen me do. I had always been the parent but today I became the child.

It took us twice as long to get home from there because I pulled over and fell apart over and over again. Mandy, who was following slowly behind in her car, would get out and give me a reassuring hug, cry along with me, talk me around, put me back together and we'd set off again. Mandy's support was the fuel I needed to get this old truck home.

When we finally pulled into the driveway, my truck's headlights picked out a familiar figure on the verandah. Steve was pacing as he waited for me. I couldn't have felt more pleased to see him. The two of us went out into the middle of the paddock and just sat there in the darkness. Steve had told me that he couldn't face talking about Lyn's accident. He had trouble talking about it even with me. So we both sat in silence for hours, crying, dwarfed under a blanket of stars.

But eventually Steve said, 'The day Mum left us, I got a really strong feeling there was something wrong.' He told me he had been working at the zoo under the backhoe when a gust of wind had come out of nowhere, blowing his hat off his head. Startled, he had jumped up quickly, hitting his head hard on the machine. He had then felt an overwhelming urge to drive off in his car. He drove for hours, not knowing where he was going. Then he'd suddenly stopped and gone home. 'If I had kept on a little longer, I would have seen her there on the side of the road. I realised later that I'd hit my head at the time she'd had her accident.'

I didn't doubt it: Lyn and Steve were as close as a mother and son could be. Born on Lyn's birthday, they had always shared a really strong bond. He was more like Lyn than anybody else.

***

Brett, the young policeman who had told me of Lyn's passing, had kept an eye on me, dropping in regularly for a cup of tea. He'd have his lights flashing so I could see him a mile away down the long drive into the property. He went above and beyond and I'll always be grateful for the friendship he extended to me. I found that I could talk to him honestly about the trouble I was going through. One day, sitting out there on the verandah, he asked me if I wanted to see where the accident had happened. I said no, that I didn't want to know. It was in the past and I desperately wanted to remember Lyn in the happy times we'd shared, not the end.

A few days later I was asked to go to the nearby police station to look over the belongings collected from the scene of Lyn's accident. The policeman on duty asked me if I'd like to take anything of significance before they cleared the wreckage away. The car, twisted and broken and scattered with fragments of possessions from our happy life together, was sitting in the yard where the tow truck had left it. It was a dog's breakfast, nothing but a scrambled mess. It seemed pointless to look over it—the thing that I wanted most of all couldn't be brought back. I don't know why I did, to be honest—all that remained were material possessions from a world where she no longer existed, things she no longer had a use for.

Fumbling through the wreckage, I caught sight of Sandra's smashed aquarium, sand and grit from it littered throughout the carnage. The shards of glass would surely have caused her a painful death. I had loved that spider; I'd had her for nine wonderful years. I picked up a few things that were salvageable: Ailac's blanket and prized toy. I also took the only intact thing I could find: a stainless steel kettle. Maybe part of me found comfort in the idea of bringing at least something of Lyn back to the home where she'd never even had the privilege of unpacking her bags.

It was just one little win against this vast loss. Her death was unjust and yet there was nothing I could do to fight it or change it. Everyone was telling me, 'Life is cruel', as if I should just accept that. But I couldn't. To work together for nearly fifty years, to go through all those ups and downs, the good and the bad, and to have that taken away in an instant just when we were about to start a new life. She didn't deserve it. We didn't deserve that. And the rest of my life would be . . . what?

I returned to Blackbutt to find Mandy waiting in the house. She'd been slaving over the stove. I couldn't cook; I had been spoilt by Lyn. I had always done the maintenance jobs, while Lyn kept the rest of our life afloat. She was our rock. Back in the day, without even blinking she could cook for an army of people, sew clothes for the grandkids, manage the reptile park's front ticket office and bottle-feed orphaned critters needing around-the-clock care. There was always a fresh chocolate slice to come home to and a hearty meal to be shared among the friends Lyn gathered to us. She was a positive influence on me like that; if it had been up to me I'd never have seen anyone. She took everything in her stride, organising me, the business and the kids. In those first few weeks without her, Mandy and Joy had stepped in to make sure I didn't have to worry about the things Lyn would normally have taken care of. But after that, I didn't know how I'd get on.

I was in a bad way following my visit to the police station, after fossicking through the wreckage that had claimed her beautiful, shining life. Everything I'd brought back was a mess, so Mandy jumped into action, placing Ailac's belongings into a shoebox for safekeeping and wiping sand from the kettle. Then I heard Mandy exclaim, 'What on earth!' in the kitchen. I was startled out of my chair, moving faster than I had in days, curious to know what had caused such a reaction when we'd all been in such a dull state of slow motion.

Just as she had been about to dunk the kettle in the washing-up water in the kitchen sink, movement had caught Mandy's eye. There was Sandra, tiptoeing over the element and bits of broken glass and sand in the bottom. I was dumbfounded. Mandy wasn't frightened, because she knew Sandra well. She'd even had one of her very own bird-eating spiders, called Samantha, that Steve had caught for her as a gift. That was normal kind of stuff in the Irwin household.

I can clearly remember the day I caught Sandra. Late one afternoon, as I headed north towards Windorah, I had grown really tired on the road, almost falling asleep at the wheel. So I had decided to pull over where I was, just north of Quilpie in the Channel Country of western Queensland. I wound into the bush a little to get away from the noisy road trains that would pass all night, and threw a swag on a tarpaulin on the ground. I had just put my head down when I saw these really big spiders moving busily around, like pedestrians in a bustling city. It was a little bit unnerving, to be honest.

The next morning, instead of just heading off, I took a really good look at these spiders and where they were living, which turned out to be holes in the ground. New, occupied holes had fresh webs at the opening, and when I dug up one of these, there was Sandra. I fell in love with her immediately. That was the first time I'd had anything to do with an inland bird-eating spider, or barking spider.

As soon as I realised Sandra was alive, I sprang into action. First I cautiously scooped her up and found her a container. Then I couldn't jump into my truck fast enough to head straight into town to buy her a new aquarium from a local pet store. A fire had been lit beneath me. I suddenly had a mission, to save Sandra, after weeks of feeling like there was nothing left in the world to hope for. I placed a ceramic water dish inside her new little house and firmly patted down a bed of new grit on the bottom. As I did, I recalled the first time she had shed her skin, all those years ago, when I had worried that she might have been dying.

She had been lying upside down in her water dish. I was so new to keeping arachnids that I thought something terrible was happening, that I'd failed in her care in some vital way. I called out to Lyn in a panic. But Lyn, ever the optimist, saw signs of life. 'She's not dead, Bob. Something's happening. Look!' she exclaimed.

As we watched in wonder, Sandra had begun to peel one leg at a time from her old skin, as if removing a pair of eight-legged stockings. She was lying in her water dish because it soaked her fragile dry skin, elasticising it enough to stretch it off her body. It was unbelievable, I had never seen anything like it. It took a long while but Lyn and I sat transfixed, glued to her aquarium, watching every last second of it until she revealed her new pale, softer skin. Over the next few days her new exterior had hardened and she had returned to feeding normally.

I let Sandra explore her new home. She immediately sought shelter under a bit of bark, cautious in this unfamiliar world. I knew how she felt. Carrying the aquarium carefully to the kitchen bench, I placed her exactly where she had lived back at our replica Rosedale house, which allowed me to sit at the same spot on our kitchen bench and marvel happily at her again.

I was elated. I felt like a little piece of me had returned from a hopeless place. When your world is turned upside down, these little signs of life can smack you awake like an ice-cold splash of water over your face. I was shocked that she was okay.

She was completely fine, no lost limbs, no shards of glass in her anywhere. Sandra had not only miraculously survived, but had found shelter in our worldly possessions. In my heart of hearts, I knew it was a gift from Lyn to make sure that I had something left that I treasured, a tiny sign that although life can be bitter, there can be sweet bits too. And they can come at the most unexpected of times.

I will forever be thankful to Sandra for turning up again. That day I began to hope that, together with my family, we would get through it. That there would be shafts of light on the road ahead for me. At any time, at any place, some small joy may still come, like a bird-eating spider hiding in a stainless steel kettle.

7
Ironbark Station

Judy Irwin

In the year 2000, thirty eastern grey kangaroo joeys came into my care, an unusually high number. I was an experienced wildlife carer but this was too many to take on by myself, and so the responsibility was shared across our small wildlife group in my local community near Toowoomba. Even between the handful of us, we were really starting to struggle with caring for this influx of orphaned and injured wildlife. The expense of their upkeep, combined with that of the other critters already in our care, was becoming more than we could handle, and we were also growing concerned about the lack of safe areas—far from busy roads and predators—where we could release them back into the wild with any kind of peace of mind. As a carer, when you've worked around the clock to give animals a second chance, the last thing you want to do is release them back into danger. But then the universe, it seemed, stepped in to help us.

'Steve Irwin has built a hack-out facility on one of his wildlife reserves somewhere out near Blackbutt,' a friend from our wildlife group told me excitedly. This property was just a fifty-minute drive from where I lived; it sounded too good to be true.

We soon learnt that the property did indeed have a large fenced enclosure built to house kangaroos and wallabies in the first stage of their re-release into the wild. A gate would eventually be opened and they'd be free to hop off into the wild when they were ready to go. This pre-release facility backed onto miles of uninterrupted bushland.

Australia Zoo invited our group out to the property to see if it would be an appropriate place to release our animals. We were told to meet the manager of Ironbark Station in the morning at eight sharp. Our entire wildlife group came along, excited. Because of the specific instructions about the time, we thought we'd been invited up for a feeding session or a special demonstration.

But it transpired that the manager—Bob, of course—had just wanted to get us in and out as quickly as possible so that he could continue working. He wasn't particularly friendly, just seemed to be fulfilling an obligation as he showed us the hack-out yard, an impressive expanse of enclosed paddock with a six-foot-high secure predator-proof fence, a dam in the middle and a big feeding shed. We all quickly dispersed after that and I headed home.

I didn't realise at the time that it had been just three short months since he had tragically lost his wife, and that he had only just moved to Ironbark Station. That explained the starkness of the home he lived in, which looked almost uninhabited.

A few days later, my home phone rang. It was Bob. I was surprised to be hearing from him. 'The zoo would like to buy the animal food for your wildlife group,' he said matter-of-factly. He explained that management had decided to assist our group. I was to give him the animal feed list and the zoo would order it in.

I was even more surprised when Bob delivered the food to my place in person a few weeks later. It was on this visit that he unexpectedly told me about his pain in losing Lyn only a few months earlier. He told me he needed something to do other than just working on his property because he wasn't coping at all with his grief. He wanted to get involved with our wildlife group as a way of distracting himself. But I was surprised most of all by what came next, because I hardly knew him from a bar of soap. 'I just need a hug,' he said as he started to fall apart. 'Please, can you just hold me?'

So I held him, a complete stranger, for what seemed like an eternity, and my heart broke for him. It was clear just how empty he was. I couldn't comprehend how he must have been feeling, but I empathised with him immensely. Every week he'd visit, and each time would follow the same pattern: he would arrive with milk powder for the animals, pour his heart out over a cup of tea, I'd put my arms around him reassuringly and then he would get into his car and drive home, crying as he reversed out of my driveway. I hated to think of him going home to that empty house alone in that fragile state.

In the months that followed we saw each other a lot. He even bought me a fridge in which to store the food, and eventually a cupboard too. For those first six months, he was a desperately broken-hearted man. The only way that he was surviving was to work twenty hours a day—even then he couldn't sleep.

I wanted to do something to help him, but the only cure was for him to grieve, to ride out those waves of pain whenever they came crashing down on his shore. Sometimes it was overwhelming and all he could do was learn how to cope when those days came. I knew he needed help with that, and that for some reason he had found some solace in our new friendship.

I started to see that for Bob, it wasn't just that he'd lost Lyn but that he also had to somehow learn to manage without her. That was where he was stuck. And so I started to loan him books to read. I had a lot of books on spirituality; it was a particular interest of mine. Spirituality had helped me with my own questions about life. I would tell him my views on death, and what I believe happens to the soul as the body dies. I thought he might find comfort, as I did, in the idea that we were eternal beings: the flesh dies but our souls live on. He studiously read all my books and we would sit and talk about it. He started to feel that nothing is ever really gone from us, and that brought about a shift in his ability to process things. At the core, I hoped to help him see that the love they shared could never be taken away from him. Just because Lyn wasn't physically around him didn't mean that her energy couldn't be felt.

Our friendship developed in this way. Then, precisely a year after we'd met, we were sitting together on his verandah, chatting, when he suddenly said something that nearly caused tea to come gushing out of my nostrils.

'Let's get married,' he said.

I was frozen in a state of shock. We hadn't talked about a relationship, or about anything like that. We were just good friends, so I was a little lost for words.

I carefully declined his offer, although I still felt that really wounded him. I wasn't looking for a relationship. I had a fifteen-year-old daughter at home, Bonny, whom I had virtually raised on my own. I owned a beautiful little house on a peaceful five acres at Cabarlah on the outskirts of Toowomba. I knew that marrying him would mean moving to Ironbark Station and taking Bonny out of the school she loved. I also knew that he was still grieving and that it was all too soon for him.

'I just need to know that there is going to be someone around,' he said. I reassured him that I would be and so we continued to see each other until Bonny finished high school. Bonny and I would visit on weekends and he would come down to Cabarlah once a week for dinner and to help out with the animals whenever he could. He didn't bring flowers for me, he brought big bunches of leaves for the koalas I was caring for. That's the way to a wildlife carer's heart. Cutting leaves for koalas in care is the most time-consuming job of all, taking hours out of any given day.

Then one weekend, while I was at Ironbark Station, the phone rang. It was Steve. 'I've called because I want to thank you for what you've done for my dad,' he said with emotion. He poured out his heart to me about the overwhelming love he felt for his dad. I was floored when the call ended. It was such a precious phone call for an adult son to have made.

He had concluded by saying he wanted to give me a car, a Landcruiser wagon, and a fuel card, to help me out. At the time I was caring for a lot of koalas and clocking up over one thousand kilometres a week to pick leaves for them, as well as making the return drive to visit Bob on weekends. On those visits I would prepare all of Bob's meals, clean the house and do the washing—the type of chores that he hated to do. Steve's phone call was a really touching moment for me, because it would have been a difficult time for the family as it was. They had lost someone incredibly important to them, the matriarch of their entire family.

Romance didn't blossom between Bob and me like it does with twenty-year-olds. There weren't any fireworks. It just crept up on us, slowly but surely. I grew to really enjoy his love of nature. I hadn't had that in my family. I had been caring for wildlife for almost twenty-five years alone, and to find a partner who cared about the same things—and in such a big way—was truly amazing. I knew no one else like him; I could ask him about any animal out in the wild and he could tell me what it was, what it ate and how it lived. Our relationship really did flourish from a shared passion for wildlife.

Bonny graduated from high school and went off to study veterinary science at university. It had long been her dream career. When she was young, I'd often wake her up by placing an echidna or a baby koala on her pillow, saying, 'You know, you're probably the only child in the whole world waking up like this today.' Meeting Bob had only furthered her passion for wildlife and he had become quite a role model.

It felt like we had reached the right time in our lives to take him up on his offer and so I thought it was about time I said so. 'If you are still interested in getting married and asked me again, I wouldn't say no a second time,' I said.

'Okay, let's do it,' he said, and he seemed pretty chuffed. But there was no engagement ring or any kind of dreamy proposal. Bob doesn't have a romantic bone in his body; those things just don't come naturally to him. Many a Friday afternoon, Steve and his family would arrive with a bunch of flowers and Steve would give them to Bob to give to me. We organised a wedding at Australia Zoo because I knew that was the only place where he felt relaxed and happy—which gave me confidence he'd turn up!

Bob doesn't like public places, he just likes to be somewhere comfortable, so on the afternoon of our wedding, Steve closed Kangaroo Heaven—the huge free-range kangaroo paddock—to the public and we were married right in the middle of it. Joy, now running the zoo's new Feeding Frenzy Foodcourt above Steve's purpose-built Crocoseum, did all of the catering. Bob wore a white polo shirt that he'd owned for thirty years. He hadn't let me buy him a new shirt for the occasion. There was no tie or suit jacket but, I guess I shouldn't complain—at least it wasn't khaki!

A few months before we were married, Bob and I had started a conversation with Steve and Terri about the ownership of Australia Zoo. 'We'd like to have the paperwork done up to legally hand the zoo over to you two,' I said to both of them. I didn't want people to think I was marrying Bob for his family's money, because by this stage the Irwins were famously successful. Bob still technically owned the original eight and a half acres after giving it to his son to manage all those years before.

Bob agreed that it was as good a time as any to sign it over. He had always wanted to do it while he was still around. Lyn had been the one who had managed the bookwork, and when she had gone, Bob hadn't kept up with that side of things. I knew it was a conversation that I'd have to initiate on his behalf. Steve and Terri had the documents legally drawn up, and he signed it all over, the whole lot.

8
Reawakening

'You'd better do something about that woman,' Steve said as we worked out in a paddock at Ironbark Station one day. We were spending a lot of time together because neither of us was coping all that well.

'I might just do that,' I replied.

It was reassuring to know that I had his approval. Steve thought Judy was pretty good to me from the get-go, and I couldn't have agreed more. I knew that just feeling as comfortable with her as I did was a good start, because that didn't come easily to someone like me who is a bit of a hermit. One of her greatest strengths is her compassion—it doesn't matter whether it's for an animal or a person, she just loves to care. She looked after me like one of her kangaroos: I needed to be rehabilitated and returned to the wild and she had a real knack for that. I warned her that I wasn't the easiest person to get along with, and I don't know if she didn't hear me, or if she wasn't listening, but I'm thankful she persevered with me. When we first met, I was just a lonely guy with a bird-eating spider and not much optimism. If it hadn't been for Judy, I wouldn't have made it through that very difficult time—it's as simple as that.

I was looking for answers everywhere and couldn't find them anywhere. On other people's recommendations I spoke to lots of people, from a counsellor to a nun, but nothing was helping. I was told I needed to accept what had happened and get on with my life. Well, that wasn't working for me either: rather than accepting, I was obsessing, and rather than moving on, my life felt like it was on hold. My brain was on a short-circuit of loss and devastation.

Judy was the first person I spoke with whose words resonated with me. I had been so angry, wanting to blame someone for what had happened, looking for a scapegoat. Judy's spiritual take on loss helped me more than I had imagined possible. I might still be walking around like a zombie if I hadn't been fortunate enough to meet her. That's one of the things I've been incredibly thankful for: to have had a teacher like Judy.

Everything in nature has energy, whether it's a plant, an animal, a river or the big blue ocean itself. What spirituality meant to me was stripping life back to its core and seeing that everything is interconnected in an intricately woven web. Everything we do has an impact on the world around us. Push and pull. Everybody has their own idea of spirituality, whether that's religion of some kind or simply tuning in to your own gut feelings. For me, spirituality was about returning to where I'd always found comfort in my life before: reconnecting with the environment. I had been so busy for so long, and worked so hard, that I had lost the kind of connection to nature I'd had when I was a little boy. Judy reawakened in me that way of thinking. I believe a love of nature is innate but that it gets lost over time. My personal opinion is that anybody who cares for animals has some basic understanding of spirituality, whether they realise that or not. All wildlife carers, without exception, are communicating with their animals and connecting with them on some level: interpreting what they need and how they behave, or just tuning in to the animal.

Judy's perspective helped me understand loss and grief from another point of view. But I don't think you ever find peace, I think you find understanding—there's a big difference. Throughout it all, the pain never left—nothing could stop it from resurfacing from time to time—but it became easier to manage. And then, slowly, after a lot of time had passed, there was joy in my life again. I woke up and it was as if the sun had come out from behind the clouds and I could see a future again. And that was all down to having someone by my side to share a future with, full of our mutual passion for wildlife. Judy and I really loved having animals around us, none more so than a baby wombat called Burrow.

***

At the beginning of the twenty-first century, northern hairy-nosed wombats were on the brink of extinction. With only around two hundred left in the wild, it became one of Steve's priorities to display them in the zoo, with the intention of raising awareness about their plight and developing a breeding program to assist in their recovery. Steve approached National Parks and

Wildlife Services to get a permit to do this, but they were concerned that the species didn't relocate well and so before they granted him permission they first wanted him to prove that he had staff experienced enough to raise wombats. If he could raise the more abundant common wombat successfully from a joey, then they would consider a project with the northerns down the track. So Steve asked Judy, who jumped at the chance to raise a wombat joey.

We didn't live in the home range of any wombat species, and Judy's wildlife rearing, although extensive, hadn't extended to wombats, so she and a friend consulted with another wildlife carer and then took a trip down south, visiting specialised wombat carers to undertake a training course in their care.

When we first brought her home, Burrow was just the size of a tennis ball, and the same shape too: she was about as wide as she was long. For a wombat, she was reasonably well behaved, but she didn't like to go anywhere without us. She would be forever trying to jump up on our laps when we were sitting on the couch, as scratches in the leather showed. Every morning she would wander into the bedroom and work her way up on to the bed between us. She became expert at this, shimmying up between the bedside table and the bed. Outside on the property, she would follow us around like a puppy dog. Before long she had really burrowed her way deep into our hearts.

After a year Burrow went off to live in her new purpose-built enclosure on display at Australia Zoo, and a rapt Steve quickly notified the department, who next wanted to know if Steve's staff could raise the southern hairy-nosed wombat, a species from South Australia. So Judy and some wildlife friends travelled down to bring five babies home, on permits issued by the department. Suddenly it was all about the wombats; they had fast become Judy's favourite animal to raise. And Ironbark Station became a nice place to be—Burrow the wombat underfoot and lots of work to do.

Ironbark Station grew over the years. Adjoining properties were purchased and a program to track koalas after their release from care was established in collaboration with the University of Queensland. With these successes, Steve eventually purchased a second property, called Mourachan, out at St George in southwest Queensland. In the end, Steve had purchased around 84,000 acres out there to protect and restore as wildlife habitat. As more land became available, Steve and Terri bought it and dedicated it to critical wildlife habitat. The station, in the area known as the Brigalow Belt, encompassed semi-arid ecosystems and had been a vital habitat for many species before widespread clearing for sheep and cattle farming had driven them to become locally extinct. Others had disappeared from the area altogether, such as the greater bilby, northern hairy-nosed wombat and the bridled nailtail wallaby.

These properties—with the model of habitat acquisition, reforestation and maintenance for the benefit of wildlife and their wild places—were beginning to set a benchmark for wildlife conservation on private property. These properties really had become Steve's and my focus: whenever Steve had any spare time we were out slashing grass, digging dams, working out in the paddocks or confronting trespassing kangaroo shooters and escorting them off the property.

With the success of Steve's television career, the zoo was now essentially focused on a more commercial platform. While their educational message was thriving as a result of that, I was starting to see that the vitally important work was taking place behind the scenes, in securing habitat for animals in the wild. I started to become aware of the value of managing land for wildlife on private property and what the individual person could do to manage land for wildlife. There was no point learning about an animal in captivity if we couldn't ensure their populations had a chance in their natural environment. Individuals out there could protect critical habitats in a similar way the government has zoned off national parks.

And it was essential work. Australia's mammalian extinction rate had fast become the worst in the world by far. No other country could even compare to the damage we'd managed to inflict in the very short time since European occupation. It's not something we purposely set out to do, but in clearing land for farming, housing and other industries, wildlife habitats were destroyed, which led directly to the extinction of animals. A lot of land-clearing may well be inevitable to support our country's population, but we have to weigh up how we're going to manage it so that progress doesn't devastate our environment. If we continue to stuff it up, it only puts our own species under threat as well. We've simply got to do things better.

Pretty much every Friday afternoon, when they weren't overseas filming, Steve and the family would come out to Ironbark for a family barbecue. Steve would cook for everyone on a forty-four-gallon drum we had out the front of the house, and they would stay for the rest of the weekend, unwinding. Steve was always noticeably tired when he arrived, looking like he had the weight of the world on his shoulders. Trying to have a conversation with him when he was like that was as good as talking to a tree. His mind would be somewhere else, full of other things.

He had ever-increasing responsibilities at that time and the stress often accumulated. Everybody wanted a piece of him. He wasn't able to just do the things that he enjoyed, that enabled him to relax. Mind you, it was self-inflicted, because the media work he was doing was a way to finance his environmental work.

But by Saturday morning, after a few hours of physically exerting himself cutting leaf for the koalas or helping me to clear lantana, he would be a totally different bloke. The dark cloud above his head would lift, and you could have a conversation with him, get him to laugh, and get inside that head of his again. As his schedule became busier, it took him longer and longer to unwind. He needed to be in the bush to quiet his mind and centre himself, away from people. The bush was his meditation, his medicine, and had been since he was a little boy.

In 2003, Steve and Terri had their second child, Robert. I was pretty chuffed for Steve, knowing how special our own father–son relationship was to me. He now had his own little mates in Bindi and Robert to keep him grounded. He was excited to be able to pass on to them everything he knew about the bush. I knew that special times lay ahead for him as a father. I also thought a bit of payback might lie ahead, if Robert was born with Steve's genes of hyperactivity.

'We named him after you, Dad,' he told me. I thought that was pretty good indeed. I was secretly punching the air.

9

The master's apprentices

'I've got the best back-up in the world.'

—STEVE IRWIN

Despite all of our work with crocodiles over the years, there was still very little known about them scientifically. How did they move about their environment? Did they return to the area they were relocated from? How many dominant males really live in one river system? Crocodiles are the unseen predator, after all. They use exceptional camouflage skills and live in a murky underwater environment. They are possibly the hardest animal in the entire world to research. You can't see them, you can't follow them, and you certainly can't swim with them. The time had come when if we didn't get these crocodiles into people's hearts and prove on paper their utmost importance to the environment then they were going to become extinct. It would only take the next bad media headline about a crocodile to bring up the discussion once again about legalising a controlled crocodile-hunting industry. And yet there was still no complete population survey of crocodiles in the wild. We simply needed more data and more scientific research in order to be influential in the management of crocodiles in our country.

By the early 2000s, Steve had his heart set on joining forces with scientists and universities to drive cutting-edge crocodile research projects. The more we knew about crocodiles, the better equipped we would be to understand, appreciate and protect them. He knew that the information produced from this kind of ground-breaking research was going to help in the long-term conservation of crocodiles around the world. He wanted to be at the forefront of bringing to light information on the species to contribute to and influence best-practice guidelines for their management in Queensland that could be widely utilised by government departments and wildlife facilities internationally.

If you don't gather as much information as possible, you can't put across a good case for conserving anything. You can't say, 'There are only ten left in this river and if we kill any more they're gone.' You can't say that unless you've got the scientific research to back it up. When we started out there was no research done at all. We worked from whatever information we could find. We certainly didn't have any firsthand information about what was happening with the species and where their populations were at. What we did know from our years of observation was that the east coast of Queensland contained very low densities of crocs.

We always feared we would run out of time with conservation. Our native animals, including our beautiful crocodiles, were dying out at such a rapid rate, and our theory was that if we couldn't get them into people's hearts, we didn't have a hope in hell of saving them. People simply weren't interested in caring for something they didn't understand. Crocodiles were seen as bloodthirsty predators that would eat you alive. So we wanted to know more about them. We wanted to start piecing together how the elusive croc had survived for so long on our planet. But to do that, Steve first and foremost needed a team of skilled crocodile catchers. A team like that didn't exist, of course, so he had to teach them first. The methods I'd taught Steve in those early years he'd not only mastered but had become a world authority in. That education had finally come full circle.

I guess Steve and I were lucky in some respects, because prior to Steve forming this group of guys and girls, we used to catch crocodiles ourselves. Just the two of us. And in some cases, just one of us. We'd already made just about all of the mistakes it was possible to make. The best lesson to learn from a mistake is to make sure you don't make it again. While we'd had to learn from scratch, we could bring this young team up to speed with all we had learnt. Then we hoped they'd take that, build on it, and get more done. In this line of work, one mistake is all it takes to cost you your life.

After years of mastering his croc-catching skills predominantly alone, Steve wanted to take a team of people into the region of Australia where his understanding of Australian wildlife had formed. To understand crocodiles, you've got to see where they live and how they interact in the wild. There is no university degree to prepare you for that kind of field-based work with apex predators.

Those trips certainly sorted the men from the boys. It was a good measure of everyone's capabilities. It was a great concept, imparting knowledge about crocodiles to a team of young people. But it was also a challenge, because you can't begin to imagine the danger involved in taking a group of people you are responsible for into some of the harshest environments in Australia to capture what can only be described as a modern-day dinosaur. Before he was able to even consider it, Steve had to make sure he could trust with his life the people he took on board. And over time, through small tests to measure not only people's abilities but their loyalty, Steve hand-selected a team of people who embodied that quality and many more.

The team he formed wasn't your average group of crocodile handlers. They were a hand-selected, eclectic mix of unskilled crocodile catchers: landscapers, bird keepers, security guards and UFC fighters. To Steve, it didn't matter who you were or what your background was, if you believed in something strongly enough then you could achieve it. And people with that attitude were the ones he wanted to surround himself with. There was no school you could attend to learn it, it simply came from the heart.

The team was to experience the mangrove environment from the time they got up to the time they went to bed. They were covered in mud, hordes of sandflies, mosquitos and everything else that comes with mangroves. But this group was prepared for that, and that's what made them really special people. Steve, without question, had succeeded in assembling the best back-up team in the world, led by his right-hand man, Brian Coulter.

The croc team

Brian Coulter, aka Briano

It was 1995 and I was just twenty-one years old when the crocodile keeper at Australia Zoo fell off a ladder, broke his arm and could no longer work with crocodiles.

'We've got to train you to be the new crocodile keeper,' Steve said to me, closely followed by the warning: 'But if you get bitten, you're out!'

Needless to say, as a young volunteer I was pretty excited to be given that kind of opportunity. I thought crocodiles were impressive, but if you had told me that seven years later I would cry over the death of my favourite crocodile, I would have responded with, 'Yeah right!'

Steve trained me up over the next four years. I followed his every move, shadowed him and strived to be just like him, because his enthusiasm was endlessly contagious. He took me on all kinds of adventures to remote places, places I wouldn't have otherwise seen. Places where you would lie down at night and see a thousand stars twinkling off in the distance. In the early days, at the drop of a hat it was just, 'Go home and get your swag, Briano, we're going on a trip.' During those adventures, Steve taught me everything I needed to know about crocodiles and wildlife. Our friendship grew as my knowledge did too. As soon as we had finished work, we'd go up to one particular area of the zoo where he had a campfire lit and we used to sit and have a can of Coke, sharing a yarn around the campfire for hours. A couple of years later, when he finally got his busted knee fixed, that evolved to surfing every morning before we started work with the rest of the team. He called them the daily 'board' meetings, and I rarely missed one. A few years later I'd come to work and it was just, 'Go home and get your passport, Briano, we're going to the airport.' There was rarely any warning about those trips. You didn't have time to get excited, because the next minute we'd be flying off somewhere in a plane for a wildlife expedition of a lifetime all in the name of International Crocodile Rescue.

As the years went by, Steve's ability to catch crocodiles had surpassed Bob's, but he always loved having Bob and his calming influence around him, especially in the frequently high-stress environments we worked in. Those trips were certainly tough going and the conditions on our crocodile camps were not for the faint-hearted. His respect for his dad was always apparent and he always sought Bob's approval no matter how old he grew to be.

While Steve was away filming one year, he asked me to capture and relocate a couple of American alligators in an enclosure. Steve instructed me to call up Bob for his assistance, because although I was confident, I was still raw and I hadn't taken the lead on that kind of capture before. I was nervous because there was a gathering of media around the enclosure filming our every move.

'Are you confident you can do the job?' Bob asked me before we got started.

I nodded my head. His next piece of advice has been etched deeply in my mind ever since. 'When you're working with dangerous animals, the most important thing is that there is only one team leader. Before you even start, it's your job to make everybody aware that you're in charge and they have to listen to you, because in this job you can't have two bosses. Because when someone hesitates, that's when accidents happen.'

Bob had a way of instilling a huge amount of confidence in me to flawlessly carry out that capture. It was a big moment for me to be given the responsibility of being the one person in charge. I looked up to Bob as a father figure. Steve was more of a big brother to me, because he wasn't that far ahead in years. They both taught me hands-on, physically showing me the way. Their leadership was something you couldn't beat. They would never ask you to do anything they wouldn't have done a hundred times themselves. If you'd worked a thirteen-hour day, then it was a guarantee that they would have worked fourteen. They really gained my respect and the respect of all the people who worked alongside them. There wasn't a person on the team who didn't idolise them.

Everything you did for Steve was a test for something far bigger later on. That something, of course, was catching some of the largest predators in Australia in their natural environment, a task you can never truly be prepared for. As time went on, our team expanded and Steve recruited more crocodile keepers, appointing me as the head of his team.

When you look at that core team Steve assembled, there was most certainly a common thread. They were guys who wouldn't think twice about going the extra mile. He didn't pick people who would only work a nine-to-five day. When you're sitting on a fourteen-foot crocodile, these are exactly the kind of people you want as your back-up team. They were the kind of people who don't expect anything unless they've worked hard for it. Because we were working with crocodiles, we had to be able to trust each other with our lives. If a guy is half asleep and not backing you up, you're going to get chomped. The bond we all formed as the years went on was an important one, and Steve was our hard-bonding glue.

Everything we know about crocodiles today grew from the moment those research trips commenced. It was Steve's foresight and desire to explore the hidden world of the crocodile that really brought knowledge about them to the fore. By sitting on the bank of a river and watching, you can't see a croc. But satellite and radio tracking and all of the underwater surveys have shown us that they are there all the time. You can't see them under there, but they are most certainly around. Only by delving deeper can you really begin to understand how they operate.

It's not like walking into a classroom. The lessons are all in observation and you need to take in everything that's said to you. In those days, it was: 'Let's go feed the crocodiles, this is how I do it. Watch me and learn.' And we were learning every single day.

In assembling the team, everything was a test from the word go. Steve was one of those guys who could work people out pretty quickly. He didn't have time for idiots or anyone with a really big ego. He wanted genuine, hard-working, conscientious people. Steve was watching individuals for a very long time, sizing them up for their work ethic and passion for the work they were doing. They were certainly on his radar long before they knew it.

In 2003, Steve decided to take around sixteen staff with him into the wilds of Australia. It was to be a training course and a classroom like no other, led by a father and son team in the far-flung location of Queensland's Lakefield National Park. The very blokes who pioneered the whole crocodile-catching thing were right there, hands-on, teaching us how to follow in their footsteps. They had both sustained injuries over the years and had crocodile teeth lodged in different parts of their bodies and we were to be the lucky recipients of those hard lessons, gaining from the mistakes they had already made. Given that they still had all of their limbs, fingers and toes, I made up my mind from a very early age that I was going to listen to everything they told me and take it on board.

'Welcome to croc school,' Steve said.

Lakefield National Park was the beginning of the real test, the training ground, and the making of the core team. Those early trips were a big learning curve for everyone.

And while a number of people came and went from the team in the years that followed, the core group remained the same, enduring many years catching crocodiles together and backing each other up.

Crocodile lullabies, Lakefield National Park

BRETTY MOSTYN, AKA BIRDY BRETT

As a young bloke, I was privileged to be able to look after Steve's incredible bird collection at Australia Zoo. I couldn't have been more excited when the opportunity came knocking one day to join the big fella himself, Steve Irwin, on a training trip that played a part in pioneering crocodile research in the wilds of Far North Queensland. It was one of the team's first trips together. For me it was like a training mission to prepare us for a proper round of research later on. It was to be an adventure of a lifetime and I was jumping out of my skin.

Not knowing what was coming up was the exciting part. I was hungry to find out what I didn't know about. Our team had freshly captured a fourteen-foot saltwater crocodile named Seven. He was such a large animal that it took the whole team to hold him down when we captured him. It was a true measure of that animal's incredible strength to see ten or more grown men and women being moved around by the sheer strength of one animal. He was growling and I was apprehensive. Via radio, Steve had asked me to stand watch over this big male croc while Steve drove his vehicle through the bush to park up beside him and keep watch over him throughout the night. Only Steve would do this; he wouldn't have slept for worrying about the wellbeing of an animal he took responsibility for after taking it out of its environment. He was waiting for a satellite tracker to arrive before the croc was to be released into the wild and become a vessel for ground-breaking scientific research. So there I was, babysitting this crocodile, when I heard Steve's next instructions over the radio.

'All right, mate, I'm just pullin' off the road now and I'm gonna start comin' in. When he starts twitchin' or lookin' agitated, you need to start singing in a very . . . well, whatever you can do. Just sing! Your voice has got to drown out my engine. I'm coming in.'

'Copy that, mate,' I replied over the radio.

Thankfully Steve couldn't see my face, because I was as white as a ghost upon hearing his instructions.

This moment became my biggest test, hands down, on that trip working with predatory animals. My boss wanted me to sing to a crocodile. I'd jump on a crocodile any day, but sing to one? It was an instruction that certainly took a lot of talking myself around.

The idea was to distract the crocodile when he heard the noise of Steve's loud engine. Possibly one of the most terrifying moments in my career to date was the idea of singing in front of my boss, the team, all of my mates. But I knew

I didn't have a choice. None of us were ever game enough to tell Stevo there was something we couldn't do for him. Whatever time of the day or night, we were up for the challenge. We'd have done almost anything to prove to him we were capable and worthy of being on his team. He had that kind of effect on a lot of people; he had the ability to instil in you the confidence that you could do anything at all. So if he wanted me to sing to a crocodile, then by crikey I was going to sing to a crocodile.

It must have been only five minutes but it felt as though I'd stood there for a lifetime running through the scenario in my mind. What the hell do I sing to a crocodile? My song repertoire was far from comprehensive. The only place I was at ease singing was in the shower. I couldn't for the life of me decide on what to sing, when suddenly common sense prevailed and I realised that it wasn't likely the crocodile would be partial to any song in particular.

The next minute, out of nowhere, the cameraman came running out of the bush, making a beeline for me. I wanted to hide, but he was right up in my face with a camera, and behind me was a river full of crocodiles. Meanwhile Steve was on the radio again.

'Okay, mate, I'm at the fifty-metre mark, you'd better start singing.' He delivered that order with as much gravity as if he'd asked me to jump on the head of a big croc. I knew he wasn't joking.

So there I was, sounding like a strangled cat, as I made my singing debut in the middle of Cape York. Singing to a large lizard capable of doing me a fair bit of damage. I awkwardly sang the only lyrics that came to mind, a fusion of a couple of Aussie bush ballads.

To my surprise, it worked. Seven kept still. This fourteen-foot apex predator didn't move a muscle. I couldn't help but think that perhaps the croc thought if he just kept still then maybe I'd stop singing.

Stevo pulled up beside me in his truck, calling out his window with the biggest grin on his face. 'Don't give up your day job, Bretto.'

We all burst out laughing.

I felt truly blessed to have found myself in a chapter on my life's journey in the presence of greatness, learning from two of the most inspirational, passionate, fearless and fair-dinkum Aussie legends. Bob and Steve instilled in me a belief that anything is possible, to believe in my dreams and destiny. They are two of the most humble blokes I've ever met. They considered themselves ordinary, but in our eyes there was no doubt that they were extraordinary.

That trip to Lakefield National Park was the beginning of times none of us will ever forget. With Steve at the helm, a superman, we certainly enjoyed a wild and memorable ride together, surrounded by an amazingly skilful, passionate and extremely hard-working team of outstanding men and women, all in the name of crocodile research.

Steve was a wonderful teacher who inspired every member of our team and in him we had a boss we treasured dearly. He was an incredible leader, gifted in so many ways. And he got a lot of that from his dad. Bob and Steve were the best of friends. Steve idolised Bob. The respect, gratitude and love he openly expressed and showed to his old mate was amazing to witness in the years that followed.

Knee-beards on the Nesbit River

Trevor Neucom, aka Trev

'I want you to design me a boot for an elephant, Trev.'

Steve knew that whatever he wanted, I could make it for him. My official role at Australia Zoo was maintenance manager of the welding team. If Steve wanted something done, he wanted it done yesterday. You didn't dare admit your lack of expertise in building something you'd never turned your hand to before. You'd just get down to business and find a way to do it. It was a boy thing, something we all had in common, to prove to a manager we had the utmost respect for that we were capable. We'd watched on as he built most of that zoo with his bare hands. He didn't need to: by that stage Steve had enough employees and capable heavy machinery to never really have to lift a finger himself. But he liked to lead by example. Whatever it was he asked, you'd find a way, because if Steve could do something, you could too.

Never having made a boot for anything before, I surprised myself by successfully devising a model of a rubber boot fit for one of the largest land animals on the planet. Something to add to the résumé, thanks to Steve! It surprisingly worked a treat, giving our much-loved zoo elephant with a sore leg a new lease on life.

It was Steve's long-haul trips to America that had me sweating under the collar as I anxiously awaited his return. He'd always come back with new ideas for the welding team. Steve never relaxed; I'm not entirely sure he was capable of stilling his restless mind. He was always coming up with new ways to improve his methods and better understand animals. The ideas seemed to flow from a bottomless pit: they just kept on coming at him like an automated tennis ball machine firing one ambitious project after another. I could only imagine those cogs in his poor brain working overtime while he sat strapped in his seat. The confines of an aeroplane would have been testing for a man who had more ideas brewing than he was capable of fitting into one human lifespan.

'Trev, I've got twenty-four hours to sit on a plane when I go to America to dream up all of the things for you to make for me when I get back!'

And this is exactly how I came to join my first fully fledged crocodile research trip with the Australia Zoo croc team to the far-flung location of the Nesbit River.

'I want you to build me a floating crocodile trap, Trev.'

Of all the weird and wonderful things Steve had challenged me to make, this was one of the most intimidating tasks yet. Over their lifetimes, Steve and Bob had fine-tuned methods of crocodile capture that were widely recognised as the most tried and tested methods around. They were the most skilled crocodile catchers of their time and over the years they had pioneered new styles of soft-mesh bag traps.

The bag traps that were previously used were effective, but now the team was forging into new areas like the Nesbit River with unfamiliar tidal environments. You had to put a lot of thought into where you put your bag traps. A floating crocodile trap would be more practical. Our existing bag traps were always worrying for a team of people if you had to set the trap in a really muddy, mangrove-lined riverbank where you sank up to your knees with each step. In certain instances there was no suitable site to set the traps because of the sinking mud or too much vegetation along the banks. A lot of time was spent trying to find locations suitable for the traps. The water level on the Nesbit varied a lot. So you had to be careful when setting a bag trap that you took into account the rise and fall of the tide, because you wouldn't want to catch a crocodile in the middle of the night if you'd set your trap down too low and the tide came in and covered the whole thing.

Steve knew we could always do things better. He was always forging ahead to make the process less stressful for the crocodile and the work environment safer for the team. The design of a floating, all-terrain crocodile trap was a way to streamline this process and make it easier. The traps travelled up in sections on the back of our rigs and would be assembled like a meccano set on location. It took many hours to get them together in Cape York's relentless heat.

I had never been in the position of having to capture a wild crocodile. As these traps were a fairly new concept, everything was experimental. You certainly couldn't have tested these out on the Sunshine Coast. We needed to work with them directly in the field, improving them with every live crocodile capture we faced.

By the conclusion of the trip, we'd perfected a new floating crocodile trap that had all of us excited about the opportunities it might give us in the future. It meant we could capture more crocodiles, collecting more data on each trip. It was like Christmas for Steve, with new toys for our cutting-edge research.

With so much equipment out in a remote part of the world, it became increasingly important to have someone on site who could fix things when they buckled under pressure. And pressure they had with the wild Top End terrain that we put our gear through—it was tough going. We traversed a dramatically changing landscape across untouched areas of national parks as large as some small countries. Up and down muddy slopes in vehicles using low range, rolling trailers down washouts, towing vehicles out of many nail-biting situations, sinking boats, winching fallen logs off our paths—there was always the chance that something would need repairing on these untamed explorations. We drove our equipment to its full capacity, and Steve drove our team even harder. This was the first time I'd had the opportunity to work with Bob and Steve together in their world, a place where this father-and-son dynamic was on fire, burning brightly in front of our team of eager apprentices.

Steve and Bob had long had a fascination with ocean-going crocodiles and this trip had taken us to the perfect location to get a closer look at them. The Nesbit River was a distinct ecosystem on the Cape York Peninsula with a river system flowing into the Coral Sea of the South Pacific Ocean. Despite being named saltwater crocodiles, very little was known about these animals' time spent basking and hunting on the Great Barrier Reef. The Nesbit area was also comprised of around thirty-nine nationally important wetland systems. We were perfectly placed in the middle of super-croc country.

This couldn't have been more apparent to the team the night we finally reached our camp on the Nesbit River. After travelling 1850 kilometres from the Sunshine Coast, we finally arrived, weary from battling the hardships of an unforgiving environment. Our team had spent days on the road in a cavalcade of utes and four-wheel drives towing the equipment necessary for the research expedition. We were a khaki-clad army loaded with crocodile traps, tents, ropes and food. We had everything but the kitchen sink in order to create a home away from home in a very remote part of Australia.

After we'd set up camp in record time to beat the descending orange fireball that was the sun, nightfall began to sink its teeth into the vanishing afternoon. The daylight had been exchanged for a swathe of stars overhead, while everything else around us was blanketed in darkness. You couldn't help but stare transfixed as you contemplated how big the universe was. The beauty of this wilderness area suddenly made the hardship of our journey feel insignificant.

The serenity was quickly disturbed by the realisation that the Nesbit River was now lapping against the banks uncomfortably close to our tents. Being a new area to us, we hadn't realised how high the tide was going to creep in. We had unknowingly timed our set-up a few hours before at the Nesbit River's dramatic tidal low, and now it was lapping at the front flaps of our tents.

Pulling out my torch to assess the situation, I pointed a beam of light slowly into the obscurity ahead and all I could see were reflective red-eye shines from crocodiles looking in. All that was visible were glittery dots in the sky and glowing eyes on the water. It was really hard to distinguish where the stars ended and the eye shines began. You could easily have imagined that the stars had fallen out of the sky and into the river. In terms of our research, this was exciting, but in terms of our peace of mind it was the kind of stuff that made the hair stand up on the back of your neck. Crocodile soup was out there waiting for us.

But we were so exhausted from the adventurous journey that we decided to stay put. Some of the boys were a safe distance back, but Bob and I were in tents the closest to the swelling river. At the peak of the high tide, if I'd made a really big step, my feet would have been wet the moment I stepped out of the tent. A crocodile could have wandered quite easily into either of our tents without even drying out; he'd have left wet footprints all over the place. I didn't admit this to the other boys at the time, but that first night I slept with one eye open wide. A few days later, Bob admitted that he didn't sleep well that night either. And that's something coming from a bloke who has no fear.

It was only a few short hours later that a disturbing noise disrupted the Cape York mosquito orchestra that was playing in my tent. Steve was animatedly banging pots and pans around our campsite like a deranged one-man band, a camp alarm clock signalling that it was time for checking traps to see what crocodile goodies may have been awaiting us from the night before. We had to get out on the river as early as we could, which was just after daylight. Some of the traps were set in direct sunlight, and Steve didn't want to leave crocodiles exposed to the sun.

As a bunch of dishevelled boys crawled sheepishly out of their tents with their eyes half closed, my torch threw a spotlight on Steve, who was looking back at me with a big grin. It was clear that he got a real kick out of unnerving the troops at an ungodly hour.

'Sorry, did I wake you?' he said.

Like a bull at a gate, he had us up long before the day had even woken up itself. This was the kind of place where Steve came alive, and we knew we had to up the ante in terms of our work ethic just to keep up with his gusto.

'Now you're up, we may as well get out on the water!'

Everyone was on standby back at camp, getting their gear ready for a day of catching crocodiles, as Steve and Bob hit the water to monitor the traps set overnight up the river. This was always a job they did together. We waited anxiously for a radio call from Steve to say there was a croc or more in the traps. When it came, we'd spring straight into gear like a well-oiled machine ready for a big day of processing crocodiles. Everyone knew their roles.

The weeks that followed saw us trapping crocodiles with the new floating traps and fitting the crocs with satellite trackers. It was a process of learning whether the translocation of crocodiles actually worked. For years, the protocol in crocodile management was relocating so-called problem crocodiles from one area to another where they would establish a new territory away from people. We were moving them around fifty kilometres to see if they'd return home or if they'd happily take up a new territory. This research was critical because it proved that crocodiles were turning up exactly where we'd first found them. The crocodiles were returning home. They were defying everything we thought we knew before, that relocating a problem crocodile was a solution. Steve and Bob turned on its head everything they'd known about crocodiles during a life of working with this species.

The last few days of the trip, working down on the edge of the river, was a time I'll never forget. Steve and I had been in and out of the water all day fine-tuning the mechanics of a floating trap. Despite my preference for wearing jeans in the stifling heat of Cape York, on this rare day I sported a pair of shorts. This amused Steve no end, as he'd never seen me in anything but my trademark jeans. He thought it was hilarious, the first time he'd seen my lily-white legs in broad daylight. He just pointed to my knees and laughed like crazy. 'Have a look at his legs. I can't stop looking at his legs. He's got knee beards. Briano, get this man some jeans!'

The three of us had a good laugh, none more so than Steve, who couldn't get through his next line of filming without laughing hysterically whenever he caught a glimpse of me out of the water.

Not wanting to give him ammunition again the following morning, I had emerged to start our final day at camp in my blue denim strides. Steve took immense pleasure in finding another window to poke some fun at me. 'Thanks for putting your jeans back on. We couldn't have taken those legs any longer.' He laughed as he bent down to pick something up. 'There's only one thing left to do.'

Steve pulled out his knife, which resembled something out of a Crocodile Dundee movie. Before I had time to say, 'That's not a knife!', Steve had hacked off my jeans from just above the knee. We stood around laughing before he shook my hand. Steve always shook hands as a sign of his sincerity about something. When he did, you knew that it was something from the heart. He made a habit of doing this with a lot of the younger boys on the team as he watched them enter into adult situations over the years like proposing to their partners or buying their first homes. He was old-fashioned like that. So it was all jokes aside while he shook my hand.

'Nice sharing crocs with you, mate. You're a bloody champion.' He said this genuinely as he ruffled the hair on my head with his hand, nearly sending my hat flying off into the water. He then addressed the rest of the team, who were looking on. 'This bloke built all of my traps. Best engineer. Best mate I've

Steve got a shock to see me turn up to the launch of his movie *Crocodile Hunter: Collision Course*. He was walking along and spotted me among fans and I made him sign my boarding pass. He wrote something rude, which was typical Steve. I've still got that piece of paper. IRWIN FAMILY PHOTO

Steve, when he was awarded an Honorary Senior Fellowship by the University of the Sunshine Coast.
IRWIN FAMILY PHOTO

One of the elephants sporting a new boot that Trevor designed. These elephants were part of the Bullen's family circus animals that were retired to Australia Zoo. They had all been together for many decades. A favourite animal of mine at the zoo. IRWIN FAMILY PHOTO

I'll always remember him as my best mate. I consider myself to have been a very privileged father. IRWIN FAMILY PHOTO

Steve touched people from all over the world. Tributes over-flowed at Australia Zoo's front entrance. GETTY IMAGES

Speaking at Steve's memorial service, held in the Crocoseum. GETTY IMAGES

Steve's truck in the centre of his beloved Crocoseum at the memorial service held for him at Australia Zoo. GETTY IMAGES

Hey Dad,
thanks for helping me to become the Bloke I am.
I love you heaps
Stevo.

Steve was the kind of guy who wore his heart on his sleeve.

Steve and his beloved companion, Sui. He loved his little mate.
GETTY IMAGES

The old sign from Cattle Creek that I made for Steve when Chilli died is now hanging up in the woodshed I built on our new property, called Camp Chilli. I treasure this gift from the Accornero family.
PHOTO COURTESY OF GREGORY JOHNSTONE

Wildlife in abundance at Camp Chilli. PHOTO COURTESY OF GREGORY JOHNSTONE

Tucker time for a koala undergoing rehabilitation with us before release back into the wild. IRWIN FAMILY PHOTO

Some friends found this sign in some long grass near Australia Zoo and gave it to me for my 70th birthday. It's the original roadside entry signage to the park. We now have this relic on display at Camp Chilli. IRWIN FAMILY PHOTO

Camp Chilli is a beautiful place to call home, with koalas and an abundance of native wildlife that comes and goes. PHOTO BY AMANDA FRENCH

Talking to local media in Gladstone about the threats facing the Great Barrier Reef. PHOTO BY AMANDA FRENCH

Out at Camp Chilli with a gorgeous baby wombat. PHOTO BY CLARE GOVER

Trevor, from the old croc crew, and me on a cattle station in Cape York. One of many adventures that we share today out in the bush. PHOTO BY AMANDA FRENCH

A highlight for me whenever I am in Cairns is checking in with the Cairns Turtle Rehabilitation Centre. Pictured here with the amazing co-founder Jennie Gilbert and her team of volunteers. PHOTO COURTESY OF CHRISTIAN MILLER

Bob and Amanda on the road. Pictured here with Buddha, a green sea turtle ready for release after some time undergoing rehabilitation with the dedicated volunteers at the Whitsunday Turtle Rescue Centre.

Bob and Amanda on the road. Storytelling in Cape York. PHOTO BY BRENDAN GRAY

Digging for wombats that had been buried alive in South Australia.
PHOTO BY BRIGITTE STEVENS

Young people are the future. That's been our philosophy from day one. Presenting an educational crocodile demo for the little ones at Wildlife HQ in April 2016. This amazing wildlife facility reminds me of the early years of the reptile park. PHOTO BY AMANDA FRENCH

Dropping in on the incredible Libby Edge and her remarkable project Eco Barge Clean Seas Inc. This project has removed over 200,000 kilograms of rubbish from the marine environment of the iconic Whitsundays. PHOTO BY AMANDA FRENCH

Imagine if we lost the Great Barrier Reef. That's something that I think we should feel profoundly ashamed of as a species: if we were responsible for the destruction of the largest living structure on the planet that is home to the most diverse communities of animals. Here, I'm at a rally in the Whitsundays as a proud spokesperson for the Fight for the Reef campaign.
PHOTO BY AMANDA FRENCH

With Sea Shepherd Conservation Society's Australian Director, Jeff Hansen, after the naming of their flagship vessel the MV *Steve Irwin* used in their direct action campaigns against illegal whaling and fishing activities.
PHOTO BY TIM WATTERS

Visiting Margit Cianelli on the Atherton Tablelands who raises Lumholtz tree kangaroo orphans. Pictured here with Kimberley, a juvenile tree roo, wearing a radio-tracking collar for a day out in the rainforest.
PHOTO BY AMANDA FRENCH

Working with Dan Mead and Brett Mostyn in Mission Beach in 2015 on a cassowary research project. It's been nice working with some of the old crew again. I feel proud to see them still in the field of wildlife management.
PHOTO BY AMANDA FRENCH

Returning to Cattle Creek 30 years on, to reunite with property owner, and good friend, Stephen Accornero. The old lean-to I built for Steve has since blown down, as you can see behind us. PHOTO BY AMANDA FRENCH

I can see a good future now, whereas I couldn't before. There's so many young Australians out there now with the environment in their heart. PHOTO BY BEN DESSEN

ever had.' Then he looked at me, laughing. 'But you've got to get an operation on those legs.'

I was thrilled, despite the fact that I needed a new pair of jeans. In his unique way, Steve was giving my new traps the seal of approval. It was moments like that one that made it all worthwhile. I believed I could do whatever I put my mind to. And when it was all done and dusted and we drove home tired, bruised and weather-beaten, it was moments like these that had me counting down the days to getting back on the road with the team again.

So now it's just a standing joke that I can't go anywhere without my trademark jeans. It's kind of stuck with everyone ever since. These days, I always wear my jeans with pride and smile at the memory of being in an isolated environment learning unforgettable lessons from Steve Irwin.

FRANK MIKULA, AKA LEFTY

'I've got a job for you to do, Lefty.'

One of the last jobs I was asked to do as a young volunteer at Australia Zoo was to rake an area required for a film set within the park. I had already stayed back after my 3 p.m. finishing time when my manager came to tell me that Steve had a job for me to do.

'Here's a rake,' he said.

We got in the car, and I thought, 'Sure, I'll do a little bit of raking.' When we arrived there, I realised there was about a hundred metres of pathway to rake. Just a few days later I realised that Steve had found out about the extra mile I had gone that day.

It was 1999. Unexpectedly a position became available for me planting trees and building fake rocks on the landscaping team.

With my career ambition to be a park ranger when I finally graduated from university, I jumped at the chance. Before too long I had graduated from doing general maintenance to working within the bird department. Birds then led to alligators, and within a few months I was working with crocodiles. My ambition had very quickly shifted from park ranger to croc keeper, and before too long I was invited along on crocodile research trips.

Before we set off, we were briefed on the extreme nature of camp life. But nothing prepared us for the reality. In those saltwater environments, the mosquitos are insane. You have to cover your skin in Aerogard, otherwise you'll just be eaten alive by mozzies. You'd wake up in your tent and they'd be hovering by your face just waiting to bite you. So the second you were showered, you would coat yourself in Aerogard. Your skin would turn to fish scales by the end of the camp.

Steve's ability to make even the smallest person feel bulletproof was amazing. The Nesbit trip was my first invitation to join the rest of the boys on a full-blown crocodile research expedition after our training expedition the year before.

One day we were following Steve to check a trap when we realised that the floating trap had sunk. We managed to get a small crocodile out of the trap, but it only had one rope secured around its jaws. Steve was pulling him to shore as if he was walking a dog on a lead. But before he knew it, he'd snapped the top jaw rope, so without a moment's hesitation, Steve jumped on top of the croc waist-deep in the water.

Without even thinking, all four of us turned and jumped on the back of the crocodile too. Steve was hanging on to its head, calculating his next move and all of ours.

'This is so dangerous it's not funny. The jaws are free!' he shouted to us.

We had to get him on to semi-dry land. Then Steve fell down a hole, with a croc sitting there in his lap.

In hindsight, throwing yourself on an unrestrained crocodile in the water seems ludicrous. Just because someone else jumps off a bridge, do you go and leap off the bridge too? Of course, human instinct says, 'Don't jump on a crocodile in the water,' but everyone did. We all had each other's backs.

Steve and Bob were skilled professionals. And Steve's apprenticeship had lasted a lifetime. I suppose that's why we leapt straight in the deep end with Steve. We were confident that he knew what he was doing. It's like being in the passenger seat next to a seasoned helicopter pilot. You want to fly with someone who is experienced and has clocked up plenty of hours. Steve was a master of his trade, a born leader and we were ready to fly with him.

Steve was always aware of everyone else's position and what they were doing, and with that, at the end of the day, everyone was going home with their limbs intact. He was very good at getting everyone to do the job efficiently.

10

The final expedition

Six-mil rope, Lakefield National Park

'Six-mil!' Steve commanded, covered in thick mangrove mud while face-down hanging on to the head of a fifteen-foot, 550-kilogram saltwater crocodile. The mud was never our desired place to restrain a crocodile, because a slippery crocodile is a dangerous one. In this pristine, untouched part of the world, we just kept pulling out bigger and bigger crocodiles from our traps each and every time. It was a good sign that crocodiles were thriving without humans encroaching in their environment as was occurring in the ever-expanding urbanised areas of the fastest growing state in Australia, the east coast of Queensland. The Queensland government's crocodile management in response to human–crocodile conflict in these parts was still in its infancy.

I took my usual position right beside Steve next to the jaw of the animal, holding it down while I observed the extreme intensity of this particular crocodile capture. It was so tense that you could have cut the already thick, humid top-end air with a knife. We were nearing the end of our time on the Kennedy River in Lakefield National Park, one of our most ambitious crocodile research trips yet. As a team, we had processed for the purpose of scientific data over fifty crocodiles by the conclusion of the trip. It was the largest number of crocodiles processed in the history of Australia Zoo's collaborative crocodile research expeditions.

As a result of that impressive outcome, the team had almost reached their limit, they were physically hurting all over. From the early hours of the morning, day after day, they'd be covered in thick mud and surrounded by a dense wall of sandflies and mosquitos. Before they could give their heartbeat a chance to return to its resting rate, they'd be off to set more traps. But nobody ever complained. We knew what needed to be done and we'd be back in the dinghies cruising along the river to start the process all over again.

Food was eaten on the run with rarely any downtime to rest. After they'd already worked for eight or ten hours solid, if there was still another two hours to go, the team would rise to the challenge. You'd say to them, 'Who's available to set that next trap?' And they'd all put their hands up. And yet you'd take one look at them when they were setting that next trap and you just knew they had reached their threshold. They'd physically had it. They'd been taught from day one, you can always do more and you can always do it better. That was the kind of work ethic they had been shown, and they continued to raise the bar.

The method of capture was a methodical process, choreographed precisely with each individual knowing their specific role. If you could liken crocodile catching to a dance, everyone knew their position, movement and footing for this daring routine. Crocs explode, tire, build up, and explode, so we'd work between those explosions. 'Building up,' the people holding the back legs of the crocodile would call out as they sensed a strong vibration through the hind legs warning that the crocodile was about to put up a good struggle. All ten participants would hang on for dear life and it was always a test of your ability to not be tossed around like a ragdoll. We'd all taken it in turns at some point to go hurtling through the air. Steve would kill himself laughing if it was me, but would find time a few hours later to seek me out and ask if I'd been hurt in any way.

The six-mil rope had one simple job at the release stage of the capture: it was the final process in setting the crocodile free. When you secured the head in order to process the crocodile, you had to first tape the crocodile's mouth shut, ensuring that the most dangerous part of the animal was secure. Once you had that tape in place, you'd cut off all of the others, leaving only one rope running along the head of the crocodile: the six-mil. You'd tape the jaw again securely over that rope, and at the same time, you'd tape an elasticised blindfold over the eyes of the crocodile to help minimise any stress on the animal. The rope ran underneath it. Everything would be set in place. It was then tied to a small polystyrene float and held by a member of the team who was a safe distance away from the crocodile.

It was only when the whole procedure was finished and we'd taken the necessary measurements of the crocodile for research and attached the satellite tracker that the crocodile would be positioned so it had a clear path to the water on its own. When everything was perfectly in position, the team would start to methodically and carefully climb off the crocodile.

Usually the first team of people to go would be the two people at the very rear of the crocodile, then the next team would go and so on until just two people were left holding the crocodile down. You'd wait until you could feel that he was settled, and then you'd instruct one of those people to go, leaving just one lone individual at the head of the crocodile with another person holding the rope in position. That last person had the job of cautiously cutting the tape on the jaw and the tape on the eyes three-quarters of the way through so that only a fraction of the tape remained. This, of course, had to be done in record time. That last person would finally leave the crocodile, and whoever had hold of the rope, the last thread that connected our team to that crocodile, would give it a firm tug and it would peel off along the jaw of the croc, taking with it the tape from around the jaw and the bandage from around the eyes. The crocodile was finally free to make its way back to the water, to again be a wild animal and possibly contemplate its alien abduction. The poly float was attached to the rope just in case things didn't go to plan and the rope fell into the water so it could easily be retrieved. That modest little six-mil rope was one of the most significant pieces of the crocodile-capturing procedure.

First, someone would hand it to the person who was on the head of the crocodile, known as the 'Head Hunter', the most hazardous position, so close to the powerful jaws of the animal. Usually that person was Steve. The rope had to be a certain length, spliced perfectly on the end so that it was neat and tidy. No daggy bits were acceptable, and the team had learnt that we were quite particular about this because it played such an important role for the crocodile to return to the wild where it belonged; we worked hard to make it as unobtrusive as possible. The team would prepare these six-mil pieces of rope at night by the fire and keep them in their pockets so that at any given time whoever was nearest to the Head Hunter would be able to promptly hand it over so that everything would run smoothly. It was a tried and tested method everyone was well versed in.

But today, with Steve at the head, I had a different plan. I had another piece of six-mil rope where I'd cut the burnt end off with a knife and had teased it out at the end so that it had frayed into individual segments about one foot long. Steve was getting impatient, still not looking up, holding out his hand and shouting again. 'Six-mil! Are one of you blokes going to pass me that six-mil, or what?'

I couldn't help myself; I passed him this piece of frayed rope, knowing very well he might not react favourably. Seeing it in his hand, Steve saw red. He looked up as if to say, 'Well, you are going to pay for that.' He was shocked to think that any one of his team would do that to him in the risky position he was in. But I knew that everything was under control; it was just one time I felt it was possible to take some of the heat out of the moment because we still had more crocodiles to process and the day grew tenser as it went on and the team grew increasingly tired.

The kind of pressure that people are placed under in those situations can make it a very risky and dangerous job. If one person in the team doesn't do their job correctly, it can have a really adverse effect on the whole team. From time to time, those things would happen and Steve would let people know in no uncertain terms that they had mucked up, that they hadn't performed as well as they should have. In these kinds of settings, Steve couldn't afford pleasantries like 'Would you mind', 'please' and 'thank you'. It had to be fast and accurate because in those jaws is enough power to kill twenty men. He felt that if anybody got seriously hurt while we were processing a crocodile it was his responsibility. Obviously, with ten or twelve people in that team who Steve was responsible for, this caused tension.

So it seemed like a good time to lighten the mood, to get Steve in a better frame of mind and to break some of that rigidity. Steve was also battling with a lot of physical pain, working with a broken neck and other injuries. While he was working with crocodiles, he tried to hide it. But anybody who was the slightest bit observant could tell that he wasn't going so well.

As soon as he saw me grinning back at him and recognised that it was my wrinkly scarred hand connected to the other end of that rope, his expression changed immediately and his frown morphed into a defeated but mischievous and childlike grin that made the stunt all the more worthwhile.

'You old bastard,' he huffed and threw the frayed rope right back at me before making a light-hearted comment to the team. 'That's the problem when you're working with the oldest living fossil.' He was, of course, referring to me and not the dinosaur he was working on.

It was a good feeling at that moment because I knew damn well that I was getting away with something nobody else would. Steve would have been thinking, *It's my old man, there's not much I can do about this. I just have to wear it.*

I knew I wouldn't get flattened, I knew I'd get away with it, but the thought had crossed my mind that he might lash out without looking first. None of the croc team laughed out loud, but behind his back they were exchanging glances and sniggering, clearing their throats to disguise any laughter. Of course I had another six-mil rope prepared and immediately gave him the real one. I tucked the frayed one back into my pocket as we continued on, a little lighter on our feet. It made the day a lot easier to get through with much less intensity.

I was camped at Camp 19, tucked up a little bit back in the scrub. In the evenings, I'd walk down and join Steve for a meal. We camped apart from the rest of the team, who were over at Camp 20, to get a bit of space, so that we could concentrate on preparing for the next day. My camp was set among the melaleuca trees with a green ants' nest I'd brush up against every other day and pay the price for. Never learnt my lesson. I almost got to know those green ants on a personal basis.

It was a comfortable night after a typically hot day in the Cape. Earlier in the night, there were a lot of people moving about in the light of the campfire as normal, cooking dinner on the camp oven, using the cooler temperature of the night to pack up as much gear as they could before the scorching heat set in by morning, when we were moving on.

Steve usually went to bed much earlier than me, but on this last night at camp he'd decided to join me around the campfire. By this time, it was just Steve and me who were up; everyone else from our camp had retired to their tents, exhausted by the events of an action-packed day. Although, he normally slept on *Croc One* anchored out in the river, Steve had been sleeping in the camp while he'd battled with constant pain. Sleeping in his swag in the camp meant that he could get up at his leisure and fuss about in the darkness without disturbing anyone on the boat when the pain became intense. But he never slept all that well; he was renowned for that. And although he was constantly battling with all of that pain, he still worked through it as if there was nothing wrong. He continued to set traps, climb trees and be as physically involved as before. And he would never, ever complain. But as someone who knew him like the back of my hand, I saw that no matter what he did to fight it off, the pain was written all over his face. I took this time when we were alone to bring it up.

'You know I can see you struggling. It's as clear as dog's doovas.'

Steve owned up to it. He knew he didn't have to keep up his guard with me. 'I think I've nearly reached my used-by date.'

He was struggling physically because he'd really knocked himself around and he rarely gave himself any reprieve from his injuries. In his lifetime he'd been snapped, gnawed, clawed, bitten, savaged, jumped on, whacked—you name it. He had scars all over him. No two fingers were the same; each one had either been broken, split or chomped. His hands were virtually scars on scars. In the end you couldn't tell where one scar started and another finished. But every single time, he knew that those injuries had been caused by his own blunders. Growing up, I'd always taught him that if he got bitten, it was through no fault of the animal but his own error. He knew what he was up against every single time. It was all a giant learning curve for him as he kept pushing the envelope with his research and natural curiosity about wildlife. And he was good at that too. Exceptional.

As the two of us took it in turns to stoke the fire from our folding camp chairs, he talked about how badly he'd treated his body and how much this was weighing on his mind with his upcoming filming schedule. In his life working with wildlife he'd had everything but the kitchen sink thrown at him. And in the end he had the kitchen sink thrown in there too. Because of this, Steve was constantly working with a lot of pain, and we sat discussing how physically demanding these last four weeks in particular had been on him, and mentally it was challenging him no end. He acknowledged that he'd knocked himself around badly and had got away with it up to a point when he was young. But it had started to catch up with him.

'I want to cut back on the filming, on all of it. I want to spend more time getting Bindi into it and being home,' he said.

I didn't get much involved in that side of things; Steve kept me pretty protected from all of that because he knew being in the public eye was never my thing. But Steve told me that he was facing an almost endless series of television projects in the months ahead. He was due to leave the bush to work on several big television specials and fly to the US to promote his shows. It was an unrelenting schedule which he told me he had little enthusiasm for despite the fact that he was aware of what it enabled him to do for the conservation side of things and spreading his message. He was physically drained already by the end of this trip, having worked at full capacity over a long time, without a break and in a very unforgiving environment. The mud, mosquitos and physical endurance of the last month had just about finished him. He made it very clear to me that he wanted a break, that it was getting to a stage where he didn't feel he had a life of his own. He wanted more time to get back to the things he really enjoyed, being a dad and being hands-on in the conservation field.

Very quickly the conversation turned to the current trip. We talked about the good times we'd had and appreciated the time we'd spent together as a family.

'How about you and that six-mil rope! You're lucky 'cos I just about flattened you.' We had a good laugh and suddenly the mood had shifted again.

Capturing a large number of crocodiles in such a short amount of time had taken us over thirty years of practice and learning from our mistakes. With the success of this milestone expedition, we reflected on how far we had come since that time way back in the 1970s when we set out to combat the stigma attached to man-eating crocodiles in order to save their lives. It was years of learning on our feet, fine-tuning our self-taught techniques, and years of our lives spent knee-deep in the mangroves and swamps of northern Australia. Steve was so chuffed to have gone from a two-man croc-catching band to a mammoth research expedition with a well-oiled team. These days he had more than his trusty Toyota Landcruiser ute and a croc-catching net. His worldwide TV success had afforded him a multitude of four-wheel drives, dinghies, a seventy-five-foot purpose-built research vessel, helicopters and the partnerships he'd nurtured so well with the government and universities he'd valuably collaborated with. This could only mean better outcomes for the animal he loved most in the world, the crocs. The experience of this team, in my eyes, was unsurpassed by anyone. He had established the best croc-catching team in the world.

'We've come a long way pretty fast. How good are we?' Steve said.

'I always told you by the time you'd reach forty you'd have probably grown a brain!' I teased in return. I'd always driven home the fact that that kind of finite direction for a young bloke doesn't come until much later in life.

We kicked back for hours longer, one of those nights I wished would go on forever. We reminisced over the early days of mishaps, close calls and belly laughter along the track. Modest times when we'd tie our clothes to a rope and leave them out in the turbulent whitecaps of the creek rapids to be washed in our makeshift bush washing machine. We remembered the animals he grew up with, like Brolly the Brolga who used to steal his marbles and he'd have to wait for them to be digested before he could play with them again. We laughed out loud remembering the time he released a taipan in my camp—and I couldn't be sure whether my venomous bedfellow had exited the tent as I crawled into my sleeping bag—and the many times he really tested my patience when he approached me in the zoo as his irritating alias 'Glen Glamour' with hideous fake buck-teeth and wig to move about unrecognised by fans. Every single time he'd get me with that bloody disguise.

In some ways I might have given Steve experiences and knowledge over the years, but by the same token I got as much back as I gave. It was never just a one-way street. In these later years, I was learning a lot more from Steve from what he had achieved with the zoo, the team and the research side of things. He'd taken our humble reptile park's message global. I probably got a lot more than most parents got out of their children. To have those memories of sharing in really unique experiences to me was pretty special. I can't think of another dad in the world who might have had an opportunity quite like that.

The hours had really got away from us as the moon shifted across the night sky, and before too long the fire had turned to coal. With a long drive ahead of me in the morning, we decided to call it a night, folding up our camp chairs before I bid goodnight to the green ants one last time and made my way to my tent guided by the light on my head torch. But before we went our separate ways, Steve and I shook hands. It was a routine thing we always did at the end of every day or night.

There was some kind of unspoken acknowledgement whenever we did that. An electricity, as two individuals became physically connected. It was a standard greeting for us, something we did constantly. If a moment was stressful or we'd had a hard time doing something that hadn't gone to plan or it was a harder day than usual, we'd just shake hands. It was always something I looked forward to.

And each time, without fail, he'd try to break my fingers. He probably could have if he wanted to, because he was gifted with arms like an orangutan from the day he was born. At the same time he'd give a satisfied smirk while crushing the bones in my fingers with his giant hands. I'd just look at him, not uttering a word. We'd go through this routine every time. There was no way I would ever give in or let him see my discomfort and yet it hurt like hell. That was always our little thing and something we shared from when he was a really young bloke. He grew to have the strength of ten men as he wrangled eleven-foot crocodiles solo that these days took a team of men to hold down.

As the early morning sun rose over the Kennedy River, the camp inhabitants began to dissipate as the team rose under the shelter of darkness to load their makeshift homes of the past four weeks onto the trucks. Over the coming days, our exhausted group would look forward to making the long journey home for some well-deserved rest, but it was only the beginning for Steve. As we'd finalised the research project and were able to make a break for home, Steve's demanding months of filming were just starting. Together with his close friend and manager, John Stainton, his film crew and his lead croc keeper, Briano, he was to continue on to the Great Barrier Reef onboard his mother ship *Croc One*. I'd packed up the last of my gear, leaving ahead of the rest of the team, doing one final check of the ropes, securing everything on the back of the truck when Steve came over to say goodbye.

He shook my hand. When we made the usual eye contact, I noticed he appeared somewhat emotional. I realised that the end of his time in the bush was weighing heavily on his mind after the conversation we'd had the night before around the campfire. Being out here always grounded him because it was like his earthwire planting his feet firmly on the soil. The far north was a place he was deeply connected to his whole life. On this particular trip there had been no film schedule, no fans, just the like-minded team of people he'd chosen to surround himself with in the wilds of Australia he so loved.

'See ya later, Bob.'

He always called me Bob; he called me a lot of other things as well, but when we were on our own, he simply called me Bob. I liked that, it made me feel pretty close to him. Because after all of these years I didn't feel like just his dad, we were more than just father and son. It went way beyond that, a long way.

'See ya, Steve. Take it a bit easier,' I said, fully aware that it was a waste of time saying anything like that, because Steve only had one way of doing things and that was flat out.

I got in the truck, shaking out the pain in my hand from that handshake, well out of Steve's view, and fired up the engine to traverse the two-thousand-kilometre journey home to Ironbark Station in south-east Queensland. I drove away feeling a portion of the weight of my son's pain as I caught him in my rear-view mirror staring blankly at the red taillights of my truck. The truck's lights were my wave goodbye. To me, he still looked just like that helpless blond-haired kid in an adult's body, who had a robust, gung-ho exterior but was soft on the inside like the sinking mud of Cape York's mangroves; that same little boy who, no matter how many times he'd beat himself up, still needed his mum or dad's reassurance when he was in pain. As a parent, when your children suffer, you suffer too, no matter how old they grow to be. I knew that perhaps it was my little secret that he wanted to travel home with everyone else. He was with a group of people he understood, who were dedicated to the vision he had, and he was working with one of the most important creatures to him on the planet.

You never expect that's the last time you're ever going to see your son, but I certainly had a feeling he sensed something was about to happen.

Travel Log: Bob and Amanda (with John)

90 km out of Kowanyama in Cape York, Queensland, September 2014

Amanda

Bob and I followed as John led the way back to the homestead along an unused dirt track winding its way through the dry cattle property we'd been camped on. In the midst of the drought, we had been anchored as close to watering holes as possible; we quite simply wouldn't have survived without the cooling effects of water in the presence of the sweltering Far North Queensland sun. Not that the waterholes were that much cooler; they bordered on bath-like temperatures. The landscape outside the window was desolate, the bush was sparse, the grass that would naturally nourish the animals had been sunburnt out of existence, and the cattle were painfully thin as a result. It was an indicator also of the financial struggles cattle farmers in the north were facing, attributable to a combination of harsh weather events and the end product of banning live export to Indonesia a few years prior. As an avid supporter of the campaign to end the cruelty, I now suddenly felt like there were two sides to the story, this was the aftermath.

I'd spent the last couple of weeks hearing personal struggles highlighting the rate of suicide in farming families up here following the foreclosure of properties by the banks. One of the victims was a young station hand whom Bob had developed a close friendship with, becoming a bit of a mentor to him. Just two years earlier Bob had returned from three weeks on this very property with him and his family, only hearing of this tragedy the day he made the long drive home to Camp Chilli. Bob was immensely troubled by his passing, wondering if there was something more he could have done, considering the friendship he had formed with him. He was so young, with immense pressures of hardship and little access to support outside of these remote areas. Sadly, his story was not an isolated event. Suicide is rife out here. There was no denying that farmers up in these remote parts of our country were doing it tremendously tough.

All of a sudden, John's vehicle came to a halt, the back of his ute looking as though it was about to come hurtling through the front of our windscreen as the dust around us exploded into the air. We came to an immediate stop, and after the dust had settled, I spotted a small poddy calf running out of the bush towards John, who dismounted from the truck to take a closer look. Bob jumped out of our vehicle to join John by the side of the gravel road.

We had witnessed the end of a recent cattle muster on the property; it wasn't uncommon after using helicopters to round up the herds from the air for calves like this to be split up from their nursing mothers. This calf had clearly been left behind, a stark reality of life on the land. When the calf saw us, she had desperation in her eyes. Her behaviour reminded me of a lost hiker coming across the first people she might have seen after days without food and water staggering out of the bush. Disorientated. Hungry. Sick. Looking into her wide black eyes, I was suddenly taken back to my time with a small elephant calf that I had helped to rescue a few years before in Sumatra. She was found wandering alone in a palm oil plantation while her herd was lying dead nearby. I could only imagine that her encounter with the first living thing that she saw would have been similar to this. Perhaps I was over-thinking the whole thing, but there was a similarity for me in this story.

John offered the calf a drink of water. She guzzled it down, nudging him in desperation for more. As I got out of the car, I saw Bob shaking his head helplessly.

Her ears were almost gone. What little was left of the ears was now oozing with infection and flies.

'Bloody dingoes,' Bob said, shaking his head.

'Too far gone. I'll grab the gun,' John said despondently, and he went to fetch a gun that he used for feral animal control from the truck.

I could feel hot tears escaping down my face. For some reason the water that fell from my eyes felt like boiling water in the scorching Cape York temperatures. I'd never seen anything killed before and I wasn't at all prepared for it. The calf was nuzzling me for some more water, which made my tears start to stream even faster. I didn't grow up in the country, and was considerably removed from the harshness of life and death in the animal world. In my world, death was boxed up and given to someone else to dispose of. My immediate, often naive response to critters suffering is to try and save them, whatever the cost. I realise it is not the best reaction at times, particularly when I've found myself working with wildlife in third world countries. Often there are no veterinarians available to save the day or in the event that there are, then they make a decision for you behind closed curtains.

As John returned from the truck, he could see that I was uncomfortable with this idea. I tried to reason with my two mates. I felt like it was me against them. And it was for obvious reasons.

'Can't we just take her up to the homestead and see if they can help her?'

'She's in a really bad way. We need to put her out of her misery, it's the right thing to do.' John said.

I continued to plead my case. As John began to soften, Bob hardened. He was silent and evidently annoyed with me. It's the worst feeling in the world to receive that look from Bob knowing you've disappointed him. He doesn't have to say anything; he just gives you that disapproving look over the top of his glasses. He walked back to the truck in a bit of a huff and got into the driver's seat, leaving John and me there to continue our debate over what to do.

For the first time since I'd met him, I felt angry with Bob. I wondered how this man with such compassion for all animals would not want to try and save this calf first. I realised, however, this was my own insecurity talking—my fear of witnessing death. If anyone was more experienced about making that call, it was Bob. Deep down, of course, I knew that.

The next thing I knew, John had the calf over his shoulders and was loading it onto the tray of his ute. He'd completely given in to me. I could see Bob through his windscreen shaking his head as he lit another smoke and watched on. It could have been just as likely that the smoke that I saw was in fact coming out of his ears, and not the cigarette he had in his mouth. Saying he was annoyed was a bit of an understatement.

At this point in time, I didn't care. I told myself that I'd cop the wrath of Bob's silent treatment later. Right now, I was immensely happy that I didn't have to endure watching the calf being put down. John started tying up its legs and securing it on the back of the tray.

'You're going to have to lie on top of it all the way back. It's not going to be a comfy ride.'

'Okay,' I said. *Whatever I had to do*, I thought.

To my surprise, Bob eventually wandered over and began helping, using his famous bush knot skills to speed up the process. No one can tie knots quite like Bob. He gave me John's radio from the truck to wear on my belt in case I needed the truck to stop at any time. If I found myself sliding off or lying in a ditch on the side of the road hidden by a veil of thick red dust, he told me to radio in. I found this gesture endearing, showing some level of thoughtfulness despite his resistance to returning to the homestead with the calf. He made one final point before he returned to his truck.

'You do realise it's pointless, don't you? They'll only shoot it at the homestead anyway.'

The next fifty kilometres were painful. It took two and a half hours to navigate our way over what can only be described as the dustiest, bumpiest track I've ever endured. I was straddled over the top of this calf as infection was pouring out of her poor ears all over me. Fine red dust was showering me as if someone was relentlessly emptying a bag of dry cement over me. The calf mooed each time the ropes pulled on her damaged little legs.

Every part of me was aching by the time we eventually arrived back at the homestead. Covered from head to toe in red dust, I looked like an Oompa Loompa straight out of *Charlie and the Chocolate Factory*, the only clean parts of me being my teeth and eyeballs, which stood out like a sore thumb in contrast to the rest. My hair had gone from blonde to bright red. I looked as though I'd just landed from a hiatus on Mars. The station managers, Andrew and Alby, came out to meet us and were amused at the sight of me. Alby just looked me up and down and burst out laughing.

'You're welcome to use our shower, love,' she said.

I am sure at this point Bob wished he'd left me back in south-east Queensland and not brought me out into a remote part of his world. Suddenly I didn't feel prepared for the harshness of the world in which he lived, as much as I relished these adventures. Not only was I a sight for sore eyes, I'd brought them home an unwelcome gift—an animal that in everyone's eyes should have been dealt with the way that they do in the country.

The calf was unloaded into the house yard where there were a number of other orphaned poddy calves being hand-raised. I was relieved to know she had another chance at life, and that Alby had a personal interest in rehabilitating calves orphaned on the station.

It ended up being another two full days on the road without a proper shower after that experience and I felt a right mess for those days. The next camp that we found with enough water to bathe in felt like an oasis. With the far north in the midst of a severe drought, most of the creeks that we'd planned to camp at on the way home were bone dry. We passed one dry creek bed after another. Now, Bob, John and I sat in the stream of water, unwinding. Like Jesus turning water into wine, the dust particles shedding off my body had quickly turned the otherwise crystal-clear water into mud. The refreshing cold water also had the healing effect of instantly lifting the mood of the previous few days. Now that the tiredness had started to subside and there was a period of time to reflect, Bob took this as a good moment to have one of his little Amanda–Bob chats with me. I felt like Mufasa and Simba down on the elephant graveyard.

'You made me a bit cranky with that calf, you know.'

'I know I did. I just wish I had a tougher exterior at times. I need to harden up, but I wasn't born in the bush! It's only now I'm learning about it all.'

'I'll let you in on a secret. When you truly care for an animal, it's not a matter of simply liking animals and taking them into your care. It's one of the most difficult jobs on the planet. And it's actually the most common wake-up call for anyone getting into the wildlife industry. You're learning to love something enough to let it go. You can't do what *you* want with that animal. You're doing what's right for that animal, which is quite often tough love. It's hard for us to understand that when we try and use our human emotions to understand the mechanics of the animal world. And when you're working with wildlife, you're facing life and death every single day. It brings you back to the appreciation that life is a privilege, because it can be taken so fast. And it happens in every species every single day.'

'I understand. It's very difficult for me to make a decision to let something die. I'm sorry that I didn't let you do what was best.'

'Working with wildlife also teaches you that animals face death differently. More often than not, animals aren't afraid of death as we human beings are. That calf would have eventually lay down and let death come to her. And her death would have been horrific out here, because come nightfall, those dingoes would most likely have eaten her alive. Sometimes you want to intervene and you can't. Sometimes it just feels very unpleasant to be kind.'

'Why did you let me rescue her in the end? And go through all of that? You could have just shot her. After all, you make the rules out here,' I said, half-smiling, already predicting his answer.

'It was a lesson that you had to learn for yourself. That animal was suffering. You wanted that calf to live because it was what you wanted. And to be a good wildlife carer, you've got to look at it from the animal's perspective, not your own.'

I agreed with everything he was telling me. And I wondered what caring for animals had taught him about his own personal journey.

'Did you develop a tougher exterior from working with animals? Has it helped you to cope in any way with loss because you were somewhat hardened by it?' I asked.

'Never. When you work with animals, you learn to know death very well. It's never easy. And it's no different from life in the human world really. We're not going to be here forever, and I think we forget that as a species. Sadly, we aren't immune from death despite the fact that we can make all of this progress as humans. Working with wildlife has taught me this, it has really driven home that we are all on this journey together. They die, we die. And yet we think we are above death. I think that's why we make such devastating decisions for our planet too. We are having the same experience on this planet whether we are human or animal. But no matter how often you go through it, it never gets any easier. Whether it's humans or animals, regardless of how often you have to let go of something that you profoundly care about, or that you have nurtured over a lifetime, it kills you. And that's the whole point. I'm not saying that you can't feel sad or that it shouldn't affect you, not at all. The day you don't feel something for that animal is the day you go and do something else. You have those feelings for a reason, that's why you work with wildlife in the first place. But the day you don't have them is the day that you get out of the wildlife industry altogether. You may as well go and lay bricks.'

That night around the campfire, I was surprised when Bob continued on with this conversation. I quietly listened. That's the thing about campfires: they're the perfect setting for a story. Staring into the flickering light is sure to get anyone talking, even a man who would quite often prefer to sit in silence for our seventeen-hour non stop journeys.

'You know what we talked about earlier? About loss?'

'Yes', I replied.

'It never gets any easier, you know. No matter how many times you have to go through it. It's just as painful the first time as it is the second time. And let me just say, a crocodile could bite off my arm, I could fall off a roof or be bitten by a hundred venomous snakes. It's got nothing in comparison to mental pain. That's by far the worst of the human experience. There's nothing that could even come close.'

As the fire crackled over the next few hours, I was taken back to a time with Bob when his entire world as he knew it changed forever.

'I spent my last time with Steve around a campfire like this. I never knew it would be the last time I'd ever see him. You never think that'll be the last time you'll see someone who was the biggest part of you.'

**A few months later we found out the calf, of course, didn't survive.*

11
Losing you

Judy Irwin

Bob had only just recently returned home from his time with Steve and the team in Cape York. It was a Monday afternoon, 4 September 2006, and he was heading out to bury a cow that had died while calving on our property at Ironbark Station. I was in the work ute on another track when I caught sight of Bob. He'd suddenly dropped to the ground with his mobile phone in his hand.

I hastily drove over to him. I thought he'd been injured. He was just sitting there propped up against his vehicle looking dazed and confused. He was slumped over and just staring at the ground, obviously in shock.

'What's wrong?' I asked.

Still staring in front of him, he said, 'Steve's had a serious accident and has died.'

It was hard to fathom. Bob was staring at the ground. His son-in-law Frank, general manager of Australia Zoo, had called. It wouldn't have been an easy job to break that kind of news to Bob. There would have been no words to lessen the blow. Whichever way it was said, it was going to shatter his world into a million pieces. And it did.

Bob suddenly got up and took off towards the bush on foot, with me following close behind. I was in a state of panic. He was deep in shock now and the reality would soon start to set in. Losing Steve would be enough to push him over the edge. He'd just come back from the brink after losing Lyn, and my concern was that he was about to spiral back down into that deep, dark hole. This could be enough for him to decide that he didn't want to go on. So I followed him as he alternated between sitting and wandering through the gully. Sometimes I was with him, sometimes he gestured that he wanted to be alone. So I just always stayed where I could see him. I didn't want him to be alone and disappear off into the bush somewhere. I was unable to say anything to him while he was stricken with pain. I couldn't even comprehend what he would have been experiencing. It was an awful feeling to watch the person you love suffering like that and not be able to do a single thing to console them or help them in any way. I didn't know what to do. It was awful.

That afternoon, as family members started to arrive at Ironbark Station, I noticed Bob disappear from the house, heading towards the sawmill shed. A little while later, I excused myself and followed him down there too. He spoke the first words he'd managed to utter for many hours. 'I want to be alone. I just need to be alone.' He sobbed painfully.

I sat there with him anyway. I didn't speak. He sat in silence for a very long time, going from bouts of pained tears to just staring. Eventually he spoke again. 'I have to go into the zoo and ask the media to leave Terri alone.' He felt this really strongly. We hadn't been watching the news or listening to the radio, so we didn't know the extent of the media circus then, but Bob just had a gut feeling that he had to go there and help. So the next morning, after a sleepless night, we drove to the zoo. Bob wanted to travel alone, so I followed closely in my car.

Bob Irwin

They say that when you have everything, you have everything to lose. And that is perfectly true.

It is incomprehensible to wake up without a care in the world and go about your day, as carefree as normal, and then get a life-altering phone call like that. All of a sudden you are looking out into a very different world. One without the person who has stood by you, been engrained in every single aspect of your life. It's impossible to digest that kind of information. Unbearable. The hardest thing for anyone in this world to have to suffer is losing your child. It's not how it's supposed to be at all. To lose someone you raised and watched grow every day. Someone you taught to walk. Taught to catch crocodiles. Taught to love.

Steve was my everything. My friend. My strength. My mirror image. He was the calming influence in my life. The joy. The key to all of my adventures. For forty-four years we had spent so much time together, and now I wasn't ever going to see him again.

Again, I thought: *why him? Why not me? Why someone with so much life ahead of them, rather than someone who's had their time?* I would gladly have swapped places with him, without giving it another thought. It just seemed so very wrong for him to go. He was just starting out as a father, the best years you could ever have. He thrived on it; he loved his kids. That was the most unbearable part of all.

When I lost Steve, a big part of me went with him forever. I certainly thought again about not continuing. I had already been through the agony of losing Lyn after forty-six years, and then to lose Steve, well, the pain was almost intolerable. I would never be the same again.

At the zoo, the media had already established themselves, setting up tents and satellite dishes, there twenty-four hours a day. News of Steve's death prompted widespread shock, and thousands of people had also visited the zoo to pay tribute, leaving flowers, candles, stuffed animals and messages of support. The zoo was like a nest of ants. We hadn't really prepared ourselves for what that was going to be like. There were people absolutely everywhere. The police had to close roads, even the main highway, to manage the traffic. We entered through a back way to avoid it all.

John Stainton had taken on talking to the media and arranging a press conference to respond to the media frenzy. It was held in the original carpark at the old entry, when it had just been Beerwah Reptile Park. Looking at the swarm of people lining the front of the zoo that day, it was surreal to think that this had led from us first opening those front gates as an excited young family all those years ago. What I would have given to go back. We knew that the media weren't going to leave us alone until someone from the family spoke, so I decided to do it.

The media demand was partly fuelled by the people watching right around the world who had loved Steve. It was clear a lot of people were mourning his loss. It was a strange feeling, to think that a portion of the pain that I was feeling, and our family was feeling, was being felt worldwide. It was very different from losing Lyn—that had been very private, very personal. This time, we had to share our heartbreak with the world.

Unfortunately, that didn't help. To be honest, the fact that so many people were grieving for my son only made me feel a bigger sense of loss, because he touched so many people, got the message out there like no one else could, and that void would never be filled. He was irreplaceable. I suppose there was some naivety on my part about the outpouring of love. My time together with Steve was pretty much always in the field, at the zoo or in the bush. I never really got involved with Steve's media career or travelled with him to red carpet events. So to me, he was just Steve my son, the boy in the bush where we were so remote, and so far from people, that I never really saw it any other way. It really startled me to see how much the world was watching. There were certainly two sides to Steve and I was definitely the part of his life that was very normal and grounded. I guess the attention that he received meant that up to that point we had succeeded in raising him to be a dinky-di Aussie who was respected for the work he did and the way he interacted with people. There's a fair bit of pleasure that you get out of that as a parent.

There are a couple of levels of how people feel about one another. You might be good mates, you might be friends, you might be in love with someone like your husband or your wife. And then there's another level, and that's the level that Steve and I were on. As time went on that grew even stronger. We weren't just father and son, and that was difficult for people to understand.

I wasn't sure that I was going to be able to get through that press conference. I just did the best I could. I didn't take off my sunglasses; they concealed the tears that were constantly streaming, and created a psychological barrier between myself and the media. The journalists were strangers, ruthlessly and publicly probing me with the kind of personal questions that you wouldn't ask even those closest to you. I had no planned speech; I never did. I just opened up my mouth and whatever came out, did. The entire croc team came out during that press conference to back me up. We weren't catching crocodiles this day, but their strength was needed just as much.

'Ladies and gentlemen, this is the first media interview that I've ever given,' I said. 'And it's not something I enjoy, but I owe it to Steve. And I also owe it to Terri and the children. First of all, I'd like to ask the media to please give Terri and the children a break. I realise you've got a job to do, but it's extremely hard for Terri and the children right now. Terri is holding up very well, considering. She's extremely concerned for her children, Bindi and Robert, obviously. And so I ask the media to give them a bit of a break, for the children's sake.'

But then the questions kept firing, one after another.

'What was Steve really like?'

'He was an ordinary guy. He was just like any other guy in the street. He just had this ability to get through to people. We weren't like father and son. We never were. We were good mates. I'll remember Steve as my best mate ever. He'd come up to the property and we'd wander off and we'd have a barbecue, maybe just wander off into the scrub and we'd light a fire. I'd have a couple of smokes, because I'm a criminal and I smoke, and we might sit around the fire talking for hours on end, about nothing really at all. And it was just so enjoyable. I'm a lucky guy that I've had the opportunity to have a son like Steve.'

It was a surreal feeling to be talking about him in past tense. He was so real to me still. I couldn't grasp that he would only be alive in my memories from now on. I didn't want to accept that. I couldn't.

'What is one of the things you hope he is remembered for?' The microphones and recorders were all pointed towards me, the flash of the cameras blinding.

I didn't have to think for a second to answer that one. 'Honesty. I told him as Australia Zoo grew, as the filming scene with Johnny grew, whatever you do, wherever you are, you will be honest. And he was.'

Another question fired. 'Did he have a deadly passion? Many people say that he was pushing the envelope too far?'

I suppose that was warranted but it really made me wonder how people with this kind of job sleep at night. In their own lives, when they reached the very bottom of the barrel, would they appreciate me knocking on their door and demanding answers to such personal questions, sleeping on their front lawn until they supplied them?

I answered the best way I could. 'Over the years Steve and I had a lot of adventures together. And there have been many occasions when anything could have gone wrong. Steve knew the risks involved in the type of work he was doing, and he wouldn't have wanted it any other way. There's never been anybody else that I know of with Steve's personality, strength and conviction. And his message was conservation. He was such a strong influence that people all over the world believed in him.'

Steve and I had discussed the risks. That either one of us could have a fatal accident from the kind of work we were doing. It was the nature of the beast. We knew through and through that our line of work was a deadly passion. Over the years we'd had some pretty fortunate escapes and survived almost certain death. Steve, in particular, had always pushed himself hard. But he did it because he had things he wanted to achieve.

We knew that at any time one of us could make a mistake that couldn't be corrected. Steve would have accepted that. He died doing the things that he loved in life. He wouldn't have wanted to have been in a car accident, or been hit by a bus or to suffer some kind of terrible illness.

Another question. 'What's the plan for the zoo now? Will it continue on without him?'

Well, we hadn't talked about it. We knew, of course, that going forward with the zoo without him would feel like moving forward without a map. But it was his home; he'd grown up there since he was a young boy. To let it go—to let his message die with him—well, that would have been such a terrible waste.

'I retired from the zoo many years ago. I still do conservation work on the property, and I'm going to help Terri wherever I can to carry on his conservation work.'

It had felt like an ambush, but the press conference was finally over. And just in time, because I was on the verge of collapsing into a blubbering heap. I had only just made it through and now I needed to go and hide somewhere far away from people.

John did an amazing job corralling the media that day and in the weeks that followed. I don't know where he found the capacity in the face of his own despair. John had been with Steve when he left us, and he wasn't handling Steve's loss any better than us. Over the years they'd become very good friends. On our behalf, he held it all together. I really respected him for that, and to me he felt just like family.

We continued to drive to the zoo every day. I didn't sleep there, I preferred to drive the hours home. The media didn't tire for a long time. Steve remained headline news on CNN in the United States for over a week and the media did whatever they could to get to us. Eventually I had to put heavy machinery across the tracks leading up to the house on Ironbark Station to prevent people driving in. But even that didn't stop them: a couple of determined journalists climbed over the gates and walked in, right up our one-kilometre driveway. I couldn't believe their nerve.

The show must go on

The Croc Team
Frank Mikula, aka Lefty

Autopilot is the only way you can describe when your physical body is driving the ship while your mind is drifting far away. That's how all of us approached the next day at work. We knew Steve would be kicking us up the backside if we just sat back and let it all come undone, so we had the collective ambition to make everything appear as close to normal as we could conceivably make it. So we busied ourselves in making sure that the crocs at the zoo were happy and healthy, and got in and occupied our minds with diligent physical work. With busy hands, you could easily disguise the shock that had set in, sending jolts of unfamiliar pain through your body every time you had a moment to stop and collect your thoughts.

The best idea was not to let your mind wander, to help it pass with action. Too many questions would enter your mind that you didn't have the answers for at this early point in time. 'Is this the end?' 'What happens now to all of that hard work?' 'Will it continue on?' The decision made by all of the croc team was that the zoo operations for now would carry on unchanged. Like nothing had happened. We'd feed the animals. We'd do the shows. We'd just pull together as a team and get it done.

But in the back of my mind I was stewing on a time of the day that was hurtling towards us at breakneck pace, an unstoppable, unavoidable event that we wished we could have put on hold while we came to terms with the reality of the past twenty-four hours. Eleven o'clock was a thick black cloud hovering above my head overshadowing every thought. Two times a day, at 11 a.m. and 2 p.m., we dropped everything to deliver the world-famous Crocoseum shows. Rain, hail or shine, we did it seven days a week, every single day of the year, driven by Steve's intent to show visitors from all over the world exactly why crocs rule. The pinnacle attraction that put Australia Zoo on the map, Steve's famous live croc feeding demo in his purpose-built, five-thousand-seat Crocoseum. But this day was to be immeasurably different. Today would be the very first show since Steve had left us. It was in the back of my mind the entire day, consuming every thought. 'What's going to happen around the show today?' It would be the first of many milestones in moving Australia Zoo forward without our fearless leader, and that was a pill that nobody was willing to swallow. The Crocoseum was the home of the Crocodile Hunter. It was his dream, his platform in getting his conservation message out to the world, and a labour of his blood, sweat and tears. To think that he'd never walk in there again was just unimaginable.

He was a phenomenal force that burned brightly in our eyes. What would we do moving forward without the star of our show now that the flame had extinguished?

And I couldn't help but selfishly consider what we would do as Steve Irwin's crocodile team without our apex leader. He was our big wise croc, right at the top of his game. Like an old, territorial, busted-up crocodile in the river that kept the wilds of the world around him in order, how would this ecosystem which he had wonderfully handcrafted continue on without him? How would we forge ahead with research and education when he was the most recognised conservationist out there? To our team, he was our leader, big brother, best mate and, without a doubt, our personal hero. He was the reason we were here, following this path that he'd led us down, unearthing our personal passions. To be given the gift of having your eyes opened to that innate soul purpose is something you simply can't thank someone for enough. Some people go through their entire lives trying to find it.

I was the last of the boys to arrive at the back of the Crocoseum after the free-flight bird show had just finished. The bird and snake shows were the warm-up, building up the crowd for the highlight of anyone's zoo visit, seeing the Crocodile Hunter. Why he was called the Crocodile Hunter, I'll never know, because his life's mission was saving their lives. Funny how I'd never really considered this before. That name was everywhere I looked in my workplace.

The typical atmosphere behind the scenes was light-hearted as we waited for our cue to perform. In fighting off a few nerves about presenting in front of so many people we'd find comfort in chatting, kicking each other in the back of the legs and playing a few practical jokes before the start of the show. It had become customary to challenge each other to get away with throwing in a few hidden lines from our favourite movie, *Anchorman*, a hilarious task to keep our mind on something else and the other boys in fits of laughter backstage.

Being crocodile keepers first and performers second, public speaking was definitely not our forte. We were there to educate people about the animals; none of us had an ambition to do what Steve could do so naturally in the spotlight. We were quite happy to be his back-up supporting his endeavours behind the camera lens. While Steve was certainly in the foreground, we were working away in the background. In doing so, our faces were plastered right around the world on his renowned documentaries, though we never grew to be comfortable with a camera in our faces. Combatting a few nerves about public speaking was always something we battled with, and Steve took delight in throwing us in the deep end. Give me a croc to feed any day. Today, looking around at my sombre team, my mind suddenly wandered to a happier time.

It was only months before that Bindi had started performing in her all-singing, all-dancing children's series *Bindi and the Crocmen*. Steve, immensely proud of his young daughter, got devotedly involved in the shows, singing, dancing, and encouraging her from the sidelines. He was the proudest dad around. One day as he was about to introduce Bindi to take the floor during a show, Steve commanded for the music to play from the Crocoseum sound department and for his croc team to dance. We were all horrified, fumbling our way through some of the worst impromptu dance routines imaginable. A horde of ungraceful men with pairs of two left feet looking well out of our comfort zones. But a week later the joke was on him. Little did Steve know that we had tirelessly practised a choreographed routine, and we bemused Steve front and centre in the Crocoseum as we broke out into still some of the worst dance moves, finishing up with hurling our smallest member, Crocs Dan, into the air and catching him, as they did with Bindi in her shows. It was one of the most priceless pranks that we had played and Steve watched on in stitches of laughter from the top of the stadium seating.

But the mood backstage was distinctly different today with nobody uttering a word. Those usual fears just didn't enter my mind. We were silently standing around, not really knowing what to say. Quiet with the weight of our own heavy thoughts.

I quickly realised that it wasn't only me that was plagued by these thoughts about the pending show. Just before it was about to start, Toby broke the silence. Toby was one of my first managers, and had taken me under his wing in the early days, teaching me everything that I now know. It was unfamiliar territory to see such a strong figure in my life crushed by the weight of this shared grief.

'No one feels that they are up to doing the show today—can you stand in for us?'

Looking down at the ground as I scuffed my boot nervously on the concrete, I'd hoped that he was directing that question at someone else. My heart sank as I looked up to see the rest of my team staring back at me with desperation in their eyes. *No pressure*, I sarcastically thought. Despite my nerves, deep down I was flattered that they had asked me to do it. I couldn't have felt more proud to be asked to represent my team at our darkest hour. I just sincerely doubted my own ability to pull it off.

Before I found my voice to accept the task, I had another willing volunteer. Crocs Dan put up his hand. 'I'll do it with you, Lefty. I'll back you up.'

So then I thought, *Okay, we'll get through this, we'll just get in there and get it done*. There was no conversation between us to plan the delivery of the show or what was going to be said, if anything was going to be said at all outside of our usual educational banter.

Then came the countdown. I stood frozen waiting for the gates to open and the show to begin. The first time today that I had no option but to stand still as the floodgates burst in my mind as despondent thoughts permeated that wall that I had previously built up allowing the inconceivable realities of our new path ahead to set in.

'Sixty seconds. Standing by . . .'

The video clip rolled; there was no turning back now.

These animated clips had been so commonplace as part of our daily show that they were just a part of the Australia Zoo furniture. On a normal day we'd almost become immune to these kinds of 'Steve-isms' littered around the park giving people a hint of that recognisable Irwin zest exploding into their zoo visit. But today I was more aware of it than I had ever been before. Steve was everywhere you looked in this place, how would we keep up that momentum without him? Surely we couldn't just take down the billboards plastering his face on every corner of this facility and keep up the pretence that nothing had happened? The sponsor-driven big screen that towered above the Crocoseum was bursting with material designed to hype up the crowd for Steve Irwin's celebrated arrival.

A sixty-second countdown launched depicting Steve preparing for the croc demo ambitiously making his way through the zoo and approaching the Crocoseum as numbers ticked over on the screen. Footage exploded in high definition of an energetic crocodile being let out of its enclosure, thrashing around and cruising on the surface of the water down the canal, nicknamed the love tunnel, which fed into the heart of the Crocoseum. Commando-style sound FX completed the package, giving it that suspenseful dynamic of his Crocodile Hunter documentaries. Steve was shown nearing the back entry point of the Crocoseum and being mic'd up for the show. He had determination in his stride as he drove his way closer to the crowd.

'Five, four, three, two, one . . .' Boom. The screen went black. The sound of the gates winding open filled the backstage area as the team behind the scenes released the crocodile. This was it.

Instead of Steve's all-too-familiar face in his trademark khakis, boots and mop of wavy blond hair detonating through the gates of the Crocoseum to his cheering fans in the crowd, on this day I was to be his substandard replacement. Today there was to be no smoke machines blaring out of the love tunnel to go with that clip that normally enhanced that element of showmanship. It would be a noticeably different show. But the show must go on, I told myself, because that's what Steve would have wanted us to do.

The crocodile was guided by the team from the back enclosures and channelled down into a pond reaching the middle of the arena, similar to what had just featured on the big screen. As the crocodile perfectly made his grand entrance, I marvelled at Steve's ambitious design in dreaming up the Crocoseum—a concept that he was told would never work, training saltwater crocodiles to travel on cue. But he proved them wrong because he was remarkably bright and had insight like no other. It was a resounding success building a sports-style stadium with the purpose of having a crocodile front and centre as the main attraction. His life's ambition was in endorsing crocodiles to have their name in lights and here they'd dazzle forevermore.

I went first to welcome the audience, and Dan brought the crocodile through second. My knees felt like they were buckling beneath me. I anguished over how I was about to get through this.

Starting to take my first few paces into the middle of our grassy stage, I felt that I had the wind knocked out of me instantly as I became aware of the audience. It wasn't the overflowing crowd that disarmed me but the sea of Australia Zoo staff lining the front of the Crocoseum looking hopefully back at me. Our peers had formed a guard of honour—a khaki-clad strong wall of Steve's greatest supporters standing there with us in witnessing the first of the milestones without him. They'd dropped all tools from right across the zoo to be there watching. Cleaners, zoo keepers, retail staff, family.

I stood out there feeling like a kangaroo in a spotlight—so many eyes on us to get through it. I knew we were doing this show on behalf of our Australia Zoo family who were grieving. I had a job to do and the reality was that there was still a large crocodile out there, so thankfully my attention quickly became focused on that. I heard Steve's words reverberating in my mind.

'Mistakes happen when people get complacent. Never take your mind off the job—no cutting corners, do everything properly. Remember that a great day can turn into your worst nightmare in twenty seconds if you muck up. Don't get bitten or you can go back to laying bricks.'

His advice calmed me, distinctively amusing but with a serious undertone. I knew that in his absence, I'd always call on his teachings whenever I needed to. Those kinds of things will be etched in my mind forever; in every action he taught me, I'll heed that advice. So in one respect, it was keeping your mind on the task at hand knowing that you don't want to slip over, fall in, do anything that would put you in danger. But on the other hand, I wanted to really make Stevo proud. Proud of his entire team stepping up and showing him, 'We've got this now, mate.'

So we did it, hands down the greatest challenge I have ever faced. Then Dan, shy by nature, completely floored me as he turned to address the audience in his confident closing words.

'Now's not the end, it's just an opportunity to take Steve's message forward, to ramp everything up and not let that message die with him. We need all of you to help us to keep it going, not to let that hard work come undone.'

Dan put his head down briefly and we both stood silently as the crowd gave a standing ovation. We knew of course that it was deservingly directed at Steve, not us.

Dan absolutely nailed it, I thought, as I stood beside my mate in awe of his words. He'd taken such a big step up to the mark expressing the thoughts that the rest of our heartbroken team were unable to verbalise. I don't know where he found the strength or words but one thing that I do know is that he did a stellar job. The world was watching, and Dan represented our entire team exceptionally well. I have never felt more proud to be part of that team than in those ten minutes in the spotlight of the Crocoseum.

When the crocodile was locked down back into his enclosure and the audience had dispersed from the stadium-style seating of the Crocoseum like a busy ant colony running out of an ant mound, I had a brief moment alone to reflect. The normal after-show feeling was overwhelmingly different. Instead of that sensation of buzzing adrenaline from having delivered yet another successful croc demo educating the crowds, proving to ourselves that we had conquered our public-speaking fears, I felt as though someone had walked right up and punched me hard in the guts, winding me as I realised that a fundamental part of us was missing. You could sense from every person watching, with all eyes on us, a feeling of immense loss. The crowd still clapped and cheered but the tears flowing from their eyes showed they were battling to come to terms with the loss of our irreplaceable Aussie legend. It was clear that their applause was a sign of both gratitude and sympathy for our entire Australia Zoo family.

That show was a marker of the first of the days we confronted without our leader. The future was coming at us no matter how much we wanted to stop the clocks, pause time, be back in Lakefield and feel whole doing the things that we loved most of all. The actuality was startling in that moment for me that we were moving forward into a future without our trusty pilot, and it was going to take some time to adjust. I knew in that instant that things were never going to be the same again, we had just seen a door close on the most exciting and profound chapter that had shaped our young years. Steve helped us as we grew from boys to men to understand the world through his unique and wonderful perspective. He let our team see who he was, and that will forever be his greatest gift to all of us. Above all else, he was real.

Brian 'Briano' Coulter

Over the years, Steve and I had helped each other through some hairy situations: he'd raced to me when I'd had a serious car accident, I'd lifted him out of the way of a charging, open-jawed salty after he'd slipped in the enclosure. 'You know, you bloody saved my bacon,' Steve said. But that was just what it was like: we had each other's backs. What we all had with Steve was certainly not the average relationship you have with your boss.

But as it turned out, no amount of first aid courses could have helped me change the outcome of that unbelievably tragic day that Steve died, filming on his beloved vessel, *Croc One*, out on the Great Barrier Reef. I would have given my right arm to change that. My wife Kate and I just felt like massive failures because we'd tried to save him, and we couldn't. I was riddled with sadness and guilt.

To go through that with him was difficult enough. It was traumatising. One of the most gut-wrenching feelings was returning to the zoo to face his family. To walk back through those gates without him was awful: I was coming back and he wasn't. I wondered how I could face them after what had happened. Would they blame us for not being able to help him?

The first person I saw was Bob. I felt physically sick when I saw him. That was Steve's father. His best ever mate. I didn't have any words to make his pain go away. But as soon as Bob saw me, he walked right up to Kate and me and embraced us. Despite his own palpable grief, he still comforted us, and helped lift the weight of sadness, despair and guilt from our shoulders. That hug went a long way for me that day. It meant the absolute world.

With Bob's arms around me, I was suddenly taken back to something that had happened a couple of years earlier. On the day of baby Bob's naming ceremony, Steve decided that he would take his new son in with him to do the croc show, for Bob's public debut. He'd done it for years previously with Bindi, so I didn't bat an eyelid. He was the ultimate father, he would never have done anything to jeopardise the safety of his children. He'd been brought up in the middle of a zoo and these kinds of interactions with animals were mild in comparison to what he got up to as a kid and out in the wild.

But the camera crew decided to make a big deal of it and the media went ballistic. Steve was suddenly painted as the worst dad in the world. He was completely devastated. He was in the running for Australian of the Year and they pulled his nomination because of the negative press. Steve understood, but he was very upset about the perception out there about him as a father.

A week or so later, Steve was doing one of his routine crocodile demonstrations in the Crocoseum when out of nowhere he started sobbing and telling the crowd how much he loved his children and how devastated he was to be labelled a bad father in the eyes of the world. He was terribly upset. I was sitting there watching, not knowing what to do, but bloody hurting for him. The next thing I knew, Bob senior walked straight out from behind the scenes into the centre of the Crocoseum and wrapped his arms around Steve. Such a public move was really unlike Bob; he usually kept out of the spotlight. But he could see how much Steve was struggling. They embraced for a long time as Steve pulled himself together, and then he addressed the audience again. 'Your family are the most important thing you'll ever have,' Steve said, visibly heartened. Bob just turned around and left as quietly as he'd arrived.

I decided I needed to give Bob the opportunity to know exactly what had happened on the day of Steve's accident. I thought there might come a time when he'd want to know some details, and be reassured that Steve had gone peacefully. I certainly didn't want Bob to think that he couldn't ask me for fear of upsetting me, or making me relive it. So after tossing and turning for many weeks, wondering how to broach the subject, I decided that the very next time I saw him I would just bring it up. I was nervous, because I didn't want to upset him any more than he already was.

A few weeks later, there was a moment alone with Bob on his verandah. 'Would you like to know how it happened?' I asked.

Bob paused, but he didn't look up from his teacup. 'No, it's not something I care to know about,' he said matter-of-factly.

We changed the subject. I understood where he was coming from. His response perfectly matched where he was at that time with his grief: quiet, reflective, processing. I felt it'd been right to give him the chance to know if he'd wanted to and now I could lay it to rest. After that, I vowed to myself I would never talk to the media about the private events of Steve's passing. Out of respect for Bob, and the rest of the family. I never did and I never will.

Bob Irwin

I really respected Briano for offering me the chance to put the whole picture together in my head, because I certainly had pieces missing from Steve's last moments. But that was intentional. I wanted to remember him exactly how I last saw him: sitting around the campfire, alive and full of enthusiasm like always. He was purely himself in that memory, and I kept it alive in my head, the two of us side by side in Lakefield National Park, doing what we loved.

People handle things differently. Some people can't rest until they know every detail, but at that particular time, I felt that I didn't need any more information. I just couldn't cope with anything else. I'd already had enough.

Upon reflection, I was probably a little bit abrupt with Briano. Perhaps I should have explained myself a little bit better but I really didn't have it together then. I didn't want to put Briano through reliving it either.

I suppose I tried to shut out a lot of the specific details because I didn't want to accept that it had happened in the first place. I had a rough idea. But the most important piece of information I already knew: that Briano had been beside him to comfort him in his final moments. It had all been over quickly, but Steve would have known he was going to die and you wouldn't wish it on anyone to be with someone in a moment like that and not be able to do a thing to change the outcome. Steve was lucky that he had somebody who he respected so much to hold him for those last few moments of his life, rather than dying alone on the bottom of the ocean. He was with a mate who loved him and whom he loved in return.

If you were ever in a difficult situation at any time, anywhere, you really couldn't wish to have a better bloke standing alongside you than Briano. I knew in my heart that he would have done everything in his power to change the result of that awful day, and I considered that to be reassuring. That was proof to me that Steve managed to surround himself with a group of very loyal people. They weren't just friends or colleagues, they were mates for life.

When I first saw Briano walk through the gates of the compound when he returned to the zoo, I just instinctively wanted to hug him. He looked terribly sad. That hug wasn't just for his benefit, but for mine as well, because in some strange way I needed to be able to thank him. As a parent, you of course want to always be there to comfort your children when they're hurt or in their hour of greatest need. But I hadn't been there, I'd been a long way away. To know that he was comforted in that way, well, that's all that I could really have asked for.

Briano could have spoken about that incident to the media, of course. He could have quite easily sold the story and made a hell of a lot of money. But Briano's faithfulness didn't waver. And the family and I respected that beyond words.

***

Steve was offered a state funeral, but our family declined, because he was just an ordinary bloke and that's how he would have wanted to be remembered. We opted to have a private ceremony at the zoo, strictly for friends and family.

The media were terribly unforgiving to have to deal with at such a time. No matter how widely known my son was, we were at heart just an average family wanting to grieve in private and they were making that very difficult. When friends and family came and went they'd have to lie down under a blanket in the boot to avoid a barrage of photographers. The media were so bloodthirsty that they even offered the funeral parlour a significant sum of money for any details of Steve's death.

The funeral was held in a private area of the zoo, inaccessible to the media, but choppers still hovered above, trying to get an aerial photo of our family and the service. We had covered the area with shadecloth suspended high on poles to provide privacy from the air, and we also set up a decoy location, with a marquee and chairs, in another area of the zoo. This was all so that we could just get on with what we had to do and lay Steve to rest.

A few people decided to put personal effects in with him. What got me the most was Steve's personal security guard, Security Dan, putting in Steve's beloved boxing gloves. A professional mixed martial arts competitor, he had been working as a cleaner at the zoo when Steve had heard about his training and sought him out. Dan was immediately offered a position as one of Steve's personal bodyguards and travelled everywhere with him, even on the crocodile research trips. Wildlife was never really Dan's forte; he was purely there to be an extra set of strong hands. But he worked as hard as everybody else, and that's what I liked about him too. The wildlife factor eventually came later.

After a while, Steve paid for Dan's flights overseas four times a year so that he could compete internationally, and in return Dan trained Steve. Steve got right into it. On our trips to Cape York there'd always be a match in the middle of the bush, complete with crocodile keepers in boxing gloves. Steve had these truly special kinds of relationships with so many people. Anyone who was close to Steve had similar stories about him helping them to realise their passion. Everybody had their own unique bond with him. He had a way of making each individual feel important, like they had their one-on-one thing.

After Dan placed the boxing gloves in with Steve, he shared a story with me. 'Steve asked me to hit him once,' he said. 'That's the kind of wild man he was, and I mean that as a compliment. He said, "I want you to punch me really hard in the stomach."'

They'd been at one of their training sessions in a makeshift gym built in an old house at the back of the zoo. 'Are you serious, mate?' Dan had replied. In all of his years of training, no one had ever asked him to do that before.

'Yeah, I mean, if you get the chance, I want you to really drop me. Take the wind out of me,' Steve had said.

So Dan did. He winded Steve, knocking him to the ground.

Once he'd got his breath back and climbed to his feet, Steve said, 'Thanks so much for that,' with the biggest smile on his face imaginable. The same kind of smile he got when he was out in the bush or when he threw himself one hundred per cent into something. That was his way. Steve didn't do the what ifs. His attitude was, 'Let's just do it and see what happens.'

'Steve had a very healthy relationship with failure,' Dan continued. 'Anyone who is successful has to. That's the cornerstone of sports psychology. If you develop an unhealthy relationship with failure, you'll never amount to anything. So not only did he not care if he failed, he embraced it. He wanted to get his arse kicked.'

That anecdote resonated deeply with me and I smiled about it, because it was a perfectly accurate description of him. We then both shed a few tears.

When it was my turn to farewell Steve, I put in that frayed piece of six-mil rope from our last crocodile research trip. I don't know why I did that. I don't even know why I still had it. There must have been a reason I held onto it, because a broken piece of rope isn't the kind of thing that you ordinarily keep. I guess a part of me wanted to send him off with the last bit of fun we'd had together; it was my last connection to that time. Just like the six-mil rope was the final step in the crocodile's return to freedom, this particular piece was the last thing connecting me to him before his own release into the wild. Because I knew that it was to the wilds of this world that he would be going.

Many of the team and I stayed right until the very last piece of dirt was gently placed on top of him. It was so final. It was goodbye.

That was a difficult day for me. I wasn't coping. I didn't want to speak to anyone, I just wanted to be by myself. I'd be talking to someone and all of a sudden I'd have to leave mid-sentence and find a corner somewhere just to hide away.

In the end, I decided that the best place to be was inside Steve's truck. I felt closest to him in there and hoped like hell no one would come and find me. I closed all of the doors and sat in there alone. Looking around the cabin, I found his hat—a green and khaki Australia Zoo–branded cap that he wore almost religiously, his mop of wiry blond hair poking out the sides. It still had his name written on the strap across the back. He wrote his name on it because everybody had the same one at croc camp and he got sick of people pinching his. I didn't tell anyone, but I took his hat home that day. I felt like I needed a piece of him with me and I didn't have much else to hang onto. So I took it home and hung it in a very special place, where it still sits to this very day.

True Blue

The Croc Team

Dan Mead

There wasn't a dry eye in the stadium as John Williamson, with his characteristic voice of the bush, narrated verses describing what Steve taught each of us about mateship and what it was to be true blue. Standing shoulder to shoulder with the complete croc team, we established a guard of honour and stood tall watching our devastated head crocodile keeper, Briano, as he symbolically packed up Steve's truck for its last voyage out of his Crocoseum. A wreath floated by in the crocodile pond surrounding an image of a more thoughtful side of Steve and inscribed with his famous catch-cry 'Crocs Rule'. The stadium was as jam-packed as I had ever seen it. Over the previous weeks we'd slowly come to terms with the difficult reality that Steve would never be coming home; now this was to be our final farewell, broadcast, true to form, into people's lounge rooms right across the world. In the same way that he engaged people in his life, over 300 million people tuned in to join us in remembering our leader, our hero.

Although I had my head bowed, I kept catching glimpses of Bob in the VIP area. He concealed his grief behind dark glasses that covered his eyes. The sadness that engulfed him had completely unravelled me, having just watched him take to the stage to address the audience with his brief but profound words.

'Don't grieve for Steve, he is at peace now. Grieve for the animals,' he said, 'because the animals have lost the best friend that they ever had, and so have I.'

Those words still haunt me. No one should ever have to suffer such a loss.

I don't think Bob had planned to speak that day, but he must have made a last-minute decision to do so. Such a quiet and private man, it would have taken such courage to stand up there and find the words to share his personal grief with the world. I felt deeply sorry for Bob to have lost his son. Their respect for one another was unparalleled. Bob was without a doubt the quiet achiever who gave Steve such an incredible platform to find his life's passion. I'm sure that Steve got his humility from Bob. That was the common thread between them. There was an obvious tightness to their relationship that no friendship would ever have. And yet Bob talks of himself as just a normal bloke, same as everybody else. But he was proof to me that normal blokes can do great things. And that's the kind of category that I put Bob in today of all days. He lit a certain fire in Steve at a very young age, a fire that went on to ignite something in me and in many others who I stood beside today, from the croc team to dozens of other zoo keepers. Bob is the kind of person who would spend the time to drag out the best in any person, no matter how much time it took to do it. He had all of the time in the world to pass on his wisdom. You couldn't help but be inspired by him. He had dedicated his life to changing the world in this way. Anyone who puts something as important as conservation first is my hero. We would always stand beside him, today, tomorrow and in the years ahead.

Briano was rightfully given the task of loading up Steve's ute with the equipment for his last croc trip into the unknown, wrapping up the end of the zoo's unified wave goodbye to the most loved member of our team. Despite the fact that his memorial included a host of celebrity appearances, today he wasn't Steve Irwin the megastar, he was just one of the rest of us as a sea of khaki uniforms grieved. Briano started the difficult process of packing up Steve's truck. Ropes, esky, crocodile nets, his axe, and a canvas to protect his gear from the elements along the rugged roads to the far north that he'd spent his lifetime exploring but would never again return to. Watching on, I contemplated each piece of the once foreign equipment I had eventually become accustomed to using. With each item thoughtfully placed on the back of Steve's Cruiser, my mind ran through almost every single memory of crocodile captures where he had bestowed on me the knowledge that I am equipped with today. I had never in my wildest dreams imagined that I'd have the opportunity to do this kind of work. My first day as a volunteer at just eighteen years old saw me filling out a job preference form in which I wrote how nervous I'd be working with crocodiles. My training flashed before my eyes, from my days as that inexperienced volunteer with so much to learn right through my highlights in remote parts of the Australian bush, to conclude with one of my greatest moments hands-down from just two weeks before: my most cherished moment with Steve at the back of *Croc One* in Lakefield National Park. I recalled it as clear as day.

Earlier, while processing another big croc, Steve had hold of one of the jaw ropes, using it to bind the croc jaws closed as it rolled. I had hold of the opposing rope and watched on as the croc started to roll the other way, causing Steve's rope to unwrap, allowing the jaws to open. With no two crocodiles ever being the same, occasionally things don't go to plan even when you're the Crocodile Hunter. Steve was used to thinking on his feet; I had watched intently on countless occasions as he adapted his plan in a split second as situations changed. As this was unfolding in front of me, I could see I was in a fortunate position with my rope where I could take a bit of control and safely bind the jaws up. The team on my rope behind me couldn't see what was unfolding and they were unknowingly pulling the ropes out of my hands, making it difficult for me to move and secure the jaws as the croc rolled. Profanities were coming from behind and from me as well as I competed to pull the ropes back in our accidental game of tug-o-war. Steve was still directly opposite me on the other side of the croc's head, watching me the whole time like a hawk. He stood close enough to jump back in at any minute but allowed me to take the lead. I guess he could see that I was able to stay calm and take control, and once the crocodile was finally secure, he just gave me a little nod, as if to say 'Well done, mate'. Everything went well from there, and as a team we successfully processed another big croc, providing us with more scientific data. It was such a thrill to be in that position and to now have confidence in my own abilities to think on the spot and lead the team out of a challenging situation.

Afterwards I ferried Steve in the tinnie that he'd taught me to drive all those years before back up to *Croc One*. As I pulled up to the back of the boat, Steve stepped from the tinnie up to the back of his research vessel. When I switched the outboard motor into reverse and slowly started to back away, Steve signalled at me to cut the engine, and he gave me a pep talk that I'll never forget.

'Dan, you did well today, you've really got this croc-catching thing sorted now. You nailed it today. I've seen a lot from you in these past few weeks, all you fellas have really stepped up and I couldn't be more proud of where you're at now. I've seen enough to know that you've got it. I'm sorry though, mate, as this means that I'm done training you. I'll have to start giving some of the newer blokes a go now. You have to know I'm happy with how far you've come. I thought we'd come up here and I'd be continuing your training all month, but I've seen enough to know that you're ready.'

After all of those years trying to soak up as much as I possibly could from him, I'd just been given the ultimate tick of approval from Steve. I thanked him with words that I didn't think were enough to acknowledge what his approval had just done for a young bloke like me. I considered how different this trip had been compared to the very first trip that I ever did with him, when he basically told me, 'You need to learn everything I do while you're here. Stick to me like glue, no matter what.' And I did. I jumped in the boat with him, I jumped in the car with him, and I learnt as we confronted whatever we were faced with. You'd think on your feet, find different ways of doing things, and muster that little bit of extra strength within yourself to lift a crocodile trap or drag a couple of boats up steep muddy embankments. I learnt more from Steve than from anyone else in my life, simply because he was prepared to throw me in at the deep end.

I wouldn't have believed that'd be the last trip I'd ever do with Steve. I always saw Steve as invincible—we idolised him, and you never expect someone you're striving to be like to disappear all of a sudden. But in hindsight, I felt in a sense as though that trip was Steve signing off and saying goodbye. Handing over the reins to the team that he'd been in a hurry over the years to impart his knowledge to. It's hard to imagine it could be possible, but I believe that he somehow knew he wasn't going to be around for long enough.

That day, securing that croc, I learnt that I could be a leader. After years of following a lot of people, watching how they do things, listening to what they say. And to learn that I was able to lead, to do things for myself and develop and do things my way with confidence was a huge life lesson. Being a good leader allows people to follow you. And I think that's definitely why we followed Steve and Bob, because they were both so confident in their beliefs and in how we were doing things. If you can be a good leader, you can help others to become better people.

That moment faded to black as I was brought back to earth standing in the Crocoseum with my best mates watching Briano load on the last of Steve's gear, his surfboard. Briano paused and looked thoughtfully at a personal effect that we all knew held a really significant meaning for him. Surfing was something the two of them shared that was always their thing.

John Williamson had the entire audience singing along. I suddenly felt a lump in my throat, which I didn't recognise, not being much of an emotional person. It was the sight of Steve's beloved surfboard with the notorious green crocodile decal etched on the bottom. It was absolutely killing me watching Briano hesitate in letting that part of him go.

I knew Briano was suffering tremendously, struggling to come to terms with it all. Watching your best mate leave our earth would be enough to make a lesser man walk away. But Briano had returned home, mustered the team and reminded us we had a job to do for Steve. And now here he was in front of his team, the zoo and the world, leading by example just as Steve had always done. I admire and look up to this bloke as much as any mentor and mate I ever had.

Briano slowly drove Steve's truck out of the Crocoseum and we followed our leader as a final show of respect. Briano driving Steve's truck wasn't only symbolic in showing a part of Steve leaving us, but also represented how Briano would now drive our team forward as one.

Briano was definitely a good boss. His style of management all just filtered down from Bob and Steve. He invested a lot of time in his team; he was constantly giving us opportunities to do things and try things, to learn and develop. And that was the greatest thing about knowing we'd be led by Briano: he put our development and training first. Even if it meant that a job would take a little longer or would require more staff, he ensured that we had ample opportunity to grow our skills. That's a sign of a really good leader—one who is aware of his team and put the development of his team first. And that was the environment in which he was taught too. Happy staff who appreciate what you do for them will always achieve more than people being dictated to.

That team was the best group of people I'll work with in my life. Steve had managed to weave together a really close-knit group of people. He had put together a group of people who were trustworthy and looked after each other no matter what. We would surf together in the mornings, fish together on the weekends and regularly get together for team barbecues. We had to trust each other, have each other's backs, which we did, and I know we always will.

11

Goodbye to croc catching

In July 2007, I led the Australia Zoo croc team back up to Lakefield National Park to continue the crocodile research project in Steve's name. It was something that I felt I had to do. It was exactly a year after we had last been up there with Steve. It was to be a very difficult reminder of everything I had lost. It was challenging for a lot of other people too, because every single year before that Steve had been there, on every crocodile capture, calling all the shots. To be going back to the same place without him was a really empty feeling. We would have to find our groove without him.

We went back to the same campsite. I was flooded with memories of Steve and that last campfire. If I'd known that would be the last time I'd see him I would have never left him there. The trouble is, you think you have all the time in the world with the ones you love.

It was strange to see how everything else could exist when he didn't anymore. The campsite still looked the same, the trees were still alive, the team was still the same core crew as before. As much as we all knew what we had to do, and what we hoped to achieve, it certainly wasn't the same.

They were good times working with those people again. It was pretty emotional at times, for all of us. When we were physically busy with a lot of crocodile catching it wasn't so bad. But other times, I'd have to have a good cry alone in the boat. As a bloke, you're not supposed to show your emotions, but I sure had plenty. But I was starting to realise that tears weren't a sign of weakness at all: they were a sign of overpowering, irreplaceable love. I learnt that from Steve. Steve showed people that it was okay to wear your heart on your sleeve. He showed a lot of people that it was okay to be passionate about the things you love.

The biggest croc we caught on that trip was a whopping sixteen feet long, a big grumpy boy. He was very uncooperative. Once we'd measured and tagged him, we moved all the boats out of his path so that he had a clear run into the water. But he decided to veer off in a different direction, launching straight off the bank onto one of our boats, sinking it immediately.

'I think we should call this one Steve,' one of the boys said. I couldn't have agreed more. The decision was unanimous. Soon afterwards, we caught him again in another trap just around the corner. His name certainly was fitting: he had a full-on nature. Crocodiles are like people in that way, no two have the same personality. We all thought that was pretty good and that perhaps Steve was somehow up there with us, orchestrating it all for our entertainment. He would have been having a good laugh, I'm sure.

Over the years, Steve had spoken quite a few times about how he'd want to be remembered. It's like he always knew he wasn't going to be around for long. And over these days I heard a lot of stories about how on that last trip Steve had really gone out of his way to thank people for their work over the years and acknowledge how far they'd come as a team. In the light of what had happened, most of the team felt that Steve had said his goodbyes. Then, before he'd left on *Croc One*, he'd called the team together to deliver a very emotional speech. He told them that it had been the best month of his life.

'Fair dinkum. I came up here busted up, with a broken neck, and the first week was just hell. All I could do was walk around. But you guys are really good. You made sure that I didn't have to lift anything too heavy, and jumped on the crocs like absolute legends, and so I was able to relax. And it felt good teaching and giving this year, rather than trying to do everything myself. My neck's still giving me grief, but you know what? It pales in comparison to the goodness that I've got in my heart from this month. There's not a team on earth that I'd sooner be with.'

He was with a group of people he understood, who were dedicated to the work that he did, and he was working with one of the most important creatures to him on the planet. Really, how much better could it be? He left us on such a high.

Steve's greatest legacy has been establishing a team of dedicated people to increase our knowledge of crocodile habits and habitats through research. This research has helped to educate millions of people about the importance of nature conservation. I knew that it would continue on without him. He had been like a rock in a pond, sending ripples right across the surface of the water. As I watched his team catch almost thirty crocodiles on that trip, I realised how capable they had become. They didn't need me anymore, they had crocodile catching down to a fine art.

So that was my last crocodile research trip with the team. A huge chapter in my life closed. Although I'll never tire of catching crocodiles, it felt like the end of an era for the team and me. I knew that the team would keep it going, and that it was their time to step up. For me, and for Steve, if you're not passing that knowledge on, then what are you doing it for? When you get to mentor someone in a field you are very experienced in, there is no better feeling in the world. Steve had, without question, established the best croc-catching team out there. That was his legacy.

On arriving home, I realised that Steve was in every part of that country for me and it was still too raw. He was in the campsite, the boat, the crocs, and the people he had taught. There wasn't a part of that country or a kilometre on the road to get there that wasn't a reminder to me of his uncontained excitement, or the experiences we'd shared over many years together. I needed some time to adjust to a world without him.

13

Camp Chilli

In 2008, I announced to zoo management that I had decided to part ways with Australia Zoo, and the media went to town on it. There were some pretty speculative headlines, saying there'd been rifts, family feuds, that I was worried about commercialisation, that I was locked out, that I'd quit.

Some of it was true. Some of it wasn't. What it came down to was that management and I weren't able to agree on certain aspects of Australia Zoo after Steve's passing. Nearly every time I went in I would have a difference of opinion with somebody on matters that I was growing increasingly concerned about. The zoo was finding its feet without Steve. While the management were understandably readjusting and finding a new balance, things were suffering as a result of that, in my opinion. It was certainly a difficult time for everybody involved, because we weren't just a business—we were a family. But I still felt there were important things that needed attention regardless of the circumstances and so I addressed them, in person and through letters.

It all came to a head in a final telephone call—that was the final push for me. I was told I was becoming a disruptive influence and that I was no longer welcome at the zoo. I felt that I had no alternative but to leave. In my opinion it had been made very clear that my influence and knowledge were no longer required. I didn't retire as was suggested to me. I resigned.

As soon as I made that decision, that was it. I downed tools at Ironbark Station. I've always had the attitude that you can't do something half-heartedly. If you're going to do something, you've got to do it one hundred per cent. That means you've got to be ruthless in order to move forwards sometimes, because being stuck in the middle is what causes unhappiness. This was one of those times for me where there could be no grey area—it was plainly black and white.

But I won't go into much more detail than that, other than to say that I made a pretty finite decision to part ways with the zoo so I could continue Steve's work the way I believed it needed to be done. But I don't think my family matters should be aired publicly and I will stand by my decision not to discuss this in further detail with the media. It's certainly nobody else's business but zoo management and mine.

At the time, I was so angry with how it had panned out that I probably didn't think things through as well as I should have. I hadn't factored in how I was going to survive without a wage from the zoo. I didn't own anything—no house, no car, no assets at all. People probably expected me to be driving around in a Mercedes-Benz due to the financial success of Australia Zoo, but everything I'd ever had I had put into the reptile park or the work that Steve and I did together. That's what I had wanted to do, that's how I had wanted to live my life. Looking back with hindsight I wouldn't change it a jot either.

After some negotiation, I came to a financial agreement with the zoo, because of my thirty-six years starting it up and the rest of it. We agreed on a modest pension that would allow Judy and me to have a house and property and a small income.

One thing that weighed heavily on me about leaving the zoo was how Steve would have reacted. To a certain degree, I felt as though I'd failed him. I was tired. I'd had enough. But I felt guilty for not trying harder. Steve had always achieved whatever was in his heart—he'd fought hard for what he believed in and stood up for what was important. I knew I could never be another Steve, but I didn't doubt that he would have hoped that I would carry on his work.

I beat myself up about that for quite some time. I wondered what he would think about his old man not being there, working as hard and as passionately as I once had for the place we built up together with our bare hands. But finally, hard as it is to explain, I was sure I'd made the right decision. In the end, I felt he would have been happy for me to carry on our work in my own way.

But it certainly felt awful to walk away from the zoo. I'd raised my family there and spent three decades establishing it from a bare block of land. I'd put my heart and soul into that place, and I think a part of me will never leave, will always be there alongside Steve. It was certainly difficult to part from my son's final resting place, the many special animals, the crocodile research and the team that I considered to be like my family.

There were personal consequences to leaving the zoo as well, among them that my relationship with Steve's children, Bindi and Robert, would suffer. Naturally that wasn't something I was happy about. I had so many stories of Steve and my adventures that I would have loved to have told the kids. I would have loved to have shown them some of those special places Steve and I ventured to together.

One of the things I found most difficult was leaving Ironbark Station. Everything I did there was for Steve and me—they were the projects we talked about, our big hopes of building a new model for conservation properties. We'd already proved a lot: that it's possible to run cattle at a profit and keep habitat for wildlife at the same time. It didn't need to be one or the other—we could create a more harmonious balance. Steve and I had turned Ironbark Station from a wildlife desert into a wildlife haven. I suppose sometimes you don't realise how deeply you are entwined with something until you leave it. I hoped the property would still be run as successfully, and with the same level of commitment, after I left.

As it turned out, Australia Zoo's maintenance manager, Trev, took over my role, which I was happy about. They don't come more dedicated than him. Trev is the kind of person who always says it how it is. Before too long, he moved to Ironbark Station and let me know how things were going. Trev was, and still is, the closest friend that I've had since Steve left. He's certainly the closest person to a son I've had in the years that've followed.

Just before we were due to leave Ironbark Station, I agreed to an interview with ABC's *Australian Story* to address my departure from Australia Zoo. The media were harassing us constantly but I wanted to get my point of view across without my story being altered in any way, as was happening elsewhere in the media. There were so many appalling versions out there about what had taken place. I simply wanted people to understand that I had resigned from the zoo, hoping that it would finally put an end to some of those rumours and allow us some privacy.

I didn't get paid for the story, despite the fact that there were a lot of other paying offers at the time. I've always had a lot of respect for the ABC, because they do their homework and I really trusted the team assigned to produce the story. Money was never a consideration. They didn't twist my words, they just let me tell it how it was from my perspective. As it turned out, that episode became one of the highest rating episodes for *Australian Story* that year, and one of the top ten for the decade. Around one and a half million viewers tuned in. That was a sign of how much interest there was in the Irwin family story. It was crazy to think that people were so interested in a time in our lives that we just wanted to put behind us.

***

The day I resigned, Judy and I started looking for a new property to move to. We had the same problem that probably everybody faces when they're trying to start a new life—nothing quite suited us. We wanted somewhere that wasn't totally destroyed by land clearing. Finally, we found a place just thirty kilometres from Kingaroy, three and a half hours' drive north-west of Brisbane. As soon as I drove through the gates of this 640-acre property, I had a really good feeling about it. The real estate agent was trying to spruik it as a good cattle block because there was no infrastructure on it at all. But we didn't want it for cattle, we wanted it for wildlife, and it was perfect wilderness country, surrounded by national park and state forest. We instantly knew this was going to be our new home.

There was certainly a lot of work ahead. We had to start from scratch and build a house, a shed—even a road to get in there. Once we'd bought it I worked twelve- to fourteen-hour days to get it to a habitable state. But I just loved it. It was good to keep my mind active and my hands busy, because I wasn't handling things all that well.

We were stuck for a name for the property, but we didn't stew on it and we knew that something would come to us eventually.

I had buried Lyn's ashes in a box in a special area at Ironbark Station, out on a big hill overlooking the rest of the property, not too far from the house. When it was finally time to leave Ironbark Station for the new property, I decided there was no way I would leave Lyn there. But I hadn't marked the spot, and after digging for hours I still couldn't find it. I got so frustrated with myself that I sat down and shed a few tears. After a while, I pulled myself together and quietly asked Lyn to help me find her. I got up again, walked three or four paces, and tried again. And there was the box, right where I'd started to dig.

Judy was really good about that; she knew that it was important for me. At the new property I found the perfect place when we arrived, and I made a special place for Lyn to rest. A place where she could keep an eye on me and give me a good kick up the bum from time to time. Lyn will always be wherever I am.

***

Soon after Steve passed, I received a phone call out of the blue from Stephen Accornero from up at Cattle Creek. I had really shut myself away from the rest of the world after Steve had left us, and it had been a long time since we had properly spoken. Stephen said he would like to come out and pay us a visit.

It was an emotional reunion for both of us. Stephen and his family represented a special time in my life that I could never have back. At the end of their visit, Stephen said he had something to give me, that he'd made the journey specifically to hand it to me because he didn't trust sending it in the post.

I was lost for words—it was the 'Camp Chilli' sign I had made for Steve when he lost his beloved companion down at Cattle Creek. Stephen told me they had kept it under lock and key in their home, not wanting anything to happen to it. I knew this memento would have been difficult for them to part with.

'Although it means a lot to us, it'll mean even more to you—you made it especially for him. We'd like for you to have it back,' Stephen said, with emotion.

I started to talk but then was overcome with tears. I was inconsolable and I felt a bit embarrassed about that. I had to walk away to collect myself.

This relic—this unassuming little sign with words burnt into it—represented such a special time in my life. I might have made Stephen and Annalisa feel guilty for upsetting me, but if I could have spoken I would have said that their gesture meant more to me than they could ever realise. It would have to be the single most important thing that I now own. I have very few things that belonged to Steve. I hung it in the machinery shed where I could look at it every day.

Once we'd finished the new house on the property, I built a woodshed out of some old timber and sheets of iron for the roof. In front of it I dug a fire pit surrounded by logs. Beside the campfire I set up Steve's fading camp chair, to permanently sit empty beside me whenever I lit a fire. I could sit there under the stars at night, the way we used to, and think about him and talk to him in my own way.

Then one night, I had a feeling that I needed to move that wooden sign. I could almost hear Steve telling me to hang it by the campfire. So I got it from the shed and hung it at the entrance to our woodshed. Before I knew it, I had my own little replica of the place that I had so adored with Steve: a mini Camp Chilli.

Without much further thought, Judy and I had serendipitously stumbled across the perfect name for our new home. 'Why don't we call this place Camp Chilli?' Judy said. I couldn't have agreed more. I wasted no time in painting a sign for the front gate with the property name. We've never called it anything else since.

Camp Chilli fast became a beloved home for Judy and me. There is no traffic; there are no neighbours. It's a very peaceful place in a remote part of the world. A good number of kangaroos and wallabies have moved onto the property since I dug out the dams, providing ample watering holes. We've got most species of gliders, from the tiny feathertails to the yellow-bellied and even the incredible greater gliders. A small population of koalas come and go. And there's an abundance of native bird species—we've seen about ninety varieties just around the house.

We also look after Skippy, an eastern grey kangaroo that we've taken into care. She was hand-raised by an elderly couple and couldn't be released into the wild.

Camp Chilli became a retreat for me in the wake of some very turbulent years. Out on the property I have special places where I like to go and hide out and be by myself, just roll a couple of smokes and listen to nature doing its thing around me. Sometimes sitting under the trees and having your feet planted firmly on the ground is the most spiritual thing you can do.

* * *

People often tell me that it's time I got over Steve's loss, but I feel I need him here to keep going. I gain strength from him, I get inspiration from him, I still have the same passion and drive that he and I both had. Steve's presence is always with me. It's pretty hard to explain without sounding odd, but it's when things get difficult that I feel him around the most. That's when I feel his energy, his drive and his passion. That's what kept me going in those really bad days, when I wondered how to go on. I got to a point where I could understand how if people have enough of those kinds of feelings, they just don't think they can handle it any longer. And he was somehow around me when I needed him, at those difficult times.

And if it hadn't been for Judy, I simply wouldn't have coped. Yet again, she helped me through a difficult time that I otherwise wouldn't have survived. There's no way to compare the loss of Lyn and Steve—neither was any better or worse. But the combination of the two losses was simply horrible. Lyn's passing certainly didn't make it any easier to prepare for Steve going. I consider myself lucky that I have had such a strong person like Judy alongside me to help me cope with that. I also consider myself really fortunate to be just as lucky a second time around with marriage as I was the first time. I'm so thankful to have someone who really cares for me and encourages me. It wasn't an easy time for Judy to have joined our family.

I hid out for a long time. I just needed some stable ground beneath my feet, to heal and come to terms with so much loss. I needed a chance for things to run smoothly again, I needed stability. I couldn't cope with one more blow. I didn't know what I was going to do next, but I knew that I had to do something. Ultimately, I couldn't sit still.

It's interesting how a single decision can alter the whole way your life pans out from thereon in. Whether it's the right one or the wrong one, just one decision can make a huge difference to where the road is going to take you next.

Travel log: Bob and Amanda on the road

Whale of a Campaign, Hervey Bay, Fraser Coast, Queensland, June 2010

Amanda

Bob didn't know me from a bar of soap so I was initially apprehensive to get in contact with him via the RSPCA and invite him to be the ambassador of a rally I was organising that highlighted the plight of the humpback whale, a species that had put my beachside hometown on the map as the whale watch capital of the world. There was nowhere else in the world like it where the whales stopped on their migration for a five-day holiday safely unwinding in our warm protected waters—and it was an experience of a lifetime for tourists to see these forty-ton majestic giants at close range. I knew of Bob, but he certainly knew nothing about me. I was just one of hundreds of ordinary faces that had passed through the Australia Zoo gates after Steve's sad passing. It was in working at the zoo that I came to know of his story and his life working with wildlife, and I couldn't think of another person in our country more dedicated than him to represent our cause. As a down-to-earth, authentic conservationist with a frank voice for wildlife, he embodied the Irwin trademark. His was the voice that would command the much-needed attention of an entire community on a day giving a platform to our whales. I ran through every name for wildlife on television that I could think of and none resonated with me more so than Bob's, especially after the Sea Shepherd Conservation Society had recently named their anti-whaling vessel *The Steve Irwin*, with Bob proudly attending the launch. But I was not holding out for a return phone call, because I had absolutely no connection to him.

We needed a big drawcard for our small local event to expose the issues the whales were facing with Japanese whalers increasingly hunting in the waters of Australia's southern whale sanctuary, a protection zone declared by our own federal government to safeguard the whales but with no tangible enforcement. The very humpbacks that were worth $70 million to our local economy were passing through these perilous hunting grounds on each migration after exciting the hordes of tourists in our safe protected waters of Hervey Bay, and we needed greater awareness of the issue. What shocked me to my core was learning that our region's iconic whale, Nala, identified by researchers Trish and Wally Franklin over thirty-years of returning to Hervey Bay, had been biopsied by so-called 'scientific' researchers, a facade for Japan's lethal whale hunt. I was told this news onboard a scientific research expedition, during a rare encounter with Nala herself watching her majestically raise her precious four-week-old calf on her back up to the surface of the water to show us. She held her high above the water in reaching distance from the boat. She did this over and over in the most beautiful display I had ever seen. For the first time in my life, I felt a fire lit in my belly as tears streamed from my eyes. I had never made the connection between our very own whales and the Japanese whale hunt and I knew that other people in our community surviving off whale tourism wouldn't either.

I was surprised a few days later while sitting at home to receive a phone call from Bob himself accepting my invitation on the proviso that he funded his own travel, a seven-hour round-trip from his home at Camp Chilli. This was to be one of my first campaigns as a public spokesperson for something I wanted to stand up for, and I knew that with his trusted name backing it, we would have a far greater chance of getting our message to the masses. The whaling issue had long been aligned with pot-smoking, bongo-playing hippie activists, and we wanted to host an event that showcased a different kind of activist, highlighting the everyday Australians from all walks of life who were concerned about whaling in our waters after we as a nation had reduced the humpback species to just a few hundred individuals in the 1960s. Whaling stations in Australia and New Zealand had killed over forty thousand humpback whales. After the decimation of their population, the hunting of humpbacks finally ceased in 1963, and two years later they were protected worldwide after a dramatic decline in numbers globally. In just fifty short years, numbers have thankfully recovered to a reported twenty thousand individuals on the east coast of Australia. Business owners, residents, tour operators and tourists would rally together with one simple message: that whales were worth more alive than served up for food. I considered Bob Irwin my key to doing this.

Although I was excited to see one of my greatest wildlife heroes arrive on the morning of the rally, by the time Bob appeared on the beach that morning my excitement had turned to despair. I greeted him with a despondent frown while handing him that day's local newspaper. After weeks of engaging various media, which up to this point had been in favour of our cause, I had experienced my first bout of public criticism in response to staging the event. An influential member of the local community had written a half-page column criticising me personally for 'ramming conservation down people's throats', depicting the event as if outraged activists were to chain themselves to paddle boards. I felt devastated thinking that the day was set to be a failure after months of tireless preparation. I suppose I hadn't considered there'd be divided opinions on such an issue. Bob took the article and read it with a disarming grin. He looked up from the newspaper and grabbed me by the shoulders as he gave me his reassuring feedback.

'Congratulations! Welcome to the world of advocacy. Don't worry about that drip! This is exactly what this whole thing is all about. Getting your message out there and standing up for what you believe in. You'll always be challenged along the way, but if you believe in something strongly enough you'll always achieve what you set out to achieve. That's called passion. You should feel really, really proud. It's going to be a great event!'

The day finished up exceeding our expectations, with thousands of people turning out to paddle out for the whales. With Bob's recognisable face behind this event, we were able to make a cohesive stand in showcasing our community as a stronghold for whale conservation in a peaceful but powerful way. Without a dollar in our budget to market the event, the community had turned out in their masses. People had donated their time, resources and money in order to stage the event, driven by one thing—that they genuinely cared. That moment sparked something within me, and Bob's words about the importance of taking a stand for what you believe in kept echoing in my mind. I felt immensely proud as I realised that I'd tapped into a world of like-minded, compassionate people; whale lovers from across our community had come out of the closet. In the days that followed, Bob was quoted in countless newspapers as a spokesperson for this event, spreading our message far and wide; he'd even written to the local newspaper in response to that critical article and congratulating the local community for being a stronghold for the whales. At the end of the night as we were packing down the tents and cleaning up the beach, I turned around to see Bob still sitting there transfixed by a movie about the cause playing on the open-air screen underneath the stars. I hadn't expected him to attend the entire event, but there he was, one of the last people on the beach, watching on as Captain Paul Watson from the *Sea Shepherd* spoke passionately about the whale war happening in the southern ocean. I went and sat with Bob on the sand, and he turned to me and sincerely thanked me for involving him in such an important day for our whales. I couldn't believe he was thanking *me* for this; it was to him that I attributed the success of the event. Just before he left, Bob told me that he wished to assist me in campaigning for other wildlife that I opted to fight for in the future.

'Whatever you're doing, I want to know about it,' he said.

Twelve months later, it was an operation to save a baby elephant in Sumatra named Bona, rehoming an abused sun bear called Johnny and getting behind the issues facing countless other wildlife groups across Australia in a similar way that Bob supported me as we travel from one end of the country to the other in an important crusade for wildlife. He has never accepted payment for his time, or even fuel for his vehicle. He'll decline an offer of accommodation despite the fact that he's covered hundreds of kilometres in a single sitting. He's driven by a genuine desire to help people who are on the frontline of saving our native wildlife. That day standing on the beach, it was Bob who taught me the importance of finding my voice to speak up for those less fortunate than me. He has taught me the importance of helping others with no expectation of any return. And although at times that has left me exceptionally busy, I'll forever be grateful for the opportunity to see the world through his compassionate, selfless eyes. I couldn't ask for a greater hero to teach me how to be a better caretaker of the world around me.

And although I had nothing in the pipeline at the time he made that offer, in the year that followed that's exactly how it played out. Animals in need kept presenting themselves to me, and Bob backed me in each situation by getting on the radio, writing letters and giving my campaigns his seal of Irwin approval. From elephants in Sumatra to cassowaries in the rainforest, Bob's name has been the catalyst in bringing a whole new level of awareness to these causes. That's led us to exactly where we are today—on an ongoing wildlife road trip. And an unusual pair we make.

14

Fight for it

After Steve died, I had two choices. I could vegetate somewhere for the rest of my days, or I could find some way to make sure that Steve's conservation message wasn't lost. It took me a long time, but I decided that it was still important for me to take the second option.

I started to receive requests to assist people in raising awareness for various wildlife issues. I was hesitant about getting involved, because I didn't see how I could do anything to help. But my hesitation disappeared altogether when I heard about wombats being buried alive. That really got me fired up. I had to do something about it.

The southern hairy-nosed wombat, a protected species, was the target of a cruel cull in the Murraylands region of South Australia. Because they dig deep burrows and holes on farmers' properties, they were considered a nuisance. And some farmers were taking matters into their own hands.

Brigitte Stevens, a friend of mine, was running the Wombat Awareness Organisation down in South Australia. She let me know that they were in the middle of digging out, all by hand, up to ten wombats that had been buried alive in their burrows. When I heard about that, I couldn't get in my truck fast enough, and I drove the two thousand kilometres down there to help. A few days earlier, farmers had driven bulldozers right through this area to block the tunnels intentionally, entombing the wombats underground. We worked like buggery to excavate their burrows, some of which were thirty metres long and three metres deep.

Even though southern hairy-nosed wombats are considered a threatened native species, farmers could seek destruction permits for the animals from the state government. While I was down there, I was keen to talk to farmers to discuss the issue from their point of view. According to these farmers, the problem was that the wombats would eat crops as they were planted, they would dig holes that their machinery would fall into, and they broke and damaged fences. But with one farmer I visited, I was surprised to learn that of his thousands of acres of land, only one tiny little corner, just half an acre, had these wombat burrows. It was affecting his fencing there. 'What do you estimate is the cost in dollar terms of the damage these wombats have done to your business?' I asked.

'Well, that half-acre they damaged is worth one hundred and fifty dollars per year,' he said.

'If I give you one hundred and fifty dollars a year, will you leave the wombats alone?' I asked.

But it was clear that he just wanted the wombats gone. He'd got it in his head that the wombats were destroying his property, and no matter how much I tried, he wouldn't come round. I was grateful for his insight but I found it really difficult to see his point of view.

I probably would have been less upset if the wombats had proven to be a really widespread issue and were then disposed of humanely. I still wouldn't have agreed, but I probably could have accepted it. But in most cases they weren't. The wombats were buried alive by heavy machinery, or farmers would throw poison or explosives down the entrance to their burrows. There were all sorts of horrible methods they used. That's what upset me more than anything else. Wombats are amazing animals that play an important role in the environment and they feel pain just as much as you or me or anybody else.

Those farmers maintained that wombats were destroying all of the country down there. But they've got to remember that the wombats were there long before they started to farm the country. They'd been digging holes and whatever else for thousands upon thousands of years. The next thing they know, along comes a farmer, who simply says, 'Well, you can't do that anymore. I want this bit of land and I'm going to clear it and plant my crops.' Nobody consults with the wombats, of course. And that is exactly where the problem lies with every single animal out there that is threatened. We continue to make decisions without looking at it from the animal's point of view—without considering that their very survival is at stake.

For most of my time down there we were on our hands and knees, covered in dirt, in the scorching forty-degree summer heat, racing against the clock to find these wombats before they asphyxiated. We were out there all day, every day, until it got dark. By the end of my trip, I was exhausted. But when I went home, it weighed on my mind that these dedicated volunteers stayed out there, continuing to dig for wombats.

We might not have solved the issue, but the story of my visit made headlines in newspapers right across Australia. There was suddenly a spotlight on the matter, and therefore some pressure on the government to do something about it. Brigitte told me afterwards that they had struggled to get that kind of attention for themselves.

I returned home to Camp Chilli considerably stressed about it. Just a few days later, out slashing the grass in the paddock, I nearly drove my tractor into the dam because I was so distracted by thoughts of those poor wombats and the work of those dedicated people. This kind of treatment of animals, burying wombats alive, was an absolute blight on humanity. The more I thought about it, the tighter my chest became. When that pain suddenly worsened, I realised I had become more than a little anxious about the topic. But I put up with the agonising tightness in my chest for another four hours, working at my usual breakneck pace. After a while the pain had become unbearable, so I went back up to the house and admitted that to Judy.

'I don't feel all that good,' I said. 'I think I'll go and lie down for a while.'

Well, I hardly made it to the bed before collapsing. I was in the grip of a major heart attack. By the time the ambulance arrived, I had lost all coordination and the ability to speak. I was completely paralysed. They rushed me to the local hospital. I could see that there were a lot of medical staff fussing around, but things were hazy and I couldn't talk or gesture at all. I saw them get a defibrillator ready to jumpstart me like I would jolt a flat battery in my truck with jumper leads.

'It's not good,' I heard a doctor say. I thought to myself, *Well, this looks like the end of the road for you, Bob.*

But I was calm. I just contemplated that it was finished for me, finally over and done with. Over the years, Judy had gifted me an understanding of spirituality where I could accept whatever came. But as it turned out, it wasn't my time. They kept me going and sent me to Brisbane in an emergency Care-flight plane for specialist care at a bigger hospital.

I woke up in the intensive care unit, once it was all over, with tubes and wires hanging out all over the place. I realised with surprise that I had survived. When the specialist came to see me, he explained just how lucky I had been. 'Well, you've lost thirty-five per cent of the functionality of your heart. It's dead and gone,' he said.

At least I had one, I thought, but I knew I hadn't used my brain. In all those long hours I had chosen to ignore vital warning signs. Working through that kind of pain had been a really stupid thing to do. The male of the species are probably our own worst enemy in that way.

'The good news is that you can survive with the remaining sixty-five per cent, but you've got to be aware that if you overdo it, and get to this point again, you might not survive the next time,' he warned.

He was absolutely right. I had overdone it all these years. Physically, I'd always worked as hard as I could. It was my only way of coping with some of the bad things that had come my way. This was probably the very wake-up call I needed.

But I don't really recommend heart attacks. I'd prefer to be chomped by a three-metre crocodile, because you don't feel the crocodile coming, you only feel it afterwards. A heart attack isn't as stealthy. You feel every part of the ambush as it comes up on you. But regardless of how agonising the pain of that heart attack was, I'd take that any day compared to the pain of losing people you love.

It took me a long time to realise that living like a hermit wasn't doing me any good, and after that very close call, it was clear that I'd been given another shot at life. I thought I'd used up all my second chances already, so I felt incredibly lucky.

When I looked in the mirror for my daily shave I saw a wrinkly old bugger who hadn't looked after himself over the years. On the other hand I saw a guy who had been lucky to have the opportunities I had, and I still had more to do. I hadn't really achieved anything at all since Steve had left us. When I started to think how Steve would have wanted me to react to not having him around, giving up wasn't something I thought he'd be all that proud of. He would have told me to get my act together and given me a bloody hard kick up the bum. He had made the most of every second of every day. It was time to take a leaf out of his book.

So I said to myself, 'You'd better get back out there, Bob,' and I did. There were lots of people out there like Brigitte who needed help fighting for the thing that was still most important to me—our wildlife.

***

Soon enough more and more people who were struggling to get support for really important environmental issues were writing to me. I realised that these dedicated individuals were scattered right across the country, fighting these little battles all over the place to protect some of our most precious native wildlife. Their work might have been different, but their stories were similar. And I started to see that I could offer them some sort of help. I might not have been able to give large sums of money, but I could help to shine a spotlight on the work that they were doing. Very few people seemed to understand that what these people were doing was really critical, but I could certainly relate to them.

Back in the early days, when Lyn and I were taking in orphaned and injured wildlife at the reptile park, things were no different. We didn't receive any support from the government back then either. At one point Lyn and I were inundated with injured wildlife that had been brought in by the general public. They just kept coming, and in the end it was like a production line for around-the-clock feeding. There were no two animals that needed the same type of care. We had tawny frogmouths with broken wings, orphaned wallabies and glider joeys all needing different kinds of milk, snakes with puncture wounds after being attacked by dogs, koalas and possums with broken legs or arms after being hit by cars, you name it.

These animals of course were in no way a benefit to our park; we couldn't even have them on display. Instead they lived in our house, filling every available space. We did it solely for the sake of the animals, to nurse them back to health, and, with a bit of luck, back to the wild. Or, if that wasn't an option and they were too badly injured, to make the difficult decision to put them out of their pain. Lyn and I paid for everything—their food, the expensive veterinary bills for medication and surgery—with absolutely no assistance from the government.

And we weren't alone. There were numerous other people out there who had taken it upon themselves to care for our injured and orphaned native wildlife. These people worked up to twenty hours a day, throughout the day and night, with no expectation of any reward apart from the hope of seeing that animal back out in the wild. The work was physically demanding and expensive and completely without compensation, not so much as a pat on the back. In a sense, they were sacrificing their own lives to give the animals a second chance. Yet in doing this work, we were all doing the job of the very government department responsible for protecting the native fauna of our country.

To me, it was no different from saying that I would go out and undertake plumbing work free of charge. To say, I'm going to go and work for whoever needs it, for all hours of the day and night and every weekend, for weeks and months and years on end, until I'm physically exhausted. And at the end of it all, I'm not going to get paid. Not a single cent. Now, why on earth would you do that? Because somebody had to. That's precisely why our family and many others out there did this work.

But not everyone shared my point of view. Queensland Parks and Wildlife Services eventually threatened to confiscate the injured animals unless we agreed to pay a royalty for them. They expected us not only to do this work for free, but then to actually pay for the privilege of it. Instead of a handshake to thank us for the work that we did, we got a slap on the wrist. That didn't sit well with me. They were simply relying on the emotion and dedication of a handful of people who were prepared to sacrifice their livelihoods for the animals.

I fought these fees for quite some time out of principle. I argued the case backwards and forwards with the department, pleading to bring some common sense to the situation. But ultimately they ended the discussion: we had to pay a royalty and that was that. But I didn't quite see it that way.

'I'm going to Brisbane to sort this out,' I said to Lyn one day. I packed up a couple of baby tiger snakes that I had bred at the park into a calico bag.

Lyn wasn't happy in the slightest, pleading with me to reconsider. 'You've lost your mind,' she said. She thought I was asking for trouble, and she was right.

I drove to the Queensland Parks and Wildlife Services headquarters in Brisbane. In my Queensland Reptile and Fauna Park uniform, I rode the elevator up to the main office front desk. 'Excuse me, sir, you can't go in there! They're in a meeting,' the receptionist called, as I marched past. I kept walking until I reached the room where these bureaucrats made at times ridiculous decisions about the natural world from the confines of their inner-city office.

I didn't say anything, I just undid the knot at the end of the bag and tipped these little baby snakes right onto the big table in the middle of their boardroom and then turned on my heels. I walked straight past the receptionist, went down the elevator, back to my vehicle and drove home to Beerwah.

By the time the hour's drive was up, I'd cooled down and was feeling some considerable pangs of regret. It was a really irrational thing to do, but you get pushed to a point where you simply can't cope with certain injustices and you need to make a statement. That was my only way of getting my point across because we couldn't afford to challenge the state government legally.

I never heard a word about that incident. I don't know what happened after I left the building. But the demand to pay royalties suddenly ceased after that. We continued to care for the animals and the issue of royalties never resurfaced. But we never got a thankyou either.

In hindsight, of course, it wasn't a smart thing to do. Thankfully, these days I've got better ways of dealing with things. I'm not quite as hot-headed as I used to be. But I can still remember and understand how difficult it is for dedicated people who are caring for our wildlife and not getting the support they need, people who'd feed the animals in their care before they fed themselves. And despite all the important work they were doing, they were finding it really hard to drum up any support or awareness. I couldn't give a lot but I could use the Irwin name to at least get them some attention for their issues.

***

I knew straightaway that I wouldn't be able to help the way Steve had—I wouldn't be in front of TV cameras. I'd never liked public speaking, I'd stuttered badly when I was young. It's no secret that I'd rather be hanging onto the back of a crocodile, covered in mud and mosquitos, than in front of a camera. I wouldn't be making wildlife documentaries or walking red carpets; my focus would be on the grassroots wildlife work. I thought my role could be to help other people get the recognition they deserved for the work they were doing that had gone unnoticed.

I began with the issue of coal seam gas. I knew a fair bit about it by then, and I just hated it. I was horrified by what these companies were doing, with no consideration of either the environment or the people who lived in the affected communities.

The companies just didn't give a damn. To them, it was only about the money.

In 2011, I agreed to join a recognised coal seam gas campaigner, Drew Hutton, in protesting the issue. I was asked to help create a road blockade aimed at stopping the construction of a sixteen-kilometre gas pipeline at Tara, just west of Brisbane. Drew and his team were determined to make some noise about an issue that was continually being swept under the carpet.

'Drew, what do you think would happen if we got arrested?' I asked.

'Well, that might get it out there,' he replied. They couldn't get anyone to pay attention to this issue. Not only would this pipeline potentially contaminate groundwater with the subsequent risks to health, but the gas company had also breached environmental permits to clear vegetation along that pipeline route. They had been granted permission to clear ten metres of remnant vegetation to put the pipeline in, but in many areas we observed they'd cleared forty metres wide over six kilometres. The company had clearly breached their environmental permit and yet the state government wasn't doing a thing about it. If any ordinary Australian had done that, broken tree-clearing laws, they'd have gone to gaol, simple as that. It was extremely concerning that the government hadn't addressed this, or the concerns of Tara's residents about the use of toxic chemicals. To not even be able to get an answer about that was just not acceptable in my opinion.

'I'll do it then,' I said.

We turned up to the construction site and I sat down fair smack in the middle of the road. We brought the whole operation to a halt for a number of hours. The site was heavily patrolled by local police, and one officer came over. 'Bob, I'll give you three warnings to move off the road and allow the traffic through. But if you fail to obey those orders, then you'll give me no choice but to arrest you,' he said.

'All right,' I said.

I held my ground, there in the middle of the road, and sure enough, after three warnings they arrested me. As they did, the first police officer said to another, 'He isn't going to resist, so we treat him correctly.' And they did.

In the police car we had a lovely chat about all sorts of different things. They were very polite and treated me as they would their own grandfather. When we got back to the police station they put me outside in a lovely little courtyard and made me a cup of tea. I watched a little water dragon out there for a while. They took my fingerprints and went through the normal procedure. But finally they wanted me to sign a document saying that I agreed to not return to protest at that site ever again. Then I would be free to go.

'Sorry, fellas, but I can't sign this,' I said. So I had to go to court.

I certainly wasn't prepared to sign a document that prohibited me from speaking my mind about a really destructive issue facing our environment.

What all that managed to achieve was widespread awareness of the real concerns about the state coal seam gas operations in Queensland and the laws governing them. The story of my arrest and the details of the issue went into just about every newspaper around the country. For a day in court and a fine of four hundred dollars, we succeeded in bringing it all out into the public arena. There were certain destructive aspects of coal seam gas that hadn't received attention before that.

Sometimes the only way you can stop something is to get out there and make the public aware of exactly what's happening. Otherwise it's just too easy for people to shut their eyes and remain oblivious to what's happening in their own backyard. As hard as it is to see at times, you need to get upset. You have to look at that awful photo or TV news story and allow yourself to get emotionally involved in what's happening. You need to get angry about the cruelty and injustices facing our wildlife. Because only then will you be motivated to do something about it. You might not be able to stop it today, but who knows what position you may be in to help, somewhere down the track.

***

After a while, I was hardly ever home. Every time I felt myself getting slack, I heard Steve's voice in my head, giving me another push. I did start to burn out, because it was constant, and draining, and nearly always distressing. I was seeing first-hand some of the worst atrocities against our environment at the hands of humans. And I was travelling long distances. There were a lot of people who needed help, and it wasn't as though I had to go looking for them either. In every part of our country, there was something different going on.

In 2011, Cyclone Yasi hit the coast of northern Queensland, causing widespread damage to the prehistoric rainforests of Mission Beach. Cassowary habitats were destroyed, along with their food sources. I was asked to become a spokesperson as we rallied enough public awareness and donations, with Queensland Parks and Wildlife Services, to establish feeding stations for the iconic birds and ensure they survived until the rainforests recov-ered. There were under 150 individual birds that remained in the Mission Beach area. What struck me most was the dedication of the local community. People who had lost everything themselves—their homes, possessions and livelihoods—were the very same people who were out there helping us feed those cassowaries.

Later that year I joined forces with the people of the Mary Valley, in Queensland, to protest against the proposed Traveston Crossing Dam, which would threaten the endangered lungfish and the Mary River turtle.

I banded together with the local community of Hervey Bay, the humpback-whale watching capital of the world, to highlight the issue of protected whales in Australia's southern whale sanctuary being illegally slaughtered by Japanese whalers, with little intervention from the federal government. I was pleased to hear that the organisation fighting for these whales, the Sea Shepherd Conservation Society, named their next anti-whaling vessel the *Steve Irwin* in Steve's honour. I visited their ship for a tour, and came close to joining them for a campaign in the southern ocean, but my dicky ticker ruled it out.

I campaigned with koala conservation groups to influence the state government for greater protection of koala habitats. Koalas face localised extinction in south-east Queensland due to widespread land clearing and development. It is a fact that one of our greatest Australian icon's future looks bleak.

I became the face of the Fight for the Reef campaign and toured the state of Queensland with the late Felicity Wishart, a pioneering activist from the Australian Marine Conservation Society, to highlight the devastating impact of dumping dredge spoil onto the Great Barrier Reef, one of the seven natural wonders of the world, which I saw dying right before my eyes.

I fought hammer and tongs alongside a steadfast individual called Colin 'Who Cares' Riddell to highlight the need for change to the Native Title Act which allows the slaughter of endangered dugongs and sea turtles. Dugongs were being drowned slowly as well as cut up while they were still alive, and our precious sea turtles were being left upside down on beaches to die from dehydration. Cruelty is cruelty; it isn't a matter of race. As a result of Colin's tireless work, the Native Title Act was changed to include Indigenous people in regards to laws governing animal cruelty.

And of course every time the state government brought up the idea of reintroducing trophy hunting to 'manage' the populations of saltwater crocodiles—after every fear-mongering media headline about a croc attack—I slammed it again to every media outlet. Nothing makes my blood boil quite like the topic of trophy hunting, after all of those years of research and our life's work in educating people on the vulnerability of our apex predators. I find it difficult to understand how anybody could get any pleasure or satisfaction from killing an animal, full stop. Not because they need to kill that animal to survive themselves, but just because they can.

I travelled up and down the east coast of Queensland, uncovering more and more of these issues, and I realised that I had only just scratched the surface. These were just the people who I had met. There would be countless more people out there doing the same sort of great work who I hadn't even heard of. I met so many inspirational Australians fighting for a better world for our wildlife: they were self-funding and building sea turtle hospitals off Gladstone and Cairns and bat hospitals in the rainforest. There was a tree kangaroo rehabilitation centre, an animal most Australians probably wouldn't even realise exists.

I came to hear of a Perth grandmother who has rescued nine hundred bears from the illegal wildlife trade in Southeast Asia and relocated them to purpose-built sanctuaries. There was a young woman at Airlie Beach who had banded a team of volunteers together to remove over 200,000 kilograms of marine debris out of the iconic Whitsunday Islands. Also, koala hospitals; seabird rescue; shark and crocodile appreciation groups; and people saving the bilby.

When my focus had been narrowly on Australia Zoo or Ironbark Station, to a degree I was clueless about what was going on out there in the wild. Until I got out there, I didn't realise how bad the situation was. You just can't comprehend how dedicated some of these people on the frontline of fighting for our wildlife and the environment are until you see it for yourself.

In 2012, Judy and I and some of our friends decided to launch our own not-for-profit foundation, the Bob Irwin Wildlife & Conservation Foundation Inc. The goal of the organisation is to advocate for wildlife and the people supporting them. It's been a collaborative effort from so many people and I am thankful to the volunteers, especially the work of our foundation movers and shakers Dennis Carroll and Graham Morrow for their years of dedication to get it up and running.

I think we often forget that unsung heroes need a little encouragement from time to time. When you've got people working tirelessly for little or no reward, a tiny bit of recognition for their thankless work can be the fuel they need to go on another six months, or another year. That's something I've really enjoyed being able to do. And if a visit from me gets them some media coverage, or if my backing can get them a bit of extra funding, then to me that's what it's all about.

It's still true that I don't like the limelight or feel comfortable around groups of people. But I get a kick out of meeting courageous wildlife people right around Australia. And they've done me the honour of allowing me into their lives and letting me get involved. I've learnt a lot from these people and from seeing firsthand the work being done out there. People always want to repay me in some way, but I feel like I get a lot more than I give. Every time these people help another injured animal back to the wild, it makes me so happy—and on many occasions I've been lucky enough to be there when that happens.

I won't ever stop supporting them. I'll keep doing it for as long as I'm here, because I'm a proud Australian. I'll continue to help these people when I can, no matter where they live in this lucky country of ours. Every little bit of work they do is important and all of these people need our help.

***

For most of the last ten years I hadn't had a lot to do with Steve's old team. I suppose I didn't want to get in the way, or interfere with the way things were. But I certainly missed it; I had very special memories of working with that great group of people. In the last few years that's changed and they've started to come back into my life. It's been really great to see them again and reconnect.

From time to time we all get together for a barbecue out at Camp Chilli or they get me involved in their current work with wildlife. It's great to see what they've gone on to do, whether that's continuing to work with crocodiles or now being leaders themselves. While most of them have since moved on from

Australia Zoo—they are now zoo curators, researchers, park rangers, firefighters, or construction workers—they carry on the legacy, spreading Steve's message far and wide in their own way. That makes me feel really pleased. A part of me wonders if that was always Steve's intention. He knew that they wouldn't always be crocodile keepers, but they would still be emulating his message about following your passion and instilling that in others.

Some of the boys are now involved in our wildlife foundation, along with other young people who now form our team. We've got a really dedicated, enthusiastic bunch of volunteers who work well together, full of ideas for large-scale research projects on crocodiles and cassowaries that they want to bring to fruition. They'll take it to new heights. In their hands, the foundation will remain a voice for wildlife, and an advocate for better management practices and guidelines for their wellbeing.

At other times it's about basic stuff: grassroots observation work, advocacy, or simply all getting together somewhere remote to camp and share ideas about wildlife conservation. There's nothing better than bringing together a group of enthusiastic, like-minded individuals for nature appreciation.

There are enough young people in the organisation now to be able to take over. It'll eventually be time for me to hand the baton on to these young people, so they can get out there and do what needs to be done. I think it's special to have young people involved in taking care of our environment, because it's not my future anymore, it's theirs. Their children and their children's children will be the ones to benefit from a healthy planet. And that's something we should all be concerned about.

Even though my time's almost done, I'll keep on going for as long as I can. I'm hoping for another ten years. For the time being I'll continue to advise them from the sidelines and encourage their interests and push them as hard as I can. The day that I can't keep up with these young ones in the bush anymore is probably the day that I'll give it away. But for now, I'll push on. Sometimes my body lets me down, but I work through it and I hide behind a tree if I'm suffering a bit. Or I find something fascinating on the ground that everyone should stop and take a long, close look at—I've got that one down to a fine art now.

Bretto, one of the members of our foundation and part of the old team at Australia Zoo, caught me in one of these moments recently when I was struggling a bit. 'You're a sneaky bugger, aren't ya?' he said affectionately.

'Oh yeah, but there's ways and means of doing these sorts of things. You'll learn that as you get older,' I replied with a smile.

***

It never ceases to amaze me when I'm out on the road how many people come up to me and say, 'But Bob, I'm only one person. I can't do anything.' Well, let me start off by saying that those people are wrong. Because it is up to every individual to do their little bit too. We can't blame the government for everything that's happened, because every single person is responsible, in some way, for the health of our planet.

When I was a kid some species of animals were regarded as common, garden variety. Those same animals are now considered threatened or endangered. This is happening before our eyes, in our lifetime. Europeans have only been on this continent for around two hundred years. We've done all this damage in the blink of an eye. Most Australians don't know that we've got the worst mammalian extinction rate in the world. We've lost over thirty species since Europeans arrived. It's not just the famous Tasmanian tiger, we've lost many more vitally important species. Even as I write this, more than seventeen hundred species of fauna and flora are listed by the Australian government as 'at risk', which means there's a chance they'll go extinct unless we do something about it. The time to act for conservation is *now*.

Back in my day we could claim ignorance, but young people today haven't got excuses like that anymore. Young people have new ideas, better technology and research available to them at the click of a button. And that's what makes me excited. With that I can see a good future now, whereas before I couldn't. Before I got involved with passionate young people I was worried, but I now have faith in the future generation to fix things. When it's my time to go, I'll be content knowing that there are a lot of young Australians who have a better understanding of what needs to be done in the future to care for the environment. My generation made a heck of a mess of things in a very short time and it's now over to young people as our future leaders to learn from our mistakes.

So when people ask, 'What can one person do, Bob?', my answer is that one person can do a hell of a lot.

Can you imagine how I feel when I find out that there's a group of little schoolkids in a third-world country, whose classroom is just a wooden hut with no walls, and yet they have a television set. And you know what they're watching? Steve Irwin. They're out in the jungle, and they're watching him and listening to his message about conservation. I simply cannot put into words how I feel about that; it just makes me feel immensely proud. It never ceases to amaze me just how many people Steve affected. Almost daily we still get emails from people all around the world who have been influenced by him. There's probably more now than there was when he was still here. That makes me feel good. How could you feel anything but proud when your son is still being remembered for something as fundamentally important to our planet as wildlife conservation? And not just remembered—he has influenced so many people to get off their backside and do something themselves. A lot of them are young people and that's exactly what we want.

I see shades of Steve in these people and many others I meet out there with that special connection with the environment and wildlife. He had a way of getting to people and he really did shout his message out there loud and clear. It is amazing to see how many people he affected along the way. My biggest dream is to make sure that message keeps going through all of these inspiring young people who have become involved in the conservation of wildlife and wild places. That's exactly how we will keep that dream alive.

In my lifetime, humanity seems to have largely lost touch with the wonder of the natural world, but when my time comes to leave this physical world I will leave satisfied in the knowledge that the planet is in good hands. I am deeply humbled to think that my legacy, and that of my son, has captivated imaginations and inspired so many to truly connect with the magic of nature. I'm excited to think that an ever-growing army of young, energetic conservationists can pick up the baton and inspire all people to value and appreciate the magnificence of this planet we call home. Nature is (thankfully) very resilient if we give it half a chance.

So for me, it all comes back to that hyperactive little blond-haired kid. Because in my eyes there was no one more concerned about the state of our planet and the animals than he was. I guess the greatest thing for me today is seeing animals like snakes and crocodiles finally falling under the banner of animal wefare. That certainly wasn't the case when we were starting out. Steve showed the world that it was okay to wear your heart on your sleeve, and to get emotional and fight for what's important. Why shouldn't you be passionate about the very thing that sustains our own survival: the health of planet Earth?

When I think about it, I really have been blessed with a great life. I've been one of those people who has been extremely fortunate to work with my passion. There are lots of things that I'd like to have turned out differently, of course, but they're just the obvious ones. We've got to accept that we can't change the past, much as we would like to. That's life. All we really can do is to make the best of what's left with the people we care about. None of us is really here for all that long in the grand scheme of things. The goal is to achieve as much as we can, and leave behind a legacy for our grandchildren in the short time that we have. What can be better than clean water, fresh air and a wealth of wildlife?

Just when we might think we have figured things out in this funny little experience called life, the universe will throw us a curve ball to make us improvise. We'll all face that at some time or another to varying degrees. When I walked away from Australia Zoo, when Steve died, when I lost Lyn, I didn't think it would be possible to survive. But throughout this journey I realised that it's possible to find happiness in unexpected places. It was at the bottom of grief's barrel that I again found the things that mattered the most to me. The animals. The environment. The people who fight for what's important.

The universe is funny that way. Sometimes it has a way of making sure we end up exactly where we belong. From time to time, I still think, 'Well, you haven't really achieved what he would have wanted you to achieve.' But I'm content with the fact that I've at least tried. The most important thing in life is, no matter how many blows you get, to always get back up, because there's plenty out there to fight for.

15

Return to Cattle Creek

After thirty long years, I made a pilgrimage back to Cattle Creek in Far North Queensland, to the place where it all began. Of everywhere that Steve and I had ventured together, Cattle Creek held a special significance because it was where our education in crocodiles really began. It took me many years to pluck up the courage to return, knowing it would be a reminder of our good times. Would it all come flooding back? Would it be too painful?

Right up until I got on that plane, I seriously considered pulling out. But Amanda insisted, and I have no doubt she would have got me on that aircraft kicking and screaming if she had to. She had tracked down the Accorneros, who I had lost touch with, booked flights and hired a car, as well as coaxed me to go on the journey in the first place. Amanda and Judy worked as a team to convince me, Judy driving me the three hours to Brisbane airport. And I was immensely glad in the end that they did, because it will certainly be something that I'll take with me when I go.

Stephen Accornero and his wife Annalisa welcomed us into their home just outside Ingham. He had aged somewhat since the last time we'd met, but his larger-than-life stature and hearty laughter were exactly as I had remembered. 'You won't believe how many crocs are around here now, Bob! You said that once you took out the CEO then the teenagers would run rampant. Well, you were right—nowadays, we see them walking across the road. They've lost all fear of people. Not like it used to be when you blokes first arrived.'

I was sad to learn that his own father, Dante, or 'Danny' to us, had passed on. He had been such a wonderful father figure to Steve throughout the many months he had camped out there alone. Stephen and Danny had become Steve's close friends in those years, and the Ingham district was never far from his heart no matter how famous he went on to be.

Stephen and I exchanged our fondest old memories over cups of tea. I noticed that his mug was covered with images of Steve. He told me he drank from it every morning.

'In an interview on the US *60 Minutes* he referred to where he first learnt to catch crocs as "downtown Cattle Creek"—an insider joke for all of us locals. After that he asked if we'd been watching. He said he liked to keep that spot as his private getaway!' Stephen said, laughing. But then his tone changed. 'You know, my dad recalled a particular conversation with Steve right up until the day that he passed. One day back then, just out of the blue, sitting around his campfire, Steve suddenly told my father that when you eventually passed on, he didn't want to go to your funeral. He said he wouldn't be able to handle it, you going before him. But Dad reasoned with him, saying, "Your old man's been there for you whenever you needed him. He wiped your backside when you were a baby, and he's done everything for ya! Isn't it right that you should pay your respects to him?" And Dad said that a couple of days later Steve came up and said he was right.'

And Stephen told me something else, something that he was initially reluctant to bring up because he thought I might reckon it was all hocus pocus. He said that Steve had often spoken about our close connection. 'Us Irwins have a sixth sense,' Steve told him, 'We don't have to speak to know what the other is thinking. We know when something is going to happen to one of us.' As Stephen spoke I thought about the time my son had been bitten on the leg and I'd unexpectedly turned up a few days later, and when his hat had blown off his head at the moment of Lyn's accident. There was an accumulation of other things like these throughout the years; I remember them all.

Stephen, a hardy cane farmer from the bush himself, had thought this might be a strange concept for a rough bloke like me to digest. But he needn't have worried—this was all something that I already knew and accepted. I had never doubted that Steve and I shared a special connection, an energy. So I didn't find it unusual at all and I was pleased to know that he had recognised it too.

Stephen asked if I would like to see some old home movies of Steve and me back in the eighties, from our contract catching years. These were those first amateur films that Steve had recorded on his home video recorder. Stephen explained that over the years he had guarded these tapes with his life, keeping them under lock and key, against a barrage of media types trying to get their hands on the earliest moments of the Crocodile Hunter. The videos had never seen the light of day. 'No matter how much money I was offered, I wouldn't even consider it,' he said. I respected that immensely about the Accornero family. They don't make them much better than that—just really good people, whom we'd been lucky to meet all those years ago. They'd let us spend a lot of time on their property and they'd bent over backwards to help us. They hadn't needed to do any of it. But they did.

I thought Stephen might have a short video or two, but there was hours of footage. I sat all afternoon glued to the television, watching tape after tape of a twenty-two-year-old Steve in navy-blue overalls and a terrible mullet haircut, his beloved dog Chilli by his side.

As self-protection, I never watch Steve on television. I choose not to remember the date he passed. So when I felt an ache in my heart the first time I heard his familiar voice on those tapes, I wasn't certain I'd make it through the stack beside the VHS player. But curiosity pushed me on—I had never seen this precious footage before. And there we were again, enthusiastically scanning the banks of Cattle Creek's tributaries from our humble dinghy, happier than a couple of pigs in mud. I laughed aloud with him as he deviously sprang a crocodile trap with me inside, as I lined it with a rotten pig's leg. 'Bloody hell, I'm ankle-deep in live rice. Get me out, turkey!' I called to him as maggots teemed into my socks.

As the tapes rolled, I watched him come of age as he honed and cultivated his skills with each capture of a gargantuan crocodile. I cringed to watch some of the outrageous things he'd done, including the bit where Cookie had nearly bitten his foot clean off. It brought back a lot of good memories, and a lot of sombre ones too. I saw him take his younger sister Mandy out in the dinghy on one of her holidays up there; he was thrilled to take her into his world, and watched her sitting up the front of the boat, grinning from ear to ear, giving two big thumbs-up, as they checked traps together. I saw his film of the little ceremony he'd held for Chilli, the camera panning across her fresh grave, a mound rising from the ground. 'See you later, my small dog,' he said to the camera, struggling to get the words out. 'One day we'll be pig-hunting together again.'

But the thing that got to me most were the videos of his captures, as he worked alone on Cattle Creek, narrating to the camera. 'Dad, have a go at this, what do you think of that top jaw rope?' he said. And, 'Hey, Dad, I've got this now,' pleased as punch after one of his first solo captures. 'You should stick to catching butterflies and lizards back at the park and leave the crocodiles to me!'

As he spoke to me through the camera, and across the years, I suddenly realised that those films had been made for me as he'd camped out there alone and I was back at the zoo. I felt the closest I'd felt to him in a long while. He'd known that I'd watch them sometime; at some stage I'd see what he had so desperately wanted to show me. And I was finally seeing it now, when I most needed to, thirty years later. He'd always sought my tick of approval, and he had it more than he would ever know. I couldn't help but respond to him as though he was talking directly to me through the screen, as if he was actually there.

Stephen, watching the films beside me in his lounge room, eventually turned to me, his voice full of emotion, and said, 'Steve always said that the tapes were made to show to you if anything ever happened to him. If he mucked up he wanted you to know what he'd done wrong! Those films were always meant for you, his dad.'

My stay ended with a visit to what I'll always know as Camp Chilli, where it all began. Even after all this time, Stephen and his wife still preserved it exactly as it had been, in memory of Steve. I was fighting off tears as Stephen navigated his Landcruiser across his family property, and as I glanced at him I could see he was too. We passed through locked gates that weren't there before, and a decoy dirt track: basic security measures the family had put in place to stop the public accessing Steve's camp and defacing it. After his death, people had discourteously gone looking.

I had finally returned to the place where I felt closest to my son. I reminisced about what we went through as a couple of pretty raw crocodile hunters, and felt proud to consider what we had achieved in the long term. The old lean-to I had built him had since blown over in a cyclone, but I didn't have a problem with that. Nature had done its thing and now it was a home for reptiles seeking shelter in the crevices of the iron sheets that lay there in a heap. I made out the two rusty nails where the Camp Chilli sign once used to hang.

Once I'd taken it all in, I made my way alone down to the mangrove-lined bank of the creek, and sat beside the boat ramp where we used to launch from, and had a quiet word with my Steve. Nothing had changed as my eyes panned across the creek, except that he was no longer around. It pained my heart to realise I had never been here without him. But as I sat there, tears rolling down my aged wrinkly face, I felt his warm presence reassuringly all around me, among the sandflies' nasty but familiar stings. His presence was really, really strong. I could hear his laughter echoing out on the water, see him climbing trees to set the bag traps, smell our campfire burning. Quietly talking to him in my mind, as I often do, I could hear him respond in my head, as clear as day, telling me that he was glad I had come back to him. 'I'm still camping out here, Dad, with Chilli by my side. It'll always be our special place. You and I will always have Cattle Creek.'

Epilogue
Amanda French

Koolatah Station, Cape York, September 2015

It's only when you've eaten your last bit of long-life cheese, and you're down to boiling stagnant river water for drinking, that you start to think of heading home. But you delay it as long as you can, because packing up camp is one of the least exciting tasks of the trip, hands down. By this stage, everything is covered in red Cape York dust. And no matter how early you rise to beat the scorching heat, it always creeps up on you. The heat is inescapable; you can't outsmart it in Far North Queensland. It's only at this point, for the very first time on the trip, that home seems too far away, as you contemplate the days on the road that lie ahead, those long stretches of corrugated gravel covered in bull dust between here and there.

The homeward stretch always feels worlds apart from the original journey north. Leaving the bush when you're only just starting to feel a connection to it never feels good. For me, I'm all too aware that I'm heading back to the city and losing some of that like-mindedness that I've shared with people out here in a very remote part of the Australian bush. We've spent the last three weeks exploring this landscape with the walking encyclopaedia that is Bob Irwin. We've had balmy nights meditating under a blanket of stars atop a sand dune, listening to crocodiles snapping up fish for dinner below us. In those moments, when your mind is empty, you start to truly understand the idea of feeling at one with nature.

Thankfully that feeling lasts a wee bit longer: when you're travelling with Bob, you don't take the well-trodden path to your destination, you always take the quietest backroad where passing another vehicle is a novelty. He likes to camp on the side of the road there and light a campfire wherever he damn well pleases. Bob will never stay at a caravan park. To him tourists are only noisemakers disturbing his sought-after remoteness. The fewer people, the more isolated, the better. This of course poses a challenge for Judy, who always manages to pack enough food to last us—because out here there sure aren't any supermarkets.

But this time, leaving this special place with Bob fills me with a particular sadness. I realise the older he gets, the fewer trips like this he has left in him. At seventy-seven years of age, it's just a fact of life that before too long he won't be scaling rocky cliffs in forty-degree heat or navigating his rig over the far north's less travelled roads.

We pack up in silence. We don't really want to leave, but it's time. We fold up the camping table—the same one he used to take out camping in the early days with Lyn—and hook it on the camper trailer. It's tied down with the same old piece of canvas Bob always uses to protect his rig from the dust on the roads. The canvas came off Steve's old truck. Before he gets into the truck to drive away, he takes off his leather knife belt, a handmade gift from Steve, and slides it beneath his seat for safe-keeping. These relics are almost sacred to Bob—he has to have them on every single trip. They're pieces of the good old days coming along with him.

A slow pace is all we can manage as we travel the fifty kilometres back to the homestead of the station we've been camping on. It's a dry thirty-six degrees Celsius outside the truck. As I look around the inside of the vehicle I laugh to myself at his devotion to Toyota Landcruisers. He drives a newer model these days, but the aesthetics of the vehicle haven't evolved much over the years. There's not too much in the way of flash screens, buttons or technology that Bob would just consider a hindrance. Technology that he can't get his head around always gets threatened to go under the back wheel of his truck. It's just a new version of the tried and tested car he's always loved. That is so like him too. He doesn't waver much from his old values, beliefs or routines. It's still meat and three veg for dinner, he'll always read a map over a GPS, and he refuses to wash out the teapot for fear it will lose the essential brewed-tea taste.

I wonder how it must have felt to pack up after one of the croc camps with the old Australia Zoo crew. How exhausted they must have been, and how much they must have looked forward to having a proper shower, to sleeping in the comfort of their own beds and not needing to compete with the sand-flies for their own skin. I also contemplate how those memories must feel to them now that the dream team has dispersed. But there's no doubt that they'll always be tied together with the most skilful bush knot of their shared experiences. Because bush knots that Bob ties rarely come undone.

We pull up at the station to have a cup of tea with the property's managers, Alby and Andrew. We park behind a cattle truck, from which one thousand head of wild cattle are being unloaded with an electric cattle prod. We always like to share with Alby and Andrew some of the adventures we've had camping on their property. We tell them about the black-throated finches we've seen, and other rare birds, and the snakes that have slithered across our path. Their focus is primarily on running cattle so they rarely venture to some of the areas we've explored, and they're only too happy to learn more about their land, the way we've been looking at it with the wildlife in our eyes.

Alby greets us at the front gate along with a horde of excitable kids who're staying with them for the school holidays. These are bush kids: they get engrossed in the cattle muster, swim in crocodile-infested rivers and travel far from their families to boarding schools for a chance at a decent education. School holidays are when they get to return home to do what they love: be in the great outdoors. These kids were living in a remote area, but were far from sheltered. Out here was the authentic school of life.

As we stand talking with Alby, a young blond boy emerges to say hello. As Alby introduces him as his ten-year-old nephew Parker, the boy's eyes fall on Bob's name embroidered on his trademark khaki shirt. 'Bob Ir-win,' he sounds out. Suddenly his face lights up. 'I know a guy called Steve Irwin from the TV! He catches these really big crocodiles. I've got all of his DVDs.'

We all look amused and Bob laughs.

'Parker, this man here is actually Steve Irwin's dad,' says Alby.

'Awe-some!' Parker slowly exclaims, eyes as wide as can be.

'I bet if you looked closely at some of those DVDs you'd see old Bob,' Alby says.

'Really?'

'Oh, yeah, I was somewhere there, scratchin' around in the background,' Bob says.

Quick as a flash Parker is off, the other kids following him, as he shouts out, 'Let's go and find Bob on TV!'

Bob lit up. Here we are on a very remote property in Cape York that sees little interaction the outside world: the mail plane delivers their food, there're no shops, and visitors are infrequent, particularly those with recognisable surnames. The impact that encounter would have had on Parker was enormous. More importantly, the impact that Parker had on Bob was even more profound. Ten years ago, as little Parker's life was beginning, Steve left this world. But his message will live on forever, immortalised in the documentaries he made and his contagious enthusiasm for wildlife.

Wherever we go, people seek Bob out to tell him how Steve inspired them to follow their passion or changed their perception of wildlife. He never reveals how difficult it is for him to hear this at times, to constantly be reminded of what he's lost. Instead he lets each and every person have all the time they need to share these stories. He always enthusiastically listens.

As Koolatah Station disappears behind us in a cloud of dust, Bob finally speaks, eyes still fixed forwards. 'Far North Queensland is where I feel most connected to Steve.'

Once the lump clears from my throat enough to let me speak, I turn to Bob and ask him something I've long wanted to know. 'Bob, would you do it all over again? Have you got one more croc trip left in you? I'm not talking about just observing them, I'm talking about catching monstrous salties again. Being in charge of the team. You're the last of the original crocodile hunters. Have you still got it in you?'

He pauses, then a smile creeps up one corner of his mouth. He rolls a cigarette with one hand, the other on the wheel. 'Amanda, there are things that, no matter how old I get, I never stop thinking about. I'm getting a bit long in the tooth now, but while I can still walk, my heart will always beat for crocodiles. Those years were the best times of my entire life. Would I want to catch crocodiles again? You betcha!'

We drove on, homeward bound for Camp Chilli, telling each other lies, getting ourselves lost at forks in the road, and writing this story.

Two Bob's worth

Sitting out the hottest part of the day in his favourite camping chair, cup of tea in hand, and mints in his top pocket where his cigarettes used to be (because this year he's finally given up the smokes). Bob took some time out to share his free-flowing thoughts on a range of life lessons acquired from his own personal journey. At seventy-seven years old, this is how Bob sees it.

A message to my grandkids

The most frequent question I am asked wherever I go is about my relationship with Steve's children, Bindi and Robert. And while I haven't seen them now for a number of years, I will always feel proud standing on the sidelines and watching them succeed at whatever path they choose to follow.

Steve was the proudest dad going around. Above all else, even wildlife, his favourite job was bringing into the world his two kids. He had the highest of hopes that because of their start to life, and all that he would teach them, they would become the greatest voice for animals. Almost from the day they were born Steve was out in the bush with them at every opportunity he got, teaching them about what's important, how it all fits together, how it all works. Of course the sad part about it is that Bindi and Robert don't have him around anymore to educate them as he had intended to do. I know Steve would have loved to be there to guide them in that way. He would have loved nothing more. It was the most important job in the world to him. His family always came first.

Going back to those very early days, I took a lot of pleasure in watching Steve with Bindi out in the bush; he was just so thrilled to teach her as she grew more inquisitive. He would have felt exactly the same way about teaching Bindi those kinds of things as I did about teaching him. He imparted as much knowledge as he could about understanding animals, tracking them, seeing how they lived, and just about respecting the environment in general. When you go out into the natural world, you might not see the animals that you expect to see, but it doesn't mean that they aren't there. It just means that you're not equipped with the knowledge to understand what's happening in their world. Steve would have thoroughly enjoyed sharing his knowledge with Bindi and Robert as they got older. It would have been a very nice time for him. Both of them are now at the age where they can understand and digest that kind of information enough for it to be really quite profound.

Because of who they are, Bindi and Robert have the power now to make a real difference. They have the ultimate opportunity to get in front of every person on a couch watching television. As Steve showed, that is such a valuable platform for raising awareness about something as important as fighting for the survival of our environment.

My hope is that Bindi and Robert will never stop learning about and teaching others what's important to get back to a healthy planet. They've already got an influential name that will open a lot of doors for them—they've got a head start that Steve worked a lifetime to build up. And if their knowledge, and the information that those children have got or had access to over the years is used to continue to positively influence people whether that be governments or corporations that have the opportunity to make decisions for everybody else, that would be my greatest optimism that they can make an impact in that arena just like their dad.

It would be really nice to think that both of them could follow in their father's footsteps. When you are a parent, you have certain opportunities to bring your children up in the way that you feel is the right way to do it, and to encourage them in whatever they want to become. But you can only influence them up to a certain point.

We all have our own ideas about what we want to do, where we want to go, where our passion lies or how we want to make an impact in our time here on this earth. While they might have that feeling now, that's not to say that it will carry on, but I certainly hope that it will. They have obviously got a little bit of their dad like that, I'd like for them of course to have a lot of that because his heart was the biggest gift that he had to give to the world. It was in the right compassionate, generous place. You can only hope that is the way that it works out for them too. Everybody's different. Our lives change as we go along. Different things influence our lives.

And while I hold these hopes for Bindi and Robert, I also have lots of other grandkids who the same advice applies to. It might not be in wildlife, or in fighting for the environment but whatever the direction is that you want to go, you have to believe that it's possible to achieve what you set out to achieve. And whether they are my grandkids, or any other young Australian out there, that's my greatest bit of advice.

'Whatever you want to do in this world, it is achievable. The most important thing that I've found, that perhaps you could use, is be passionate and enthusiastic in the direction that you choose in life, and you'll be a winner.'
—STEVE IRWIN

Passion and enthusiasm

You have to believe that it's possible to achieve whatever you set out to achieve. When I gave up life as a plumber I made a really clear and definite decision that I wasn't going to live a life I no longer had a passion for. Some people make that decision at eighteen, and some people make it at eighty. The saddest thing is when people have a dream but never act on it at all.

If you have a dream, you should try to achieve it as much as possible. Everybody has that ability. It doesn't have to begin with a drastic change as it did for me, and it doesn't matter who you are, where you come from or what your background is. If you give it all you've got then anything is possible. Begin with just a firm personal agreement with yourself and one simple step forward in the direction that you want to go.

Fathers and sons

I get really embarrassed when people write to ask my advice about how they should raise their children, because I made mistakes just like everybody else. I may have been the catalyst for getting Steve involved with wildlife, but it was something that came so naturally to him. His interests were aligned with mine and that made it a lot easier to encourage and nurture his aspirations. The moments that Steve and I had together were certainly special and I'll treasure them for as long as I live. But I was no different from any other dad. In those really early years, I could have done a lot better—I should have spent more time with my kids. I was so focused on work and my other responsibilities. I was just an ordinary dad raising a son the way I thought I needed to.

The Australian bush

The most rewarding and exciting part of my life has been the Australian bush. It's not everybody's cup of tea, but for those who do get out into remote parts it can be very rewarding. You see life stripped back to its simplest form, see how nature is intricately interconnected and where we fit as a species within that interlocking jigsaw puzzle. I wish all Australians reconnected with the natural environment as often as possible. The bush opens up our eyes to the fact that everything in nature is a living entity fighting for its survival. Observing the world around you is a very gratifying way to link your soul to the earth.

Respecting apex predators

The biggest animals, like the crocodile, that you most fear are in fact the very animals that we rely on the most. On our planet today, sixteen of twenty-two species of crocodile are skinned for leather. Every year over eighty million sharks are finned alive, and one-third of species are now endangered, many of which are endemic to Australian waters. Big cats, bears and seals are hunted and turned into clothing, aphrodisiacs and trophies—they too are just one step away from extinction.

These animals are the heads of the food chain and as they're driven closer and closer to extinction, every other living thing on this planet will be adversely affected—including us. We can all make a difference by simply not purchasing any wildlife products, no matter how they are packaged or marketed. Next time you see someone wearing seal-fur boots, shark-tooth jewellery or carrying a designer crocodile-skin handbag, think to yourself how much more valuable that would have been to the wild animal who owned it.

Every single animal in the wild is part of a balanced system. Take out the dominant croc, and catfish numbers explode. Animals regulate our environment, which provides us with the oxygen we breathe and the food we eat. They are the natural filters of our very delicate climate.

Steve's catch-cry 'Crocs rule' was so important because it's true. Crocs, sharks, tigers, lions and bears rule their environments and we need them to. When we interfere with that balance and promote ourselves to the top of the food chain, we are playing a dangerous game. They are keystone species and their very role is to create stability in the ecosystem. Right now the most dangerous animal on this planet is you.

Leadership

The most important asset to any business, big or small, is its staff. You can't be successful without competent, passionate and dedicated people. Invest above all else in the training of your staff and you will not only have willing and dedicated employees, but will be helping to create empowered people who will contribute to the future. Nourish the training and experience of a good leader well enough that they can leave, but also respect them enough that they don't want to. Corporate history is vital to the longevity of any business, wildlife group, sanctuary or workplace anywhere. The most important thing that I've found is that if you lead by example you'll have willing and hard-working employees who'll go the extra mile.

Motivation

What keeps me going is knowing that the people who've gone would expect you to. They'd still want you to achieve what they would have wanted you to achieve when they were alive. That's not always easy, not when you're reminded what might have been. It's important to remember that although you can eventually learn to accept what's happened, because you can't change it, that pain can resurface at any given time. It never goes away.

At those times, motivation comes from the acceptance that soon enough our time will be up too and that our goal isn't in fact to live forever but to leave something vital behind. Leaving the world in a better state than you found it has got to be the ultimate purpose of our existence. We've got to place the highest value on leaving behind a better future for our children.

Friends

True friends are like finding a piece of gold. It's absolutely essential, from time to time, to surround yourself with like-minded people who harbour similar passions. True friends challenge you and prompt you to strive for your dreams. Steer clear of people who try to hold you back or bring you down. You have absolutely no ties to people like that and always have a choice to simply walk away. Life's too short to worry about bullies.

A letter to my dad

Mandy Irwin

When I was in high school, I had to do an English assignment on someone famous.

'Why don't you do it on your dad?' my teacher asked.

'Huh? He's not famous!' I said, amused at the thought that he could be labelled as anything but plain old Dad, who sported a very daggy white towelling hat wherever he went and rarely wore a shirt.

'Yes, he is. He owns a reptile park, and he's a very interesting person indeed.'

I couldn't for the life of me work out what was so exceptional about that. But I did what she asked and I based my project on my dad: Bob Irwin, Proprietor of Queensland Reptile and Fauna Park. Dad then packed me off to school with a freshwater, non-venomous keelback snake in my school bag, which to me seemed like a perfectly normal thing to do.

'What are you doing bringing a snake to school?' my teacher asked, startled at the sight of a pillowcase with a knot tied in the end writhing around on her staffroom desk.

'It's part of my assignment,' I replied, puzzled by her alarmed reaction.

It took a lot of persuading her that I could confidently handle a snake before I was eventually allowed to use it in my presentation. The rest of the class sat around enthralled to see a snake at school as I rattled off every known fact about them. If I knew any subject, I knew my snakes, because my dad taught me to know all about the kinds of things that slithered and hissed.

At the time, I didn't see that my childhood was different from anyone else's. It is only fairly recently that I have figured out how much both Dad and Mum shaped me into the person I am today because of the journey they took us on when they gave up the security of a successful business in Melbourne to dedicate their life to wildlife. In hindsight, I most certainly had the best upbringing a kid could ask for. What other children get to play with and learn about nearly every Australian animal imaginable? We had emus, brolgas and an assortment of snakes. Mum and Dad treated them no different to how they treated their own children. We were one big eclectic Irwin family, and no two days were ever the same in our household.

I instinctively trusted whatever Dad said. Like going swimming in the newly tiled saltwater crocodile pool, one of the first cemented ponds Dad built at the park. There was a female salty in there called Sweetie. It was the middle of summer, stinking hot, and in those days we didn't have a swimming pool for humans.

'Go and take a swim in Sweetie's pool, I've just cleaned it out. I've just had a dunk in there myself!' Dad said. 'Just keep an eye on her, Grub. Sweetie's up in the back corner sittin' on the leaves. If she starts to move towards the pool then get out quick smart!' he added.

'Okay, Dad,' I trustingly replied and I had a beautiful swim, though it was quick. I was in and out in two seconds flat.

I trusted Dad with my life. I suppose I shouldn't have; there were times when I witnessed him hanging out of a large freshwater crocodile's mouth and countless other close calls with potentially deadly animals, but I did that without ever blinking an eye. Because that's the kind of guy our dad was. With him around, nothing ever fazed me, and I look back now as an adult and I wonder where that kind of trust is born, given the circumstances we were faced with. You knew he wasn't going to give you a bum steer; that he'd never let us do something that he wouldn't do himself. And the animal kingdom picks up on that too. Animals seemed to give him their trust in return, allowing him the chance to observe and care for an assortment of weird and wonderful creatures so that he could share his findings with others. Dad and Mum handed that gift down to Steve, Joy and me. I can't imagine a life without animals around me. I think it would be an awfully empty existence, singular and selfish to consider only the wellbeing of our own species.

I certainly got my patience from Mum. I can remember seeing many tools sent flying while Dad was working out in the shed. Patience was famously not his virtue, but when it came to wildlife, he had all the patience in the world.

I love you, Dad, with all of my heart.

In leaving Melbourne, you sought out togetherness for a young family, and you more than succeeded at that. Our tight-knit family unit was testament to that with endless laughs around the dinner table, crowded at times with an army of interesting friends that you attracted with your big heart. I am so thankful for the childhood that I had. I miss those days of togetherness now that it has all but come undone. In our household, there was rarely an argument. When we struggled financially, as a kid I was oblivious. I never witnessed a bad word spoken between you and Mum. If there was, we didn't see it because it was never around us kids. I have so much respect for that.

I can still remember that horrible phone call the day we lost Mum, and then a similar one six and a half years later when we lost Steve too. Two beautiful, honest, loving people who should never have been taken from this world. I have a huge hole in my heart where they both should be that will never heal until we can all be together again, with Trinni and Curley Bird and Brolly too.

I'm so glad you're still here, although I am aware how difficult it is at times for you to comprehend the cards that you have been dealt. But you are strong, and you have taught us to be strong too. You have taught us to keep fighting for the things that are important and following what's in our hearts.

In my eyes you're the man who started an empire. If you had not dug that first hole, if you'd not cemented in that first fence pole, if you'd not had the foresight that you could achieve your dreams when everyone else said it wasn't possible, then I wonder where I would be today, and so many others who have passed through the front gates of what is now Australia Zoo. You didn't build a zoo but a classroom for many people to learn something important about animals and about themselves in the process. You are an inspiration to all of us that anything is possible. When I think about it now, my English teacher was right to say you were a person of interest. You're not quite a celebrity, because that's just not your thing at all. Your motivation has only ever been for helping animals. I understand now how rare, remarkable and big-hearted you truly are. The world has a lot to learn from you and your compassion. How lucky we have been to call you Dad. These days, I wish I could give up work and keep following you on all of your many adventures on the roads less travelled. One day we will, Dad.

Mum and Steve would be so proud of you. We all are.

Acknowledgements

When Bob and I first ventured into the great Australian outback at Broken Hill, the owner of the very property that we were there to see, Steve Radford (aka Dot), gave me some sensible advice which gave wings to this book. Over dinner one night, looking out at another breathtaking Broken Hill sunset, he said to me, 'You ought to write down his stories, you know. You're the only one who could do it. When I was younger, I too had a mentor like Bob and my greatest regret is not recording some of those stories to relive today.' That sparked me to begin writing down Bob's anecdotes and advice for my generation about the preservation of the environment. If it hadn't been for Steve Radford, many of these stories would be lost forever. I have only wanted to record them in Bob's voice.

Thanks a lot, Dot; these stories were recorded on paper because you started the cogs turning to preserve Bob Irwin's legacy. The legacy of our hero.

* * *

Bob would sincerely like to thank everybody who generously had input into this book; each conversation, no matter how short, has greatly influenced this story. It truly has been a collaborative effort that wouldn't have been possible without the following very special individuals:

Judy Irwin

Without you, Judy, this project quite simply wouldn't have been completed. I would probably have got halfway through it and decided to throw in the towel. Over the years, I have been thankful to have you as my sounding board and that has been fundamentally important to me. But I owe you a lot more than that. The very fact that I am still sitting here writing this book, I attribute to you. I'm sure you thought when you first met me, 'I can save this human,' and you have succeeded. Thank you for getting inside my head and giving me a greater insight into life itself. I really do appreciate having you around me and the friendship we share.

My family

MANDY JOHNSTONE AND FAMILY, JOY MUSCILLO, BONNY CUMMING, GRAEME HAKKAINSSON

As a parent, I've always felt it was my responsibility to ensure our children had as good a life as possible. And although you wouldn't exactly call it a normal existence, I know we achieved a great life for our children. What we have received in return is a wonderful family and I will always treasure those times we have shared. I know now that the glue in our family was mostly Lyn. She was the strength behind the family, even though she was only knee-high to a grasshopper. Since she left, I'll be the first to admit, it's been hard to replicate that. It's only in recent history I have realised just how essentially important family are. That was the mistake I made early in the piece. I thought I could cope better on my own, and I'm certainly thankful to all of you for being there through thick and thin. Thank you, Mandy, in particular, for your time spent on this book.

The Croc Team

BRIAN AND KATE COULTER, FRANK MIKULA, DAN MEAD, DAN HIGGINS, BRIAN HERBERT, BRIAN WATSON, TREVOR NEUCOM, BRETT MOSTYN AND DAMIEN MORRIS

One of the highlights for me in writing this book has been unearthing your anecdotes and being able to reminisce about one of the most satisfying chapters of my life. It has been an honour working with you over the years and watching teamwork play out at its best. What we learnt out there wasn't just about crocodiles, but important life lessons. I hope that no matter where the road takes you from here, from time to time you'll heed some of that advice. Thank you for the opportunity to reconnect and for sharing your personal stories. To those whose names are not mentioned, you know who you are.

Mates for life

MAUREEN & PETER HASKINS, NOEL & JILL PECK, STEPHEN & ANNALISA ACCORNERO, ANGUS YOUNG, JOHN CANN, TREVOR NEUCOM, KEVIN & VAL WRAYFORD, NEVILLE BURNS AND BRETT SMITH

Good friends are hard to find. Even rarer for me are people who have shared my likeminded passion for the environment

and that's the kind of category in which I put you all. No matter how many years it is between the times we meet up, I always get a really good feeling. Thank you for your warmth, hospitality and encouragement throughout the process of writing this book.

A special thankyou also to Alby & Andrew Davies, Mandy Lake, Margi Brown and my good friend and all-round healer John Rogers.

The Bob Irwin Wildlife & Conservation Foundation Inc.

Graham Morrow, Dennis Carroll, Julie & Warren Lohmann, Bonny Cumming, Judy Irwin, Gregory Johnstone, Ben Dessen, Tom Lawton, Dan Mead, Brett Mostyn, Amanda French, Bob's Army Volunteers

I found out a long time ago that it doesn't matter how good you are, if you haven't got good people around you, you can forget about it. What we have now is what I consider to be a really loyal group of passionate young Australians committed to the protection of our environment. Thank you for being an inspiration to me to keep on doing what I do and for being the backbone of our advocacy always. You have given me hope that the story will continue on.

Behind the scenes

Jane Palfreyman, Emma Rusher, Siobhán Cantrill, Aziza Kuypers, Andy Palmer, Felicia Rusher, Debra Budge

Thank you to our wonderful publishers, Allen & Unwin, for your belief in this book and the ongoing encouragement you've given me over many years in telling this story. To the various

people working around the clock, in particular Siobhán Cantrill, you truly have been an amazing team to work with, and for someone who's not all that comfortable in the spotlight, it has been a surprisingly comfortable ride to go back in time thanks to all of you. To Jane Palfreyman, I sincerely appreciate the trust I have been able to put in your wonderful team. It's only thanks to your unconditional dedication to bringing this book to life that it has been possible. Emma Rusher, thank you for weaving this web together and for your invaluable contribution to this book over many long years. We finally did it.

Bob to Amanda

It's interesting that you meet people in your life, at different stages, and instantly you're aware that person is going to be a big influence somewhere down the track. I realised from the very beginning that if I could get Amanda involved in my work, then she would play a big role in my life and help me to keep it all going. The more time I spend with her on the road, the more involved she becomes and I've realised how important she has been as the glue to put this whole picture together. She works very well with people, and some of the things that I've done over the last seven years I wouldn't have done without her. She's the one who's pushed, shoved, questioned and done all things necessary to make it all happen, and let me tell you, at times it's not easy to travel with me. If it wasn't for her, many of these projects, including this book, would never have come to fruition. Amanda, you never cease to amaze me because you continually prove you can do it. You are a true exemplar of the adage that if you believe in something strongly enough, you can achieve it. I only hope you'll continue to follow your passion.

And, lastly, Amanda to Bob

You are my wildlife hero and my like-minded friend with whom age is no barrier. You understand what makes me tick and have encouraged me to realise my dreams on so many occasions. And here we are now, having completed your book. I cherish the opportunities you have given me to see parts of this country that I am so proud to call home and experience a compassion I have witnessed in no other job. How lucky am I to work alongside you out in the field and soak up all I can about an industry I am deeply passionate about. Those experiences are worth more than money can buy.

Both you and Judy have given me confidence in my abilities, hope for a better world and an understanding of how important it is to stand up for what you believe in. And because I have the last say here in this book, you're going to listen to me for a change!

You have inspired, encouraged and supported me, and so many others through your life journey in very profound ways. You continue to say you have failed, but in our collective eyes, you have succeeded by giving us a glimpse into the world around us. That is your greatest legacy and it is one that makes a lasting impact on every person who crosses your path. It's now up to us to keep on fighting battles for animals, as they can't speak for themselves. And I promise you, it's down to you that we'll keep it all going.

Amanda French is a Queensland-based media and communications specialist across various wildlife causes. Amanda has worked both in the field and remotely in developing campaigns and providing support to domestic and international wildlife projects such as Bona the Sumatran elephant in Indonesia and Australian not-for-profit organisations Free the Bears Fund and Quoin Island Sea Turtle Rehabilitation Centre.

Amanda also works with Australian naturalist Bob Irwin to provide support to many Australian wildlife organisations through Bob's public advocacy. Together they have clocked up more than 20,000 kilometres on the road to tell their stories and inspire others.

Amanda's work within the wildlife arena was told on ABC's *Australian Story* in March 2013.